Consuming Work

Consuming Work

Youth Labor in America

YASEMIN BESEN-CASSINO

TEMPLE UNIVERSITY PRESS
Philadelphia

TEMPLE UNIVERSITY PRESS
Philadelphia, Pennsylvania 19122
www.temple.edu/tempress

Library of Congress Cataloging-in-Publication Data

Besen-Cassino, Yasemin.
  Consuming work : youth labor in America / Yasemin Besen-Cassino.
    pages   cm
  Includes bibliographical references and index.
  ISBN 978-1-4399-0948-5 (cloth : alk. paper)
  ISBN 978-1-4399-0949-2 (pbk. : alk. paper)
  ISBN 978-1-4399-0950-8 (e-book)
  1. Youth—Employment—United States.   2. Part-time employment—United States.
3. Youth—United States—Social conditions.   I. Title.

HD6273.B47 2013
331.3'470973—dc23   2013012826

Printed in the United States of America

102714P

To Zeynep and Edip Besen—with love and gratitude

Contents

Acknowledgments

This book would not have materialized without the help and support of many family members, friends, and colleagues. The project took root during my graduate study years in the Department of Sociology at the State University of New York, Stony Brook. I thank Tim Moran, Naomi Rosenthal, and Nilufer Isvan, who read early versions of the manuscript and offered valuable advice.

James B. Rule has been an amazing adviser throughout the project. He patiently read through the manuscript, offering important and timely feedback. I am thankful for his encouragement and guidance. I have also been fortunate to work with Michael Kimmel throughout this project. He has been a wonderful mentor. I am truly grateful for his theoretical guidance, moral support, and kind encouragement.

My colleagues at Montclair State University have been most supportive. Jay Livingston, Benjamin Hadis, Sangeeta Parashar, and Gil Zicklin facilitated the survey process. I also thank Janet Ruane, George Martin, and Peter Freund for their support and encouragement. Susan O'Neill helped me enormously by printing and photocopying surveys. I also thank Laura Kramer for her guidance and mentorship.

Scott Harris, Mary Gatta, David Rosen, and Gregory DeFreitas read earlier versions of various chapters. I thank them for their excellent theoretical and methodological suggestions.

I thank the wonderful team at Temple University Press. It was a true pleasure to work with Mick Gusinde-Duffy, Micah Kleit, Joan Vidal, Gary Kramer, and Lynne Frost; they made the process very enjoyable. The three anonymous reviewers offered a number of valuable comments.

Generous grants from the W. E. Upjohn Foundation supported the research in Chapter 7. The Faculty Scholarship Program and a Career Development Grant at Montclair State University also helped support this project. The 2012–2013 Distinguished Scholar Award of Montclair State University generously provided a research leave that enabled timely completion of the manuscript. I thank Marietta Morrissey and Willard Gingerich for facilitating the research leave and for providing valuable research support.

Early versions of Chapters 3, 4, and 7 originally appeared in several academic journals. An early version of Chapter 3, published as Yasemin Besen-Cassino, "Exploitation or Fun?" *Journal of Contemporary Ethnography* 35, no. 3 (2006): 319–340, is used with the permission of Sage, Inc. An early version of Chapter 4, published as Yasemin Besen-Cassino, "Pay or Play?" *Regional Labor Review* 9, no. 3 (2006): 30–40, is used with the permission of *Regional Labor Review*. An early version of Chapter 7, published as Yasemin Besen-Cassino, "Cost of Being a Girl," *NWSA Journal* [now *Feminist Formations*] 20.1 (2008): 146–160, is used with the permission of Johns Hopkins University Press.

I dearly wish my grandparents Saffet and Sadri Saptir could see this book. I miss them enormously. I thank my parents, Zeynep and Edip Besen, who have supported this project from its inception. They fostered my intellectual curiosity throughout the years and created and sustained a vibrant environment for discussion and the exchange of ideas. I only hope that I can adequately emulate the creation of that environment of loving encouragement and rich discussion. Without the support of my parents, this project would not have become a reality. I dedicate this book to them.

Dan Cassino has lived and breathed this project for the past decade. He has been a wonderful partner, coparent, and collaborator. I extend my special thanks to Dan for his endless support. Julian Eren Besen-Cassino was born during the writing of this book. He is a wonderful addition to our family and a constant source of inspiration and joy.

Consuming Work

1

Consuming Work

Introduction to Youth Work in America

It's a very American illness, the idea of giving yourself away
entirely to the idea of working in order to achieve some sort
of brass ring that usually involves people feeling some way
about you—I mean, people wonder why we walk around
feeling alienated and lonely and stressed out.
>   —David Foster Wallace, *Infinite Jest*

The boundaries between work and non-work are becoming
more fluid. Flexible, pluralized forms of underemployment
are spreading.
>   —Ulrich Beck, *Risk Society: Towards a New Modernity*

The paradise offered by the culture industry is the same old
drudgery. Both escape and elopement are predesigned to lead
back to the starting point.
>   —Theodor Adorno and Max Horkheimer,
>   *Dialectic of Enlightenment*

On one snowy day in an affluent suburb of a major metropolitan area, a
winter weather advisory was in effect. With low visibility and slippery
roads, snow had taken over the suburbs. On this bitterly cold day, Josh,[1]
like many other teenagers, traveled many miles to get to work. Despite experiencing car troubles, nearly having a car accident, and spending hours in heavy
traffic, he arrived at the coffee shop where he works part-time only—to do a
double shift, carry heavy loads of garbage in the cold, and deal with a hectic
day of selling hot beverages to shivering customers.

Even though his school was in session, he chose to come to work instead of
going to class at the local college, where he is getting his degree in theater and

---

[1] All the real names and identifying characteristics of the participants have been changed. All the
names used are pseudonyms.

humanities. When I asked him why he chose his work over his studies, he told me they need him here: "Nobody notices when I am not [in class]." Unlike at school, they notice him at work. He feels needed—like a hot cup of cocoa on a cold day.

Josh, like many other teenagers, works "part-time" while still in school, but do not be fooled by what he calls "part-time" work. "Part-time" sounds like a few hours of work scattered throughout the week, but he was at the coffee shop every day of the past week. Even on the days when he was not scheduled to work, he stopped by to hang out with his friends. He did not just stand idly by; he also helped the friends who were working. He is one of many young people who fold sweaters in clothing stores, pour our morning coffees, wait on us in restaurants, and serve us in many service and retail sector jobs. Yet Josh differs greatly from our traditional conceptions of young workers. For most of us, the terms "child labor" or "youth labor" evoke images of unventilated sweatshops in the developing world or the chimney sweeps of Dickens novels. Generally viewed as distant practices of the developing world or our historical past, child and youth labor is rarely associated with enterprises of contemporary United States. Yet contrary to popular belief, not only is youth labor widespread in the United States; it is an important element of our modern economy.

With his spiky blond hair, fashionable clothes, and brand-new cell phone, Josh looks nothing like the chimney sweeps of Dickens novels, nor does he fit the conventional definition of a service or retail worker in our contemporary economy. Typical service and retail sector jobs in which young people are employed are what Arne Kalleberg (2011) refers to as "bad jobs": routine jobs with low wages, part-time hours, few or no benefits, no autonomy, and limited opportunities for advancement (see also Levy 1998; Williams and Connell 2010). In our current economy, there is great heterogeneity among part-time jobs (Kahne 1992; Kalleberg 2011; Tilly 1995). Some new concept part-time jobs, especially in the fields of publishing, entertainment, and teaching, offer "good" part-time jobs, with higher-than-minimum-wage hourly wages, ample fringe benefits, and numerous opportunities for advancement.

The workers who are employed in these jobs are typically assumed to be desperately poor to want to work under such conditions. However, today's young labor force is dominated by more affluent youth. According to the U.S. Bureau of Labor Statistics's *Report on the Youth Labor Force* (Herman 2000), the labor-force participation rate of youth is the highest (71.6 percent) in the highest socioeconomic group and is lowest in the lowest socioeconomic group (40.6 percent). (See Figure 1.1.)

Youth who come from a higher socioeconomic status are not only more likely to work; they dominate the current composition of the youth labor force. Youth from upper and middle socioeconomic status backgrounds con-stitute the majority of the current youth labor force (44.0 percent and 11.9

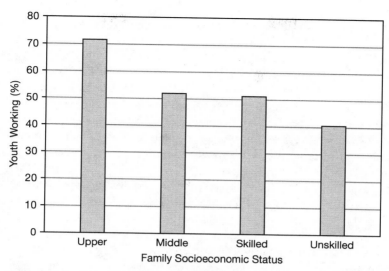

FIGURE 1.1 Percentage of Youth Working, by Socioeconomic Status

percent, respectively), and only 23.9 percent of working youth come from the lowest socioeconomic status backgrounds. (See Figure 1.2.)

Thus, contrary to popular views, the majority of youth who work do not come from economically deprived backgrounds (Herz and Kosanovich 2000; D. Johnson and Lino 2000). What sets the current youth labor force apart and renders it unique is its unprecedented and counterintuitive composition.

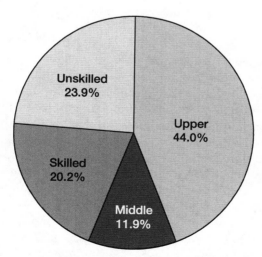

FIGURE 1.2 Composition of Youth Workforce, by Socioeconomic Status

Furthermore, because the youth labor force is dominated by youth from higher socioeconomic backgrounds, it is important to understand what motivates these young people to work. Service sector jobs, especially in the retail industry, where most young people are employed, generate some of the worst jobs (Williams and Connell 2010). According to the U.S. Bureau of Labor Statistics (H. Shaefer 2009), with wages averaging less than $10 per hour and limited and often nonstandard hours, these workers do not earn enough money to support themselves (Williams and Connell 2010). Many scholars have argued that these workers must be desperate to take these jobs (Ehrenreich 2001), yet many of these retail and service sector workers are not desperate; rather, they are so-called decommodified workers who are able to maintain their standards of living without relying on their incomes (Holden 2003; Williams and Connell 2010).

Although commonsense explanations reduce the motivation of youth to enter the labor market to their economic need, these explanations are simply not applicable to these decommodified young workers. These economic reductionist explanations do not really explain *why* young people like Josh give up their free time to work at demanding jobs for little pay if they do not truly need the money. It is important to acknowledge that some youth do need to work out of economic necessity, but they constitute only a minority of the current youth labor force. For a more comprehensive understanding of the current labor force, it is important to focus on all youth and understand their reasons for working from *their* perspective. It is expected that economically deprived youth would work in low-paying jobs with odd hours and no benefits, but why would affluent youth give up their free time to work in demanding jobs that pay only minimum wage?

Today, almost every student in the United States works sometime throughout their school careers (Manning 1990; Mortimer 2003). Currently, the U.S. Department of Labor defines "an employed person" as a civilian over sixteen years of age who does a minimum of one hour of work for pay during the reference week or fifteen hours or more of unpaid work at home or at a family business. The Fair Labor Standards Act of 1938 establishes the minimum age of child labor for nonagricultural employment as sixteen. According to U.S. federal law on youth employment, sixteen- and seventeen-year-olds can technically be employed, but they are banned from working in certain industries that the secretary of labor finds detrimental for this age group. Fourteen- and fifteen-year-olds, on the other hand, are banned from almost every industry, although they are allowed to work in retail and food services and gasoline services. There are also restrictions on the total number of hours they are allowed to work per day and per week and on the time of the day the work is performed.

For many young people, work starts much earlier than the federally mandated age. Some youth working as early as age twelve in freelance jobs, such as babysitting, snowplowing, or yard work and slowly move into more formal service and retail jobs. In our predominantly service economy, young people have established themselves as central actors. Today, 13.6 percent of our entire labor force is composed of workers between the ages of sixteen and twenty-four (U.S. Bureau of Labor Statistics 2012b). Young people have become such an integral part of our economy that we rarely notice their sociological significance. In their landmark book *When Teenagers Work*, Ellen Greenberger and Laurence Steinberg observe, "The large teenage, part-time labor force that staffs the counters of fast-food establishments, waits on customers in retail stores, assembles parts in industrial settings, and cleans motel rooms and office buildings has become such a familiar part of our social landscape that we may fail to note its unique character or to ponder its social significance" (1986: 3).

Even though youth are essential parts of our economy, their motivations have been largely neglected, and their experiences have received little attention. Prior studies on youth employment approach the topic from the perspectives of parents, educators, administrators, and employers. However, the central actors—namely, young people themselves—have been left out of the study of youth labor. Especially given the new and unique composition of the American youth labor force, capturing their perspective and understanding of why they do what they do is very important to our understanding of youth labor (Besen-Cassino 2008; Liebel 2004).

Although young people have always worked in the United States, youth employment has been recognized as a social issue only since the 1970s. Starting in the 1970s, historical inquiries began to document the prevalence of youth work throughout our history (Coleman 1984; Engel, Marsden, and Woodaman 1968; Goldstein and Oldham 1979; Johnson and Bachman 1973; Lewin-Epstein 1981; Ruhm 1997; Shapiro 1979). For much of our history, young people have worked on family farms. Because farm work among young people was so prevalent, schools adapted to the farm schedule. Even though farm work constitutes a small minority of our current workforce, schools still remain on the farm schedule, offering summer vacations. With the rise of industrialization, many young people shifted their labor from family-owned farms to factories, working alongside adults (Bills 2004). Glen Elder's pioneering work *Children of the Great Depression* (1974) documents the widespread nature of youth employment outside the family farms during the Great Depression. Youth employment, however, was not limited to economically challenging times. Mary Engel, Gerald Marsden, and Sylvie Woodaman's (1968) study of the Boston metropolitan area and Bernard Goldstein and Jack Oldham's (1979) study of New Jersey both demonstrate the widespread nature of teenage employment. Overall, this first wave of research documents the existence and prevalence of youth labor in the United States and establishes youth employment as an important area of sociological inquiry.

After the establishment of youth labor as a social issue, the second wave of research focuses on the advantages of work. This strand of research argues that working while still in school offers a wide range of benefits for young people, such as helping youth find future better jobs (D'Amico and Baker 1984; Meyer and Wise 1982; Stephenson 1980; Stern and Nakata 1989), reducing school dropout rates (D'Amico and Baker 1984; McNeal 1997), helping improve school attendance (Marsh 1991; Mortimer and Finch 1986), and improving academic performance (D'Amico and Baker 1984).

For young people who do not intend to go to college, working helps them not only find jobs more quickly but also perform better in their future jobs. Researchers in this era also argue that work teaches youth important skills, such as discipline and development of work ethic, which can be applied to an academic setting. According to many of these researchers, by providing necessary economic resources and work-related skills, such as scheduling, improving discipline, and meeting deadlines, working helps keep teenagers stay in school and focus on their studies. Ronald D'Amico and Paula Baker, however, show that although early work experience benefits non-college-bound youth, these positive effects are not present for college-bound youth. Finally, research from this era finds that working helps teens develop emotionally. These studies show that working improves teens' self-esteem by providing a sense of accomplishment. It also helps them transition into adulthood more smoothly.

This era of optimism is followed by a third wave of research that focuses primarily on the disadvantages of youth employment. In this era, many scholars question the potential negative effects of work, particularly on academic progress, psychological development, and risky behavior. Researchers argue that working while still in school lowers academic success (Marsh 1991; Mortimer and Finch 1986; Steinberg and Dornbusch 1991; Steinberg, Fegley, and Dornbusch 1993), interferes with emotional and psychological development (Greenberger and Steinberg 1986; Mortimer et al. 1994), reduces interactions with family and friends (Greenberger and Steinberg 1986; Finch et al. 1991; Mihalic and Elliot 1997; Paternoster et al. 2003), and increases the likelihood of risky behaviors, such as substance abuse (McMorris and Uggen 2000; Mihalic and Elliot 1997; Steinberg, Fegley, and Dornbush 1993) and crime (Hansen and Jarvis 2000).

Researchers in this era argue that working while still in school lowers academic success and decreases the likelihood of finishing school. Although previous studies do not take into account the intensity of work and number of hours that young people put in, this new wave of research argues that work intensity is a central factor in evaluating outcomes. Noah Lewin-Epstein (1981), for example, shows that working more than 19.5 hours per week interferes with academic progress by taking time away from academic studies. Although working fewer hours can have positive effects, higher-intensity work interferes with academic success. On the basis of their study of California teens, Greenberger and Steinberg (1986) show that working during teen years also interferes with the psychological and emotional development of teenagers in a number of ways. Further studies also demonstrate that working, especially long hours, harms relationships with family and friends by taking time away from peers, family, and extracurricular activities.

Researchers in this era also show that working increases the likelihood of risky behavior among teens, such as alcohol use, drug use, and involvement in crime. However, there is little consensus about the direction and the magnitude of these effects. Barbara McMorris and Christopher Uggen (2000) find that working as a teenager increases alcohol use, although they state that these effects are short-lived and do not cause serious effects on alcohol consumption in adult years. Sharon W. Mihalic and Delbert Elliot (1997), however, argue that teenagers who work during high school report higher levels of alcohol and marijuana use in the long-term, when they are twenty-seven and twenty-eight. Working long hours seems to increase the likelihood of risky behavior, but scholars disagree on the context in which—and extent to which—work results in such behavior. David M. Hansen and Patricia Jarvis (2000) show that working in a family business, for example, actually decreases the likelihood of risky behavior.

Today, research on youth employment moves away from evaluating the positive and negative effects of employment to instead problematizing the working conditions and structural inequalities faced by these young workers. Contemporary inquiries do not view young people as passive recipients of work's effects but rather as active, central actors with their own agency, motivations, and aspirations (Besen-Cassino 2008; Liebel 2004). Emerging research also focuses on the context and conditions of work. Although some jobs and work conditions can be beneficial for working youth, some might be harmful, depending on the job content, working conditions, and job intensity. Therefore, the new wave of research explores the differences between various kinds of youth jobs and examines their conditions. The new wave of research also points to the effects of race, gender, and socioeconomic status in determining access and working conditions. Such factors determine the types of jobs that youth take, which, in turn, determine their relative effects on individuals.

This book looks more closely at the main actors of youth employment, exploring the causes of youth labor from a sociological perspective. It answers the recent call for actor-centric research and fills this gap in the literature. The aspirations and motivations of youth cannot be adequately explained by leaving out the central actors in the process: young people themselves. In this book, I aim to answer *why* youth choose to work in the United States while they are still in school, from *their* perspective. The goal is to offer a sociological answer to the question of youth employment rather than reduce social behavior to a matter of economic gratification. This is not to say that economic gratification does not play a role in their decision to work: It is undeniable that economically deprived youth are most in need of work while still in school. However, such youth constitute a minority among the current youth labor force. For the overwhelming majority of the current youth labor force, the explanation of need fails to account for their propensity to work. In fact, a high proportion of youth who come from relatively affluent backgrounds give up their leisure time to work in highly mechanized and demanding jobs with odd hours and very low pay in addition to attending school full-time. If, in fact, economic need drives young people to work for money while they are still in school, why do affluent youth work? Are they working only for the money, too? Or does work fulfill other functions?

Methods

To answer these questions and capture the *lived experience* of work, I begin with nonparticipant observations. For the purposes of this study, I focus particularly on sixteen- to twenty-one-year-old full-time students who work while attending school. Because of corporate policy (my ethnographic site allows only students over eighteen years of age to work) and ethical reasons, my in-depth interviews focus particularly on students between the ages of eighteen and twenty-one. To remain consistent with this early ethnographic work, my later interviews focus primarily on eighteen- to twenty-one-year-old students as well. However, to offer a broader understanding, my quantitative analyses include a wider age group that includes sixteen- and seventeen-year-olds. Because my analysis shows no significant differences between high school and college students in terms of their work decisions, it makes theoretical and empirical sense to include this group as well. In the gender chapter, I also include data from younger students (ages twelve to sixteen) to better capture how early work experiences translate into later inequalities. My focus in this book is particularly on student laborers: full-time students who work while still in school. I have included nonstudents in some chapters only for comparison purposes. In this book, I focus primarily on working for pay outside the home. Although there are many types of work, I follow the U.S. Department of Labor's definition; therefore, unpaid labor, household chores, and agricultural labor remain outside the scope of this study.

My ethnography of youth labor started in 2001 at two different branches of a national coffee chain, Coffee Bean,[2] located in upper-middle-class suburbs of a major city on the East Coast. This particular coffee chain has been identified

---

[2] The name of this coffee chain has been changed.

by young people as one of the most desirable places to work, and the two par-ticular branches I picked employed predominantly young, full-time students. Between 2001 and 2004, I carried out extensive ethnographic fieldwork in two branches of this coffee chain, both of which are located in predominantly white areas with median annual incomes between $90,000 and $100,000. With their economic and ethnic/racial composition, these suburbs offer representa-tive examples of white affluent suburbs. Although my research sites are not representative of all youth jobs, and it is important to acknowledge the idio-syncrasies of all jobs, I believe the sites provide typical examples. The coffee shop I studied is similar to the environment of many youth jobs, but other occupations—such as those involving fast food rather than coffee, or those that are located in urban areas—may differ substantially and deserve separate ethnographic attention.

Throughout the duration of my ethnography, I observed workers of Cof-fee Bean in one- to eight-hour shifts, taking detailed field notes that focused on describing the tasks performed, recording the interaction and dialogue between coworkers, and capturing their interaction with the customers. My observations included both weekday and weekend shifts; morning, afternoon, and night shifts; opening and closing shifts where the managers were pres-ent and other shifts where they were not; and shifts where young people were scheduled to work together and shifts where they worked with older employ-ees. I started to record these observations first as a researcher sitting at a close table at the beginning of my ethnography, but with the help of key informants and time, I gained the confidence of the young workers and started to hang out at the counter with other friends, sometimes just observing them from the side and sometimes helping them. In addition to recording nonparticipant observations, I also conducted forty semistructured, in-depth, face-to-face interviews with college students employed at these coffee shops and similar venues. My respondents included employees of Coffee Bean at the time of the interview as well as past employees I contacted through key informants. Sixty percent of my respondents were female, and 40 percent were male. The major-ity of my respondents were white (except for one Asian American employee and one of Indian American origin). I had secured contacts with two key informants through the university, both of whom worked at the coffee shop. These key informants then provided me access to the other workers.

My face-to-face interviews varied in length from one to two hours. Most of the respondents were interviewed again at different intervals. I interviewed some at the coffee shop before or after their shifts, during their breaks, and at the nearby university, where many of them were full-time students. These interviews included detailed questions about their work and school experi-ences as well as their family lives, leisure activities, and consumption habits.

They were complemented by innumerable informal conversations, most of which took place in various corners of the coffee shops and at the young people's schools. I interpreted these interviews in the light of my extensive field notes. All the names used in this book are pseudonyms; all other identifying characteristics have been changed for confidentiality purposes.

In addition, between the years 2007 and 2008, I conducted a second wave of interviews with a wider pool of full-time college students who worked at different jobs. During this time, I conducted approximately fifty originally designed surveys and semistructured interviews at two universities (one public and one private). These universities were located in two towns in an East Coast state different from the one where I conducted my first set of observations. These locations were very similar to the locations for the earlier interviews in terms of their demographic makeup. Both were in predominantly white suburbs, with median annual incomes between $90,000 and $100,000. In these interviews, young people were asked about their work, school, and consumption habits as well as their views on different brands and stereotypes associated with different brands and their social and political views. In questions regarding consumption, I focused mostly on clothing, accessories, books, music, technology, food, and drinks. I inquired about how often these items were consumed, how much was spent on them, and which brands were found desirable.

The transcription of these interviews resulted in about 3 single-spaced pages each, totaling roughly 170 pages of text.

Finally, to document the effects of the most recent economic changes on youth employment, I conducted a third wave of seventy-five interviews and surveys in 2011. These interviews and supplemental surveys provided in-depth information on the lived experience of jobs from the perspectives of the young people. These original data offered an in-depth understanding of why they do what they do, to use the phrase coined by sociologist Jack Katz. This final wave of the study inquires about investigated some of the same issues that the previous waves of interviews dealt with. However, since the last wave took place after the economic recession, a key component of these interviews was to ask about the job-interview process and job searches with the intent to capture the effects of the economic recession on the ability to find jobs. Furthermore, unlike my detailed ethnography, which focused predominantly on white, affluent workers of Coffee Bean, in the second and third waves of my data collection, I included a more racially, ethnically, and socioeconomically diverse group to allow for comparison.

I also relied on two large-scale surveys—the National Longitudinal Study of Youth (NLSY) and the World Values Study (WVS)—to contextualize these individual stories. I used advanced statistical techniques to uncover patterns in these data sets, the details of which are discussed in the chapters that follow.

These data sets helped me contextualize the interviews and also offered cross-national comparisons. Although the in-depth interviews helped me decode the meaning of jobs from the perspective of the actors, the large-scale surveys helped me generalize the findings.

Youth Labor Force Today

According to the U.S. Bureau of Labor Statistics's *Report on the Youth Labor Force* (Herman 2000), 57 percent of early teens (fourteen- to fifteen-year-olds) work. Most teens start in freelance jobs, such as yard work, snowplowing, or babysitting, before moving on to more traditional employee positions. By the time they reach fifteen years of age, 38 percent have employee-type jobs, almost a 50 percent increase from the proportion of fourteen-year-olds in employee-type jobs. By the time youth reach eighteen years of age, almost everyone has worked sometime throughout school (Manning 1990). The largest category of employment is in the retail field (45 percent), where most youth work in eating, drinking, and restaurants (29 percent), with other retail jobs making up the remaining 16 percent. Retail is followed by the second largest sector of employment: the service sector (29 percent). Although retail and service are the dominant sectors in which youth are employed, smaller numbers work in agriculture (6 percent) and construction and manufacturing (12 percent), with the remaining 6 percent in other sectors. By the time they are older (ages sixteen to nineteen), based on 2005 data from the Current Population Survey, two major sectors of employment emerge: service (38 percent) and sales (38 percent); two-thirds of all older teenagers are employed in retail, food, and food preparation (Hirschman and Voloshin 2007).

Gender composition is approximately equally split, with females slightly more likely to work among early teenage years (59 percent to 55 percent, respectively), but these gender differences even out with time. By the time youth reach age fifteen, there are almost no gender differences in rates of employment.

Although gender does not make a substantial difference, marked racial and ethnic differences emerge among the youth workforce. White youth are more likely to work than African American and Hispanic youth. Although 64 percent of white youth are employed, the employment rates of African American and Hispanic youth are substantially lower: 43 percent and 41 percent, respectively. Finally, socioeconomic status makes a difference. Youth from higher socioeconomic status backgrounds are much more likely to work than youth from lower socioeconomic status backgrounds. Although employment rates increase substantially with age, as young people shift from more informal, freelance-type jobs to more structured, employee-type jobs, the inequalities and divisions discussed here remain fairly consistent throughout.

Young people have been a constant and vibrant part of our labor force. Today, they constitute 4 percent of our overall workforce (Hirschman and Voloshin 2007). Their labor-force participation rates have steadily increased over previous decades, peaking during the 1980s and stabilizing since then. Recent studies show that labor-force participation and intensity of work has remained relatively stable since the 1980s (Bills 2004; Warren and Forrest 2001). The recent recession, however, has shown a marked decline in youth labor-force participation rates; the labor-force participation rates of sixteen-to twenty-four-year-olds hit a record low in July 2011, as they found themselves in competition for jobs with older workers who had been laid off from higher paying jobs. Data from the U.S. Bureau of Labor Statistics (Morisi 2011) confirm that even summer employment rates, which used to be much higher than school-time employment, are substantially lower now, with many students unable to find summer jobs. However, the inequalities in the labor force, especially those based on race and ethnicity, persist (see also Current Population Survey 2005).

In the past, service and retail jobs were easy for young people to get, but even these are no longer as readily available as they used to be. Oftentimes, young people are in competition with adult workers, senior workers, and immigrant workers for these jobs. As recent research documents, socioeconomic factors play a major role in obtaining these jobs. Many employers prefer young workers with more upper-middle-class presentations and consumption habits.

The Suburb Is the New City

American suburbs have provided the backdrop for this research, because that is where many of the service and retail jobs that employ young people—especially those with higher socioeconomic statuses—are located. In general, suburbs have received limited academic attention; extensive studies of inequalities and work have focused on inner cities as the hotbed of multiple layers of inequality, such as class, race, and gender. Suburbs have always been the neutral ground, portrayed as having no class, race, or gender—just picket fences and neat yards. In the past few years, many jobs, especially service sector jobs, have left the inner cities and found homes in the suburbs. With this increased job availability, suburbs became the new cities in a way—turning into centers of service and retail jobs.

Suburbs are also important not just because they house available jobs but because in recent years they have been criticized for a lack of social interaction. As Donna Gaines (1998) shows, suburbs are centerless entities with limited common spaces. They offer few spaces for social interaction and limited opportunities to meet new people. For young people, suburbs are social wastelands. Victoria James (2007: 36) says that "the radius within which children roam freely among their homes shrunk by almost 90 per cent since the 1970s." Because many young people have limited opportunities to socialize with their friends without parental supervision, shopping malls, strip malls, and shops had provided sheltered spaces for youth to hang out without adult scrutiny. However, in recent years, young people hanging out without a specific activity has sometimes been associated with gang activity and has become the target of public suspicion (Abbott-Chapman and Robertson 2009; White 1999). Many suburban communities feel suspicious of young people congregating in public places, and many local businesses enforce rules to discourage such gatherings. For example, many malls and movie theaters do not accept unaccompanied teenagers, while some demand adult supervision for minors or define a "gang" as any group of more than three minors without a parent or guardian present. These rules allow management to kick teenagers off the premises without having to prove that they have engaged in any inappropriate activity, further narrowing the potential interaction space for these teens.

These jobs newly located in the suburbs—coffee shops on every corner, retail stores at every strip mall, clothing stores at the large malls—provide social spaces where young people meet new people and socialize with their friends. By taking jobs at these stores, young people carve out spaces for themselves, away from adult supervision and public scrutiny. Jobs enable these young people to see their friends away from their parents and other adults. They are also largely devoid of scrutiny: In the eyes of the local residents, they are not idle teenagers causing potential trouble, but responsible youth transitioning into adulthood.

The story of these affluent youth takes place within the context of affluent suburbs, with their available jobs and without unsupervised places for youth to meet.

Why Service and Retail Jobs?

In today's economy, understanding service and retail work is essential. With the continuing decline in manufacturing jobs, service jobs have become ubiquitous in our economy (Korczynski and Macdonald 2008; Macdonald and Sirianni 1996; Williams and Connell 2010).

As Ödül Bozkurt and Irena Grugulis observe, "Retail work is in many ways the new generic form of mass employment in the post-industrial socio-economic landscape. If the factory and the assembly line came to represent the quintessential workplace under industrialism . . . [the workplace] of the post-industrial era may be Wal-Mart, rather than Google" (2011: 2). Service and retail work are, indeed, socially significant and central in today's economy. More than 10 percent of the total labor force in advanced economies today is composed of retail workers (Bozkurt and Grugulis 2011). With the growing significance of retail in today's economy, we have seen a growing interest in the sector. Many scholars have studied the fast-food industry (Leidner 1993; Ritzer 1993), call centers and customer service (Callaghan and Thompson 2002; Taylor and Bain 1999), and working conditions for these sectors (Ehrenreich 2001). However, few of these studies focus on the *lived experience* of the retail workers. As the cultural understanding of "retail workers" has become synonymous with unskilled, low-paid automatons working in standardized, routinized jobs, few researchers focus on the inner differences.

"Despite the popular cultural shorthand used to depict retail workers as automatons who cannot wait to get out of these jobs if only the opportunities were there, retail work is widely diverse. The labour market spans a range from attractive, middle-class dominated 'style' labour markets . . . to the poorly paid shift work offered by mass retailers" (Bozkurt and Grugulis 2011: 5). Although all retail work is typically depicted as poorly paid shift work at mass retailers, great variation exists within the category. Retail work today also includes many boutique retailers, high-end establishments, and specialized services. As a result, many retailers require "soft skills" for their employees, such as certain appearances (Korczynski and Macdonald 2008; Warhurst, Thompson, and Nickson 2009; Williams and Connell 2010), personality traits, and people skills (Moss and Tilly 1996; Wilson 1996) with the intent to extract maximum efficiency and high productivity (Leidner 1996, 2006).

Because of this, young, attractive, middle-class students become some of the most desirable workers (Gatta 2011; Nickson et al. 2011). As employers demand certain characteristics, the workforce responds: Alongside many economically disadvantaged youth looking for work are many affluent teenagers competing for the same jobs.

Consumption and Work

Work is also closely related to consumption. The intertwined relationship of youth, work, and consumption is well-documented. Throughout our economy, young people work to sustain their consumption habits. These consumption habits have changed drastically over the past few decades. For many years, youth have been avid consumers of small-ticket items, such as gum, candy, hair accessories, lip gloss, CDs, comics, and blue jeans (Best 2009). However, in recent years, young people in North America and western Europe have started to purchase more substantial consumption items ranging from cell phones to computers and other electronics. This consumption has paralleled the large increase in their disposable income. Driven by this increase, more corporations started targeting young markets (even teen and tween markets) as consumers with their own money and consumption habits. These prospective customers are even more alluring because of their relative lack of existing brand loyalty. Naomi Klein (2002) observes an important difference in the way youth are targeted by corporations and advertisers: branding. As Amy Best (2009: 257–258) points out:

> Young people today are becoming adults in the age of competitive advertising and accelerated meaning where the image matters more than the product, in a new branded world of hyper-marketing where segmented marketing has prevailed over mass marketing, endless corporate sponsorships and partnerships that are thought to have eroded the public sphere and civil society and created a crisis of democracy. Indeed, one of the enduring features of the market that makes it so resilient is its adaptability as it relentlessly commodifies cultural forms, either folding them into already existing markets or carving out new ones.

Today, few spaces exist without the reach of the market: Virtually every part of young people's lives has been commodified and branded. The important part of consumption is the meaning and identity. Many successful corporations marketing to young people do so by imbuing commodities with social meaning that resonates with young people. Markets assign social meaning to different products and brands. By consuming them, young people form and market their identities (Best 2009). To borrow from the Frankfurt School, it can be argued that youth form their identities based on the resources offered by the cultural industries. The meaning of cultural objects is ascribed through the production process by the corporations and by the consumption process. During the exchange, in the words of Stuart Hall, meaning is encoded in the products in the production process. These products are recoded in the consumption process, during which a new layer of meaning is attached to the products. When Apple makes a phone, it is not marketing the product just by pointing out its function but is trying to show the kind of person who would use such a product. When the phone gets to the public, it acquires another level of meaning, which may or may not be what the original marketers had intended; this meaning is especially important to young people. Even countercultural movements utilize consumption items to express their individual views. Dick Hebdige (1979), in his study of Mods, shows the use of such objects as clothes, records, and hairstyles as identity markers to convey oppositional cultural ideas. The modern counterparts of these Mods might show off their identities by wearing specific brands of shoes, clothing, or audio equipment. Similarly, Sarah Thornton (1995) shows that youth develop subcultural identities through the consumption of a wide range of objects. In recent years, the already complex relationship of youth consumption and identity has become even more complex against the new backdrop of late modernity. With increasing mobility, globalization, and increased production and consumption speeds, production and consumption are less tied to traditional institutions and organizations and more to "lifestyle choices." These lifestyle choices are expressed through the consumption of cultural objects offered in the commodity culture (Bennett 2003). Identity and social status are less fixed and more fluid: They are constructed and reconstructed in everyday lives (Bauman 2000; Slater 1997). Youth spend increasing time and effort constructing their own identities and transforming their images through endless consumption. Don Slater observes, "Modernity dismantles a stable social order which provides fixed values and identities. . . . [T]he individual's boundaries, sources of meaning, social relations and needs become blurred and uncertain. This is the context of consumer culture: it floods modernity with a torrent of values, meanings, selves and others, both filling in the cultural deficits of the modern world and constantly intensifying and exploiting them" (1997: 99). Against this backdrop, and armed with ample disposable income, young people search for their identities and selves. This world that young people live in is increasingly defined by consumption. As a result, youth attribute meaning to objects they consume. Best's (2006) work shows that young people attribute meaning to their cars, with a car becoming a way to create visibility, mobility, and freedom. She shows that youth are increasingly drawn to markets not just to create and reinvent their individual identities but also to gain access and membership into groups. Because their identity and group membership is strongly entrenched in their consumption, many young people find themselves in a cycle of work and consumption (Schor 2000). Even traits or items that are not consumer goods can become part of this exercise in self-branding. Dan Cassino and Yasemin Besen-Cassino (2009), for example, show that young people consume political ideology as an object of consumption. In their analysis of the 2008 presidential elections, they show that young people relate to politics as if they are consuming a product, and they perceive political parties as brands and lifestyle choices.

This book studies the consumption of work and branded work experiences as markers of identity among youth. Within this postmodern landscape, work has transcended from supplying the means to consume commodities to being an object of consumption itself. Just as objects of consumption have become increasingly branded, jobs themselves have been branded as well. Brands are not only status markers but also identity markers. As Klein observes in *No Logo*, "Brand X is not a product but a way of life, an attitude, a set of values, a look, an idea" (2002: 23). Many commodities in the past few years have been presented and marketed as concepts: the brand as experience, as lifestyle (Klein 2002). Why not jobs? Just like an object of production, jobs can be consumed and can be branded. In fact, more than consuming a product, taking a job at the desired brand creates a higher level of brand loyalty, a firmer identity, and a stronger commitment to a subculture. Therefore, work experience is not only a leisure activity and a social space to see friends and socialize but also a branded experience to be consumed by young people.

Work and Leisure: The Binary Opposition?

Traditional accounts define work and leisure as being in opposition: Leisure is whatever you do when you are not working. Typical studies of youth employment, therefore, view youth labor as an activity motivated primarily by consumerism (Gaines 1998; Greenberger and Steinberg 1986; Hine 1999; Schor 1993). As Juliet Schor argues, "In middle-class homes, much of this work is motivated by consumerism: teenagers buy clothes, music, even cars. Some observers are worried that the desire to make money has become a compulsion, with many young Americans now working full-time, in addition to full-time school" (1993: 26). Hence, the employment of teenagers during their free time from school is often assumed to be a way of acquiring money to support their often-conspicuous consumption patterns: splurging on clothes, magazines, music, and cars. Although part-time work during school is a way to support consumption habits, youth consume more than clothes, magazines, music, and cars. Work is not just an activity that facilitates the consumption of such items but is itself consumed as a leisure activity. The consumption of the work experience, although not unique to the youth labor force, is often obscured by its role in facilitating material forms of consumption. The work experience of many young people today points to a more fluid relationship between work and leisure rather than a rigid binary opposition. As articulated by Theodor Adorno and Max Horkheimer, "Amusement under late capitalism is the prolongation of work. It is sought as an escape from the mechanized work process, and to recruit strength in order to be able to cope with it again" ([1979] 1997: 137). In one sense, leisure is presented as a binary opposition to recharge and recover from work, yet at the same time the leisure time is bombarded with images and products of capitalism. This fluid relationship of work and leisure proposed by Adorno is observed in the experience of youth work today. He argues, "At the same time, the difference between work and free time has been branded as a norm in the minds of people, at both the conscious and the unconscious level. Because, in accordance with the predominant work ethic, time free of work should be utilized for the recreation of expended labour power, then work-less time, precisely because it is a more appendage of work, is severed from the latter with puritanical zeal" (Adorno 2001: 189).

Therefore, the division between work and leisure is an arbitrary one, with the widespread nature of the division obscuring young people's true motives for working. Even in definitions of work used by the U.S. Department of Labor, which reflect the popular understanding of the concept, work is an activity done outside the home for pay: An economic motive is assumed. In the popular culture, as explicated by Adorno, work and leisure have been seen as mutually exclusive: Work is the role in which the individual functions as a producer, while leisure is the role in which the individual functions as the consumer. For young people, the traditional role of work is filled by school, while what is technically a job takes on social, rather than economic, value. Throughout this book, I explore this intertwined relationship between work, leisure, and consumption for young people.

What the Young People Think: The Affluent Worker

When I ask Kimberly, an eighteen-year-old student, to describe what an average worker at the Coffee Bean is like, she tells me:

> A typical [Coffee Bean] employee usually comes from a middle-class background or higher-class background. If in the higher class, they would probably be in their late teens and early twenties, as they are college students trying to get money for school costs. Also, while an employee here could have a family, typically they would be single or have a girlfriend or a boyfriend. Gender here is usually evenly split; however, most employees [here] are white. Most often, the people who work here are car owners, probably live in an apartment. . . . A typical [fast-food] employee is almost certainly a teenager who has the job for extra cash to buy things like CDs, car[s], and such. The typical worker here would work for minimum wage or something close to that. Unlike a [Coffee Bean] employee, a [fast-food] employee can be of any race or ethnic background. Typically, these employees are of a lower-income household, because if they were of higher income, they would not be working there in the first place. Most likely the typical employee here is of lower education or has something like a high school diploma.

Even though both the job she has and the fast-food job she looks down on are low-paying, low-skill, standardized, routine jobs, Kimberly and the other young people I spoke with make a sharp distinction between them. Youth working at more upscale establishments are associated with a more affluent lifestyle, and socioeconomic status plays a big role in getting these jobs. These jobs are not simply a means to an end: Even if they pay similar wages, they are very different, and the people working at these places are socially, economically, and demographically very different from each other. To borrow from

Proust, work becomes "the infinitely varied art of making distances." Retail and service jobs that were classified as homogenous units are in fact branded and are infinitely different in the conceptions of young people. Coffee Bean, just like the upscale products it sells to a more affluent consumer, also offers jobs for a more affluent group of workers. The young people I spoke with have told me that youth labor is much different today. Many economically disadvantaged youth who need these jobs are either shut out of the labor force or they are stuck in undesirable jobs, whereas affluent youth dominate the workforce for the desirable positions. Many work at Coffee Bean to be associated with cool brands, to hang out with their friends, and to get discounts. Throughout this book, I explore work from the perspective of these and other young people and I aim to capture their lived experience of work.

The Plan of This Book

In Chapter 2, I start at the beginning of the job experience: the job search. First, I focus on the actual jobs and explore how brands are marketed to young people. Using interviews with young people about their experiences with job searches, job interviews, and job advertisements, I explore how corporations market these jobs to affluent teenagers as fun and cool, as if they are products. Available jobs are branded as leisure activities young people, pastimes that are fun rather than work. Physically demanding, low-paying jobs at odd shifts are marketed as glamorous products to relatively affluent young people in the suburbs, who could not care less about the monetary gratifications and fringe benefits. Oftentimes, affluent young people have an advantage in getting these jobs, as they fit the "look" of the corporation.

Second, I turn my attention to how young people find jobs, contrasting their experiences with existing theories on how adults find jobs. Unlike traditional methods of finding jobs, such as using networks, contacts, or job ads, young people "shop for jobs" the same way that they shop for products. Rather than focus on the economic benefits and working conditions, they make work decisions based on brands they consume. Many also choose to work in places where their friends work. These methods highlight the unique nature of the young labor force in the United States and emphasize the social role and the social function of work for young people.

In Chapter 3, I develop a theoretical framework for why so many affluent, suburban young people work part-time. For that purpose, this chapter traces the work experience from the perspective of the employees. In doing so, I highlight the context of disconnected suburbs as the background of social poverty. I show that it is not economic poverty but social deprivation and lack of connections that drive young people to work.

Using in-depth ethnographic interviews with young people as well as a detailed ethnography at a national coffee chain, I explore the social meaning of these jobs from the perspective of the actors. This chapter examines how workplaces provide a common social space for young people: a social center in centerless suburbs. They provide social spaces to enable social interaction and create opportunities to meet new people. This chapter also shows how this work becomes a branded experience.

By working at different corporations, young people become associated with those brands. Therefore, working in more socially desirable corporations provides social status, and the work experience is consumed as a social product.

Although previous chapters focus on the United States, in Chapter 4, I situate the unique case of American suburban youth employment in a global context. This chapter has two goals. First, I aim to contextualize the detailed, qualitative findings of previous chapters using more generalizable, large-scale data from the World Values Study. Using the WVS, I explore the reasons for labor force entry for young people in the United States. Second, I compare the United States with other industrialized countries. This chapter shows that the American labor force is unique for several reasons. First, the practice of young people working while still in school is far from ubiquitous: It is not as widespread in other industrialized countries. In addition to high labor-force participation, the current demographic composition of the youth labor force is also unique. In the United States, the youth labor force is dominated by affluent youth, while in other industrialized countries, economically disadvantaged youth are more likely to work. Most importantly, in this chapter, I show that motives behind the decision to work are different. In the United States, young people work for social reasons, such as meeting new people. In other industrialized countries, economic factors determine young people's decision to work.

These social functions of work described in the previous chapters are linked to another central sphere of young people's lives: schools. In Chapter 5, I explore the role and perception of schools in providing social contacts and social space for suburban youth. First, using the WVS, this chapter shows that one of the reasons young people choose to work in the United States as opposed to other industrialized countries is due to their lack of confidence in the education system. Parallel with the in-depth interviews, many young people believe that schools do not fulfill the social function they previously did in providing a common social space, common vocabulary, and opportunities to meet new people. Many young people perceive schools as large, impersonal, bureaucratic organizations, where they fail to meet new people. Many after-school hobbies and extracurricular activities are not considered to be cool enough for image-conscious youth. Work provides not just a common social space but a branded one. Based on large-scale, cross-national data as well as in-depth interviews, this chapter explores youth perception of schools and the declining confidence in the education system in preparing young people socially as well as the consequences of the perceptions of schools in the United States.

In Chapter 6, I focus on inequalities in the workplace, discussing the effects of socioeconomic status and race on the youth labor force. Currently, socioeconomic status and race play a great role in young people's access to good jobs and desirable workplaces. Many economically disadvantaged youth—the ones who may need to work to support themselves and their families—have difficulty finding jobs. While affluent teenagers flock to these jobs, less affluent teens are kept out of the workforce, finding themselves in competition with a larger pool of applicants. Furthermore, many employers prefer more affluent teenagers with more fashionable self-presentations. In this chapter, I discuss the role of race and socioeconomic status in hiring and aesthetic labor considerations.

In Chapter 7, I focus on another form of inequality in the youth labor market: gender inequality. Young people of both sexes work while still in school in seemingly comparable jobs. These equal labor-force participation rates, perhaps, project the image of a "gender utopia," in contrast with the gendered workplaces of adult labor. In fact, in the service sector, young women are seen as better employees who have more soft skills and are less likely to cause problems. On close examination, though, we see that the youth labor force is where the gender wage gap originates. Using the National Longitudinal Study of Youth and in-depth interviews, this chapter shows that when teenagers are twelve and thirteen, they experience gender equality in pay, but when they reach fourteen and fifteen, the first gender wage gap emerges, and it only widens with age. The youth labor force offers laboratory-like conditions to study gender inequality in pay, because it naturally controls for many typical explanations of the gender wage gap. These explanations of the gender differences in pay point to differences in human capital, such as differences in education, experience, and skills, particularly in relation to maternal and domestic duties of women. By focusing on twelve- to sixteen-year-olds, we can eliminate such confounding variables, because boys in that age group rarely have more education and experience than girls do. Furthermore, maternal and domestic duties are not applicable to the majority of the girls in that age group. In this chapter, I show that although individual, human capital differences play little role in the pay gap, the types of jobs young people are employed in are central in determining how much they are paid. Girls tend to be concentrated in freelance jobs, while boys tend to be concentrated in more formal jobs. Even within the same types of jobs, girls tend to be concentrated in more traditionally feminine jobs that require more social skills, while boys are concentrated in more masculine jobs that pay more. Overall, in this chapter, I discuss the role of early work experience as the source of gender inequality.

Finally, in Chapter 8, I discuss the implications of my findings for future research and explore the new direction of youth employment. In this chapter, I also discuss the effects of the recent economic recession on youth employment and offer predictions for its future.

2

"Would You Like an Application with Your Coffee?"

Right after he settled into his dorm room, Josh, a nineteen-year-old student, went into town to "shop for a job." His rule was that if he liked to shop there, he would also like to work there. He walked around the college town, looking for stores where he shops. After a day of shopping for jobs, he walked into the coffee shop. As he was buying the coffee at the counter, he started chatting with Jenna, the shift manager. Jenna, like Josh, was a nineteen-year-old college student; they even went to the same school. After chatting for a few hours, Jenna asked Josh whether he wanted a job at the coffee shop. As Josh put it, "I came to get coffee but got a job with it." Even after changing his major from social science to theater, Josh continued to work at the coffee shop.

Monica, another college student, found her job in a different way. Monica had no intention of getting a job. Growing up in a gated community in an affluent suburb as the only daughter of doctor parents, she did not *need* to work. She did not think she would need to get a job to meet people, because she went to a nearby college. However, when she started school, she discovered that the large, impersonal classes provided little opportunity for meeting new people. She also had trouble getting together with her old friends, because most of her friends were working after school. "They [her friends] had no time anymore," she remembered. After school, her friends went directly to their jobs, and that is where they socialized. So, if she wanted to see them, she would need to get a job in the same place; she added, "Besides, it [work] was all they ever talked about." The workplace not only became a social center; it also provided a common vocabulary and dictated the topics of discussion. Without being a part of that environment, Monica felt left out of conversations. To hang out with her friends, she joined them in working at the same branch of the coffee shop. From that point, every day after school, you could find

Monica there. Sometimes she was scheduled to work, and sometimes she came to hang out with her friends who were working that day. Whenever possible, she tried to coordinate her shifts so that she was working with her friends.

Josh and Monica offer two examples of typical paths to youth work. They did not send out résumés or search for work with the aid of public or private agencies, unions, or—possibly—schools; they either shopped for jobs or found them through their close friends.

"If I Shop There, I'll Work There"

During my freshman year in college, I remember searching for jobs myself. As a sociology major, I was already tutoring small children in English as a second language and mathematics. Despite the flexible hours and good pay, I wanted a "real job." Many of my friends had already started working in employee-type jobs and started comparing brands. I, too, wanted to work at a "cool place." In Turkey, at the time, American chains, such as McDonald's and Pizza Hut, were desirable places to work, because they represented Westernization and modernity. That is how I chose my first nonfreelance summer job, interning at the Coca-Cola Company. I was overjoyed to work for minimum wage and be at the office all day, giving up my entire summer vacation. I was working for Coca-Cola and I proudly carried my backpack with the corporate logo all summer. I gladly gave up my flexible, higher-paying job as a freelance tutor to be a part of a global brand. In fact, when I applied, I did not even inquire about the pay or time commitment.

Many young people today approach the job-hunt process similarly. Most of the young people I interviewed said they did not search through job ads or rely on secondary sources, but rather approached the jobs directly like products; only three people out of the seventy-three I interviewed in 2012 said they used job ads, and two out of those three said the ads were on social-networking sites. Their initial encounters with jobs show a fluid definition of consumption and work. Most young people said they did not really think of the objective benefits of the job so much. In the adult labor market, objective concerns, such as the pay, benefits, job requirements, amount of work, and work hours, typically play a substantial role when an applicant is deciding where to work, but this does not seem to be the case among young people. Most of the young people I interviewed focused instead on the brand. Shopping at a particular store was a central consideration in determining the place of employment. Bigger chains and franchises were more desirable than mom-and-pop stores or freelance work. Although some of the participants in my study acknowledged that the demands of the job might be lower and the working conditions a little easier in individually owned mom-and-pop stores or in freelance work, they still preferred to work in larger retail establishments that had desirable brand associations. Because of child labor laws, young people are allowed to work in freelance settings—babysitting, doing yard work, and the like—before they are allowed to work in employee-type jobs. Once they are able to find employee-type jobs, many leave freelance work altogether. This trend also points to the centrality of social concerns in young people's job hunt: Freelance work may offer better working conditions and even better pay on a per-hour basis than corporate jobs, but it is generally solitary, denying any chance at socialization at work and lacking any sort of branding. Even within these corporate employee-type jobs, some brands are more popular. In the interviews, such brands as Apple, Anthropologie, Aeropostale, Hollister, Forever 21, Urban Outfitters, Coffee Bean, Express, Gap, Swatch, Mac, Sephora, American Apparel, Victoria's Secret, Bath and Body Works, Abercrombie and Fitch, and American Eagle were mentioned as the most desirable employers. These were followed by niche markets of Barnes and Noble and Best Buy. Based on subculture and interest, music stores, bookstores, tattoo parlors, and skating and skiing shops were also deemed valuable to people within various subcultural groups.

Positions at these employers generally have comparable pay and working conditions, but among young people, they were seen as very different. What separates the desirable places to work from the undesirable ones? Just like products, the jobs themselves are *branded*. The branding is not intended only for the consumers; the branded jobs are also marketed to the potential employees. Even when working conditions are comparable, many young people gravitate toward jobs with better branding. Just as consumption of these brands distinguishes them from others, working at these jobs creates a similar association with these brands. Monica told me she would not work just anywhere. Individually owned family businesses or mom-and-pop places were out of the question when she was looking for jobs. Although many small businesses may have offered more money and easier working conditions, Monica said, "It's not the same." In addition to not having a large group of her friends also working there, these small businesses did not have the right brand or the desirable image she was looking for. She told me that the place where she did choose to work was just "cool."

When I asked why she preferred one brand over the other when they offered comparable wages and working conditions, Brianna, a nineteen-year-old college student, told me, "[I] shop there." Like Josh, her motto was "If I shop there, I'll work there." Many other interviewees echoed the same sentiment. Shopping at the store and being a regular consumer is seen as an advantage in getting a job, with even some of the existing employees, who may do the interviews and see frequent customers as good potential employees. Throughout the interviews, young workers repeated, "I go there a lot," "I shop there," and other similar statements when asked why they chose to work in a particular place. Another nineteen-year-old college student, Lucy, told me that in her job search, she only went to the places where she was a regular customer and asked which businesses were hiring. She remembered having to wait for a few weeks to get her current retail job, where she had worked fourteen hours in the week prior to our interview, including nights and weekends, but in her view, it was worth the wait. She said that that particular retail job was the only place she could be happy working. Although studies of adult employment do not even include past visits to a company as an option for why someone would take a job, this scenario came up again and again in my interviews. Abby, an eighteen-year-old female student at a private college, said that she decided that she wanted to work at the particular department store while she was shopping there. In fact, she told me shopping at the store was a way for her to "find the job." That particular high-end department store, where she sold designer handbags, was the only place she would even consider working. Even when she did not buy anything there, she would regularly check out the new merchandise and window-shop there. She was already spending so much time and money at the store that she decided to start working there. As an employee, she proudly carried the shopping bags that the department store used and was happy to be seen there and associated with the brand. The particular brand, or image, of the store was an essential factor in her decision to work there. If she did not like the store, she would not have been able spend forty-five hours a week working there, including nights and weekends, during a particularly busy sale season for the store. Although she came from a family with annual income of more than $100,000, she believed that her job was worthwhile.

Julian, a nineteen-year-old student, said his work decision was based on his consumption habits as well. He noticed that he worked out at his gym so often that he decided to work there. The ubiquitous gym chain, where he had worked for thirty hours in the week prior to our interview, including his weekends, was already where he spent his leisure time with his friends. Therefore, his consumption habits justified his work decision.

This is only one supply side of the issue. Sophia, a twenty-year-old college student majoring in liberal arts, told me that management at a fashionable retail chain where she worked part-time saw being a consumer of its product and shopping at its store as a major advantage in hiring decisions. In fact, management had recently hired a part-time student employee who was a regular shopper: "She used to come to the store with her mother every week." She spent close to $2,000 one month in clothing and all the staff knew her. When she applied for the job, she was hired immediately: She knew the products well and was committed to the brand. Many corporations take the same approach when hiring employees.

In these job searches, we see a blurred division of leisure and work. Instead of showing a traditional binary opposition between work and leisure, these concepts are intertwined. Enjoying the product and shopping at the store emerge as prerequisites for getting a job in some cases and provide a great advantage for many applicants in the job market.

The second dominant job-selection method young people mentioned was to take jobs where their close friends worked. Mark Granovetter (1983) points out the "strength of weak ties" in referring to the type of relationships people have to help them find jobs. According to his research, professional workers do not find jobs through their close friends, but through their acquaintances and people they are associated with through work. Even though such relationships might appear to be "weak" or distant, these weak acquaintances are the means by which people find employment. Unlike Granovetter's professionals, young people emphasize finding jobs not through mere acquaintances but rather through friends, particularly their *close* friends. According to Fiona, a twenty-year-old college student, working with friends made all the difference. She found her job at a sit-down restaurant chain, where she had worked for the six months at the time of our interview, through her closest friends. Most of her friends were working at the same branch of the restaurant already, and they vouched for her. In addition, she was friends with the supervisor, so she did not even have to go through a formal interview process. She said that with her busy schedule of school and two extracurricular activities, she would not have time for her friends if they did not work together. In the week prior to the interview, she said that she did not have any time to see her parents or her grandparents and had spent only five hours doing homework. However, she said that she had socialized with her friends for the twenty hours she had worked over the past week. Her time at work *was* her leisure time with friends.

These findings mirror the national trends. Based on the national sample used by the National Longitudinal Study of Youth, similar patterns emerge for young people between the ages of sixteen and nineteen. As shown in Table 2.1, youth employ two dominant methods to find jobs. The most frequently used method involves contacting the employer/business directly about potential openings (not responding to a "help wanted" ad), with 41 percent of all youth finding jobs this way. The other method, which is almost equally widespread, involves finding jobs through friends (39 percent). These findings show that the descriptions given by the participants in my study are fairly typical. Methods often used in the adult labor market, such as contacting public or private agencies, school or university employment centers, unions, or companies that have placed job ads do not appear to be widely used methods among youth. In fact, none of these methods was practiced by more than 1 percent of the sample. Even responding to job ads was rare, with less than 1 percent of respondents saying that they had done so.

This is not to say that young people ignore job ads entirely. Twenty-eight percent of all youth report passively viewing job ads as a method they have

TABLE 2.1 Methods of Finding Jobs for All Youth
in the United States

	All Youth
Contact employer directly	.410
Contact public agency	.067
Contact private agency	.016
Contact friends/relatives	.390
Contact school/university	.080
Answer job ads	.098
Contact professional organizations	.003
View ads/Passive job search	.283

Source: U.S. Department of Labor, National Longitudinal Study
of Youth 1997.
Note: All numbers are reported as proportions. $N = 875$.

employed in a typical job search. However, this passive review of ads fails to
translate into active inquiries. Although many report looking at the ads, less
than 1 percent identifies answering these ads as a method of finding jobs.
Therefore, ads act as a means of obtaining information about available jobs,
but not as a means to get a job. This finding parallels my ethnographic observations of how youth, on average, find jobs: by either seeing the jobs like products and directly approaching them or by working at the places where their
friends work.

This is not to say there are no inner differences in finding jobs. If we divide
the youth sample into subcategories based on race, gender, and class, some
small differences emerge. As shown in Table 2.2, white workers are more likely
to directly approach employers than nonwhite workers (42.2 percent and 40.2
percent, respectively), while nonwhite workers tend to be more likely to find

TABLE 2.2 Methods of Finding Jobs for Youth in the United States,
by Race

	Nonwhite	White
Contact employer directly	.402	.422
Contact public agency	.080	.050
Contact private agency	.014	.019
Contact friends/relatives	.402	.374
Contact school/university	.094	.061
Answer job ads	.086	.114
Contact professional organizations	.004	.003
View ads/Passive job search	.241	.340

Source: U.S. Department of Labor, National Longitudinal Study of Youth 1997.
Note: All numbers are reported as proportions. $N = 875$.

TABLE 2.3 Methods of Finding Jobs for Youth in the United States, by Gender

	Male	Female
Contact employer directly	.416	.405
Contact public agency	.051	.084
Contact private agency	.018	.014
Contact friends/relatives	.420	.359
Contact school/university	.067	.093
Answer job ads	.099	.098
Contact professional organizations	.005	.002
View ads/Passive job search	.260	.307

Source: U.S. Department of Labor, National Longitudinal Study of Youth 1997.
Note: All numbers are reported as proportions. N = 875.

jobs through friends (40.2 percent and 37.4 percent, respectively). There are similarly slight gender differences as well (see Table 2.3). Male and female youth are equally likely to approach jobs directly (41.6 percent and 40.5 percent, respectively), but male youth are more likely to find jobs where their friends work (42.0 percent and 35.6 percent, respectively).

These differences appear to be slight, but differences based on socioeconomic status play a big role (see Table 2.4). Youth from the highest income quartile are the most likely group to contact employers directly (53.7 percent, as opposed to 36.8 percent to 42.2 percent in other income quartiles). This shows that youth from the most affluent backgrounds are the most likely to shop for jobs, whereas less economically advantaged youth resort to other means of finding work that may not be so dependent on the perceived brand of the workplace.

TABLE 2.4 Methods of Finding Jobs for Youth in the United States, by Income

	Lowest Quartile	Second Quartile	Third Quartile	Highest Quartile
Contact employer directly	.422	.368	.377	.537
Contact public agency	.090	.063	.057	.052
Contact private agency	.030	.006	.019	.022
Contact friends/relatives	.349	.385	.390	.299
Contact school/university	.090	.103	.050	.060
Answer job ads	.084	.098	.113	.119
Contact professional organizations	.012	.000	.000	.000
View ads/Passive job search	.271	.316	.283	.291

Source: U.S. Department of Labor, National Longitudinal Study of Youth 1997.
Note: All numbers are reported as proportions. N = 875.

Perspective of the Employers:
Why Hire Affluent Youth?

Jules, a twenty-year-old female student, recounted:

> During my senior year in high school, I decided to find my first job.
> Many of my friends were working at the mall close to my home. So
> I decided to find a job in retail [at the same mall]. I applied for a job
> at Seymour&Smith,[1] because I knew people that worked there, and
> I also really liked their clothing. Working at Seymour&Smith gave one
> status back in the day. It was cool and the hottest place. If you told
> someone you worked at Seymour&Smith, they held you to a different
> standard. . . . Since this was my first job, I had nothing on my résumé.
> The hiring process for this job was fairly easy. I showed up to a group
> interview and answered meaningless questions. I still remember being
> asked, "What is your favorite animal?" There were no questions like
> "How would you contribute to our company?" "Do you see yourself
> working here in five years?" . . . I had no experience. All I had was per-
> sonality and appearance; that's all I brought to the table.

Mary Gatta's (2011) ethnographic study of high-end boutiques and clothing stores documents that employers in such stores emphasize having the right
look. The first job interview described is typical of those that many young
people undergo. Unlike in traditional jobs, job experience, skills, and education have little place in the hiring process. Many young people I interviewed
agreed that their interviews included little discussion of their education, experience, or skills. Jenna remembered that in her initial interview, they talked
about her favorite music, consumption habits, and hobbies. She did not find
this line of questioning strange: She believed that by asking about hobbies and
consumption habits, an employer could learn more about a person. When she
interviewed Josh, she also asked about his favorite band (Radiohead), as she
believed this information helped capture employees with the right look and
personality.

Today, many service sector jobs base their hiring decisions on the images
that potential employees project. Working in the service sector involves selling
not only your labor but also your personality and emotions during your shift.
In *The Managed Heart* (1983), Arlie Russell Hochschild talks about emotion
work, where workers are expected to adopt the appearance and language of the
corporation instead of expressing their own. After all, corporations are selling
not just products but also images and lifestyles.

---

[1] The name of the clothing store was changed.

Jenna, the supervisor who hired Josh, later remembered the day she met him. She said that with his piercings, tattoos, and Radiohead T-shirt, he looked like a cool person: the type of person whom she would want to hang out with. After she saw his theater mask–shaped accessories and chatted with him about his passion for acting as she served his coffee, she realized they shared very similar interests and asked him whether he would consider working at the coffee shop. "You always want cool people to work here," she told me. As she remembered, he had the "right vibe." His previous work experience (limited) and job-related skills (also limited) were not relevant to the conversation.

An overwhelming majority of corporations are selling not simply a service but a certain *branded* service. Employees can be trained in the actual conduct of the job, but it is much harder to train someone to project the desired image, so finding someone with the right image becomes the employer's main focus. From coffee to clothing, more and more corporations are marketing not just their products but the type of experiences, lifestyles, and statuses that consumers would like to capture. An integral part of the experience is the employee, who serves as the face of the corporation in the service sector. This recent trend has put different demands on the potential employees,

> lead[ing] to the development of what is termed "aesthetic labour," involving the manner in which employees are expected to embody the product in industries such as service and hospitality. . . . This labour refers to the hiring of people with corporeal capacities and attributes that favorably appeal to customers' senses and which are organizationally mobilized, developed and commodified through training, management and regulation to produce an embodied style of service. As a part of this process of embodiment, employees are expected to both demonstrate soft-skills associated with personality and attitude to "look good" and "sound right." (Nickson et al. 2011: 69)

In this case, Josh was a perfect fit for the coffee shop. He looked good and sounded right: His appearance, clothes, interests, and taste in music coincided with the image of the corporation, as least as it had been internalized by the other workers already there.

The young people I interviewed at Coffee Bean agreed that the coffee shop had a look and personality, with mostly white, middle-class, affluent youth working there. Matt, a nineteen-year-old college student, told me, "A typical [Coffee Bean] employee is usually a person who seems experienced and wants to be there and definitely not a little kid or someone who is incompetent. They tend to be nice and want to make the experience a convenient one. They are normally knowledgeable and very presentable, because they are always in uniform and always looking perfectly groomed. They act like they are classier and upper class, because they kind of are." In Matt's view, the coffee-shop workers not only had a "look" but had a look that was based on their economic status.

Also present in Matt's description of Coffee Bean's employees was the young people's desire to work there and their enthusiasm for the brand. Instead of simply tolerating the work experience for the money, the employees seemed to genuinely enjoy their jobs, something reflected in young workers' interactions with the customer. What Matt noticed was that the coffee shop, like many corporations, tried to hire workers who were excited to be there. After all, they would sell not just coffee but the coffee *experience*. Workers who wanted to spend time there would theoretically inspire the customers to want to spend time there as well.

Typically, service sector employees have been characterized as inter-changeable workers reciting scripted texts and performing automated routines while wearing identical uniforms (Leidner 1993; Ritzer 2000). However, these uniform, predictable routines no longer describe much of the service and retail job market. Many higher-end brands are moving away from this traditional model into branding and marketing an "experience." Even when many fran-chises look identical in all locations, they try to make it seem as though each store is individual, unique, and custom decorated. Recent research refers to this trend as the style labor market. Dennis Nickson, Chris Warhurst, and Eli Dutton (2004), in the context of Glasgow, identify a trend for cities to rein-vent, brand, and market themselves as postindustrial with a vibrant leisure experience. Today, many high-end restaurants, boutiques, retailers, cafés, and bars have adopted similar strategies to attract customers (Gatta 2011).

Parallel with the style labor trend, recent research points to an emerging heterogeneity in the labor market (Gatta 2011; Glazer 1993; Tannock 2001). Because many employers are looking for specific types of employees, retail and fast-food jobs that once required no skills and experience are becoming increasingly competitive. Looking good and sounding right become central concerns in selecting employees, even for low-paying, low-benefit positions. While service and retail jobs are getting more competitive in hiring, traditional hiring criteria, such as work experience and job-related skills, are becoming less relevant. In remembering Josh's hiring process, Jenna said his previous work experience was not important for her, nor was his experience with coffee. She believed that as a college student, he could easily learn how to make coffee and serve beverages. However, his appearance and persona could not be easily replicated.

In marketing an experience and projecting a lifestyle, the employees become the central actors. Young workers in particular have become essential, sought-after vehicles to create the ultimate product experience. Who better to represent a brand than vibrant, youthful employees—especially ones who are enthusiastic about the product and want to be there? Young people have always been a strong supply of labor for the service sector, but with the rise of the style labor market, they have become the faces of the corporation. As Nickson and colleagues (2011: 69) observe, "Students are deemed to be particularly attractive retail employers due to their flexibility, cheapness, and highly developed soft skills" (see also Canny 2002; Curtis and Lucas 2001; Nickson et al. 2004).

In creating a brand experience, now young workers are required to look and act a certain way to project the desired image (Gatta 2011). According to Nickson, Warhurst, and Dutton (2004), the success of the corporations depends on the images their employees present to the customers. These researchers show that employers expect their employees to "look good and sound right" to help corporations create the desired images and experiences. This focus provides many corporations a competitive edge in the crowded retail and hospitality market (10). The need for potential employees to look good is not at all new to business (Gatta 2011). More than fifty years ago, C. Wright Mills (1956: 175) described the "charmer" type employee, who "focuses the customer less upon her stock of goods than upon herself. She attracts the customer with a modulated voice, artful attire and stance." (1956). Although the general idea is not new, the models of business described here take this a step further. It is not sufficient to look attractive; employees must also look *fashionable*, which requires young people to invest in their clothing, accessories, and makeup. Lynne Pettinger's ethnography of the London retail sector supports this phenomenon. She finds that in the branding of the stores, the appearances and self-presentations of the employees are central. She argues, "Fashion orientation is one facet of brand strategy and the ability to present a fashionable appearance is one of the skills needed by sales assistants in many stores" (Pettinger 2004: 468). Wearing the clothes and accessories sold in the store not only helps create a fashionable image for the corporation but also helps potential customers aspire to the projected lifestyle. Jules remembered (from her retail experience at a high-end clothing store targeting teenagers) that style and looks were very important to the corporation. The employees were allowed to wear jeans, flip-flops, or sneakers, and every week they were asked to wear a certain color polo. The desired look did not include nail polish, tattoos, or piercings. She also observed that everyone working at the retail store appeared physically fit, had straight teeth, and looked very clean-cut.

Attractiveness is important, of course, but so is self-presentation. A young person who works at Abercrombie and Fitch or Hollister would be very different from one who works at Hot Topic. David Wright shows that "physical attractiveness, particular style of dress, and types of physical comportment all contribute to the production of the retail space as meaningful and aesthetically pleasing to the customer" (2005: 305). To borrow from Pierre Bourdieu, bodies of these young workers become the vehicles of retail success. Employee bodies are shaped and molded to project and maintain the image of the corporation. This focus goes beyond projecting a fashionable image. By using the products sold and adopting the company's interests, young employees help create a bond with the customers and relate to them more easily. As Sophia, a social science major, recalled, hiring the teenager who spent so much money at the clothing store where she worked was not just an impulse decision. She believed that the customers would find her more relatable and feel comfortable asking her questions about the products.

Sophia is not alone in making such decisions. In addition to aesthetic considerations, a critical part of creating that image and branding is hiring actual and potential customers. An uncontroversial example of this might come from Wright's ethnography of bookshops, in which he shows that workers in bookstores are expected to read and enjoy books: "People come into book selling because they like books, and in my experience of interviewing several hundred people, the 'click' point in an interview is when you find out that someone is genuinely passionate about reading or books on any level. It might be that they read, it may be that they write or review or anything else, but they'll have an engagement and that's the people worth having. If they don't have that, they are not worth having in a bookshop" (2005: 305–306). In creating the "right look" and projecting the correct image of the brand, using the product goes a long way. In the case of retail, for example, young and attractive workers wearing the products that they are selling help better market the products and create the desired image for the store, the products, and the brand. Acting as consumers also ensures that the workers have in-depth knowledge about the products and can relate to the customers as peers and not just as employees. Such in-depth knowledge of the products also helps create and sustain the enthusiastic work environment. When Josh came into the coffee shop, it was obvious to Jenna that he was a regular. He had a regular drink he always ordered, and he was looking forward to seasonal products. According to Jenna, this kind of knowledge and dedication to the brand cannot be learned or taught.

In some stores, the employees are expected to show not only interest in and knowledge about the products but also an appearance that reflects their interests and knowledge. Prue Huddleston quotes the manager of a sporting goods store, who says, "Like they do the sports themselves, for example, we've got people who are interested in skateboarding, cycling, climbing, that sort of thing, it's a lifestyle thing, and of course, those are the sort of youngsters we get coming here looking for jobs" (2011: 115). In such settings, it is very important for youth to project their brand knowledge. For example, Jacob, who worked at a tattoo shop, said that he was hired because of his elaborate, visible tattoos, which helped him relate to the customers. Oftentimes, new customers asked him about his tattoos, and he thought that his tattoos showed that he belonged in the shop.

An essential component of creating an interest in the brand is through employees' consumption of the product sold. Many clothing stores, for example, require that the employees wear the clothes that they sell. Huddleston (2011) shows that in some designer fashion outlets, even part-time employees are expected to purchase merchandise to wear on the shop floor. Given the high-end nature of many of these brands, and the requirement that they wear current merchandise rather than anything that is from last season or on sale, stores generally offer substantial discounts on merchandise to employees—discounts that, not coincidentally, serve as incentives for customers to become employees. Julie, a nineteen-year-old college student, told me that she had always wanted to work at the popular clothing chain where she was employed because most of her outfits were already from that store. Her interest in the brand was not limited to the required "uniform" for the shop floor: She also wore the clothes outside the workplace. In fact, with the generous store discount she received as an employee, she shopped there even more than she had previously. Jules, too, had similar motives: The 30 percent discount she was getting at the clothing store was a great incentive for her. She loved to shop for clothes, particularly at the clothing store where she worked. Ultimately, though, she said she regretted working there, because she ended up spending so much money on clothes just because she had a discount. In the end, it becomes a vicious cycle: Young people seek jobs where they are already consumers, and their consumption habits are exacerbated by the fact that they work there, with the goods that they already wanted becoming more attractive because of their employee discounts.

The relationship between the worker and the product is complex and requires further research. Pettinger's (2006) work on retail shops, especially, points to a more interactive relationship between workers and the products that they are supposed to be selling. The workers are not simply selling the products but rather mediating the relationship between the customer and the product (Gatta 2011).

Job Ads: Marketing of the Jobs

In 2002, Coffee Bean launched a new advertisement campaign that read, "Would you like an application with your coffee?" Unlike the company's typical ads, which introduced and marketed their new products, such as coffee beans and coffee-flavored beverages, this campaign marketed a different product: a job. The job ad, placed strategically right next to the large selection of stuffed animals, mugs, and gourmet coffee beans along with other products, deviated considerably from the traditional conceptions of a job ad. The text was displayed over a background of a cozy armchair and a table with a coffee cup located conveniently on it. In this way, jobs were marketed as a product that young people could get along with their coffee. Materials marketing other products in the shop, such as baked goods and chocolates, used the same phrase. Furthermore, by featuring the image of the comfortable armchair and the coffee, the ad was trying to associate the job with a particular kind of environment. Yet despite the fact that this was a job advertisement, the ad did not contain any information on the pay rate, working hours, or benefits. In this way, the coffee shop targeted suburban students, marketing these jobs to them almost as a product to be consumed, as an enjoyable experience similar to their experience as customers sipping their caffeinated beverages in the comfortable, oversize armchairs. For the company's potential employees, therefore, money may be of less importance than the experience itself. Not coincidentally, the ad accurately described how Josh got his job at the coffee shop: with his coffee.

Employers' desire to attract certain kinds of young people is reflected in many of today's job ads targeting young people, especially in part-time retail and service jobs. To capture the marketing of jobs from the perspective of the corporations, I collected a variety of job ads from stores mentioned by young people as desirable places to work for the past year. Over four months straddling 2011 and 2012, I visited the ten largest malls in New Jersey, located throughout the state in different suburban locations. Some of these malls have all the familiar shops located in malls across the country; at least one is known for high-end shops, including several clothing and accessory shops where the average purchase exceeds one thousand dollars. Over the course of these months, I systematically visited these malls during different times to collect job advertisements displayed on shop windows. To eliminate seasonal bias, I included all seasons as well as holiday and nonholiday employment. These job ads are important, because they reflect the attitudes and views of the employers and corporations in terms of how they see these jobs. The visual and verbal cues are also valuable, as they are the first factors that the potential employees—especially students—see when they are looking to apply for these jobs, and are therefore essential in defining the social meaning of these jobs. Because of the substantial overlap in the stores within these malls, the resulting data set consists of approximately 100 corporate-produced employment display ads (ads that were obviously created by the individual stores, some of them fairly crude, were not included). Limited hiring due to the continuing economic recession may be driving down the number of ads seen, but the goal of the data collection was to capture a cross-section, a task best done by completing the process over the shortest possible time frame. These ads were then coded on the basis of their content, especially how the job was marketed. Mention of discounts, fashion, opportunity to hang out with friends, fun, coolness of the brand, and monetary considerations, such as pay, benefits, opportunity for advancement, and flexibility, were the major coding categories.

Among these ads, only a small number mention pay, benefits, working conditions, or other economic concerns. Four common themes emerge from this detailed content analysis of job advertisements.

First, just like the 2012 Coffee Bean advertisement, many of the ads emphasize the importance of friends and hanging out with them. One of the job ads reads, "What is it like to work at Coffee Bean? It is a lot like working with friends. For one thing, the people who work here are not employees, we're partners." Instead of working conditions, pay, benefits, or advancement opportunities, the central focus in the job ad is the opportunity to work with friends: The workplace provides an opportunity to socialize. Similarly, some of the ads market the friendly environment and the family-like atmosphere at the store: "Join Our Fashion Family," a Banana Republic ad reads. Some stores emphasize the enjoyable social environment by evoking images of fun. A Spencer's ad from 2012 emphasizes this aspect of working at its store by saying, "Join the Party!" Apparently, working at this store is just like going to a party. In the interviews, young people repeatedly said that they were looking to spend time with their friends at work; these workplaces want to provide that opportunity.

Second, job ads emphasize the coolness and desirability of the brand. A 2011 Old Navy recruitment ad says, "Cool jobs are in our jeans." The products, the ad is saying, are good, so the job is cool. Therefore, if you like their jeans, you should take a job there, so you can be as cool as the jeans are. Many of the ads specifically mention the fashionability of the products. A 2012 ad from Old Navy says, "If you love fashion and fun, you're in the right place." By doing so, the corporation markets the store as not only selling a fashionable brand that young people will be associated with by working there but also being a fun place to work and hang out in their free time. Some stores emphasize that these jobs as fashionable. A 2012 job ad for H&M tells prospective employees, "A great job is always in fashion." In other words, we're fashionable, and if you work here, you can be, too.

Third, the job advertisements market the job by drawing similarities to the products sold in the store. A 2012 Old Navy ad creates parallels between the job and the products the corporation sells. "Try us on," the ad reads, suggesting that young people can try on the job just as they try on the clothes in the store. This parallel between the product and the job appears in ads from numerous clothing stores. A lingerie store, Soma, advertises a job in a 2012 ad by saying, "We're looking for a perfect fit." Similarly, an Ann Taylor ad from the same year uses a similar approach, saying that its store is "The Perfect Fit." Cotton On's 2012 ad also makes the comparisons between the person and the product: "I Am Cotton On, Are You? Be a Part of the Crew! Join Us Today!"

The similarities drawn between the job and the product reinforce the marketing of the jobs and the perceived link between the products and the workers: If you like consuming these goods, you will like selling them.

Finally, in line with the importance of discounts, as discussed in the interviews, many of the ads refer to employee discounts while ignoring other benefits. This goes back to the idea that consumption and work are intertwined. Many young people say that being a consumer of the brand is the first step to working for the company. By working there, young people are entitled to discounts, which further bolster their consumption habits. Express, for example, emphasizes the employee discounts in a 2012 ad that reads, "We're looking for people with style, people who love fashion and people who want an Express discount. We're looking for people like you."

As discussed above, stores may have an interest in attracting workers who already like and use their products. "Must Love Make-up," a 2012 Bare Escentuals ad reads. Similarly, a 2012 Ann Taylor ad asks potential workers whether they "Have a passion for fashion?" A DSW ad from 2012 simply says, "now hiring shoe lovers." Arden B, in a 2012 ad, similarly looks for fashionable people, asking mall shoppers to "Join the Arden B fashion team." Sephora is more blatant in a 2012 ad, in which it recruits for a "Dream Job. Obsessed with beauty?" The most recent 2012 H&M gets right to the point: "You Obviously Like Shopping Here, Why Not Work Here?"

In many instances, the corporations market these service and retail jobs as being more glamorous than they almost certainly are. A Finish Line recruitment ad from 2012 shows the picture of two basketball players and tells viewers that it is "Always Looking for Talent." The parallel being made between working in a sporting goods store in the mall and playing for a professional basketball team is questionable at best, but the message is clear. NY & Co uses a similar message in a 2012 recruitment ad that shows a fashionably dressed Manhattanite and reads, "New York is hiring."

By working at these stores, young people can become associated with cool brands, and by receiving employee discounts, they can continue to shop there, creating a whole new level of brand loyalty.

Although employees' brand loyalty may not be as strong as those customers who take on corporate tattoos, working does strengthen this loyalty and provides an insider status to the workers. If customers are trying to be associated with a desired brand, workers are associated with it even more strongly. As a 2012 Cache recruitment ad puts it, "Cache Careers: The only thing that is more amazing that shopping at Cache is working at Cache."

Overall, the content analysis of the job ads shows that the job ads that target young people portray the positions marketed as cool, fashionable, and desirable. By working, young people will have the opportunity not only to associate with cool brands but also to hang out with their friends.

The Hiring Process

For many retail and service jobs, hiring today is based on appearance, fashion, and social skills (Gatta 2011). Nickson and colleagues (2004) demonstrate that among the employers in their study, 99 percent said that social and interpersonal skills were key; 98 percent emphasized self-presentation. In the same study, only 48 percent of the employers mentioned skills as being important factors in their hiring decisions. Knowledge and skills for these kinds of positions are job and brand specific. Many employees will be trained on the job anyway; therefore, the ability to carry out job-related tasks takes a back seat to intangibles that cannot be easily learned. Gatta's ethnographic study of high-end retail shops in New Jersey includes in-depth interviews with employers about the characteristics they look for in a job candidate. One employer describes the interview process:

> Usually people will fill out applications in our store. If I am there, I'll take note of my impression of them. If they seem cheerful, fun, animated when speaking to me, full of personality, well-spoken, I will take note of their name. I'll call these people first. . . . When I meet with an applicant the most important part of the conversation is when I am asking them about themselves. They can recite their resume to me, but really being able to carry themselves as a person is more important to me. (Gatta 2011: 58)

This idea that social skills and people skills are more important than the actual résumé resonates in the interviews I conducted with the participants in my study. Some young people I talked with, such as Jenna and Monica, had been involved in the hiring process, not too long after having gone through it themselves when they were hired. They, and others like them, agreed that social and aesthetic considerations were more important than job-related skills. Monica remembered that she had no idea how to make coffee before working at Coffee Bean; she did not even make it at home. That said, it did not take her long to figure out the process once she was hired. Making coffee is exactly the sort of skill that workers can acquire on the job. In fact, according to Monica, it might even be better for job applicants to not know it before being hired so they could learn to do it the correct way on the job. Social and personal skills, however, are harder to learn or change, making the employers' evaluations of these skills more important in their interviews with prospective workers.

All this means that it is essential for employers to be able to quickly evaluate the social and personal skills of prospective workers. Gatta's work shows that much of the hiring process is based on individual "gut feelings" and first impressions. Borrowing from Malcolm Gladwell (2005), she argues that employers make decisions in an instant based on their initial reactions. Gladwell talks about the importance of subconscious impressions and cognitions in making what he calls "two-second blink" decisions. Because first impressions are central in getting these limited positions, many employers make decisions based on the first impression. As Warhurst and Nickson show, much of what the employers are looking for is the style that the corporation wishes to project: "For employers, human capital is no substitute for cultural capital as manifest in deeply embodied dispositions" (2009: 10). However, because such decisions can be considered "blink decisions," there is a great deal of subjectivity in hiring. As Jenna said, when she talked to Josh, she just knew he was a match for the coffee shop. But how can we tell who the right match is?

Although it may seem that such decisions create situations in which otherwise-qualified people are unable to find jobs or are even discriminated against on the basis of seemingly irrelevant factors, some scholars argue that these sorts of decisions are actually democratizing. Unlike differences in education, networks, and work experience, which are relatively more difficult to acquire upon request, aesthetic labor—those personal and social skills that are a vital part of work in these jobs—can technically be acquired. Oftentimes, however, that is a difficult task. Although Warhurst and Nickson acknowledge that a focus on aesthetic labor would not eliminate class distinctions, they advocate training in aesthetic labor as "an appeal for equity and pragmatism" (2009: 11). They argue, "Twenty thousand people are unemployed in Glasgow but there exists 5,500 unfilled jobs. Our contention is that a proportion of those jobs are likely to remain unfilled unless long-term employed people are equipped with aesthetic skills. Such jobs, such as hospitality, clearly demand employees to affect the appropriate role-required body dispositions, adopting 'masks for tasks' or simple 'surface acting,' and the unemployed should be aware of this need" (Warhurst and Nickson 2009: 11).

In a Goffmanian sense, the way the workers present themselves is essential to getting hired. More than experience and education, the workers' self-presentation—whether their clothing, speech, interests, consumption habits, and mannerisms reflect the company's actual or desired image—determines whether they will get a job. Potential employees who use the store's products and have more stylish clothes and hair inevitably have an advantage over those who do not. In that sense, the need for aesthetic labor in the market has helped young people immensely. After all, many corporations are looking for young, eager, happy dispositions. However, not all young people have the same access to these sorts of resources. To borrow from Bourdieu (1984), presentations of self are not devoid of class. Class inequality is often reflected in a person's appearance, speech, and self-presentation. The ability to have fashionable clothes, hair, and accessories, as well as to be a customer of a particular store, is closely tied to the workers' economic backgrounds.

Bourdieu's *habitus* is reflected in the hiring process. Habitus refers to a "set of dispositions, reflexes and forms of behavior people acquire through acting in society" (Bourdieu 2000: 19). Through everyday social interactions and social practices, the rules and behaviors are internalized. When employers make these rapid hiring decisions, they necessarily include a lifelong set of internalized social expectations. These expectations are not devoid of class inequality, but rather act as markers of affluence. For workers, therefore, changing their self-presentations is not as easy as it sounds, and often youth from lower socioeconomic status backgrounds are at a distinct disadvantage. None of this is to say that the hiring process for higher-level positions is not also subject to rapid decision-making processes. In any interview, self-presentation is important. What is different about the jobs I am discussing is that there is no filter of résumés, educational qualifications, or work experience to ensure that all the interviewees are at least minimally qualified. For these young workers, their immediate self-presentation is their only qualification.

For youth from less privileged backgrounds, the meaning of these jobs is different. Although middle-class youth see these jobs as social venues and status markers, many low-income young people need these jobs to help support themselves and their families. But because of the requirements of aesthetic labor, the low-income youth who may need the jobs most have the greatest difficulty getting them. Service sector jobs that used to be available on every street corner are becoming less available to young workers who truly *need* them as more affluent teenagers seek out these jobs for social reasons, and employers, given a choice, would rather higher young people with more desirable self-presentations and fewer demands for wages, benefits, or better working conditions. In her detailed ethnography of inner-city youth, Katherine Newman argues that service sector jobs that were once in abundance are now difficult to come by. She observes, "Jobs, even lousy jobs, are in such short supply that inner-city teenagers are all but barred from the market" (1999: 62). These low-income teenagers are unable to find these jobs for several reasons.

The most obvious reason is that there are simply fewer entry-level jobs available in inner-city regions. Although many businesses were previously located in the cities, recent years have seen many of these jobs relocate to the suburbs. Among the young people I talked with in the suburbs, none complained about a paucity of jobs, pointing instead to how close and abundant they were. Because many of these jobs are selling images and experiences, their efforts are better served by locations in affluent suburbs than in urban areas. This parallels the emergence of the suburbs as the center of many service sector jobs. The physical separation of the jobs from the young people who need them means that many of these low-income teenagers now need to travel to the suburbs to find these jobs, making transportation a major obstacle and potentially giving employers yet another reason not to hire them. Stephanie, a nineteen-year-old college student, told me, "The locations are even different, because Coffee Bean is very selective about the area they put themselves in. I can go to a nice area and find a nice coffee shop . . . yet I can't go to a bad area and find a restaurant I would want to eat in, let alone a coffee shop. So, I guess location has a lot to do with the types of people you get." In Josh's area, there were so many branches of the coffee shop that availability was not even an issue. In fact, if the branch he initially applied to had not worked out, three others were close by.

Second, because many middle-class, affluent teenagers want these jobs for social reasons and status considerations, middle-class self-presentations have become central in the hiring process. Along with aesthetic-labor expectations, many economically disadvantaged youth now feel the need to change their images for job interviews: "If you come to an interview talking that street slang, you lost your chances of getting that job. I think if you want a job, you gotta speak appropriately to the owner, to the employer" (Larry, quoted in Newman 1999: 73). These teenagers have accepted the rules of the game: If they want a job, they have to present themselves like the middle-class youth they are competing against. Even though many economically disadvantaged youth may not be thrilled about the situation, they accept the aesthetic-labor requirements as a part of the hiring process: "Unfortunately in corporate America, you have to talk their language. That's part of life. When you try to get into something, you have to become a part of that organism. You can't get into it being who you are. Once you are in it, you can be what you want to be. But in order to be in it . . . [y]ou gotta become a part of it. How you dress, how you speak, how you present yourself" (William, quoted in Newman 1999: 74). Interestingly, looks become an accepted part of the job and a reflection of personality and character. As William observes, "What my boss looks for . . . she looks at character. She looks at how they present themselves. She looks at how they view things, you know, life themselves, other people" (quoted in Newman 1999: 74). Presentation of self becomes a sign of character, work ethic, and personality. Unfortunately, appearance is often highly correlated with income, and the evaluation of such characteristics is highly subjective.

Although low-income youth understand and accept the rules of aesthetic-labor expectations, not all can achieve the desired results. After all, changing self-presentation is not always cost efficient. To borrow from Erving Goffman, presentation of self in everyday life is like a stage performance, where individuals are like actors putting on a show. The actors have the ability to choose their stage, props, and costumes to determine how they want to present themselves to the intended audience. This performance of self in everyday life bridges the gap between structure and agency. Through changing their images, these young people have the agency to find jobs and transcend structural boundaries. However, their performances are also bound by structural constraints. The "props and costumes" in this case are restricted by the teenagers' socioeconomic status, with affluent youth being better able to put on a performance. Affluent applicants inevitably have access to more fashionable clothes, hairstyles, and accessories. The advantages of socioeconomic status are not limited to these consumption items alone. Class inequality is also reflected in the speech, mannerisms, and general self-presentations of youth. In *Distinction* (1984: 11), Bourdieu argues that "symbolic goods especially those regarded as the attributes of excellence, [as] the ideal weapon in stages of distinction" are often the attributes possessed by the ruling classes. These individual symbolic goods constitute cultural capital. Bourdieu (1984) asserts that differences in cultural capital are not simple lifestyle choices: they reflect class inequality. We rarely think twice about the social significance of such choices as we internalize these cultural markers at a young age.

> These differences in manner constitute a set of secondary properties, revealing different conditions of acquisition and predisposed to receive very different values in the various markets. Knowing that "manner" is a symbolic manifestation whose meaning and value depend as much on the perceiver as on the producer, one can see how it is that the manner of using symbolic goods, especially those regarded as the attributes of excellence, constitutes one of the key markers of "class" and also the ideal weapon in strategies of distinction. (Bourdieu 1984: 66)

In this way, the manner and behavior of the workers are closely tied to their socioeconomic backgrounds.

How Youth See the Jobs and Brands

Young people repeatedly emphasize the importance of the brand over the job itself and over making money. For many suburban teenagers, a job goes beyond making money. It is a way to be associated with a product.

Will, a nineteen-year-old male, pointed my attention to this phenomenon. Referring to Coffee Bean, a brand he perceived as cool and sophisticated, he said, "A typical [Coffee Bean] employee is someone, usually a teenager or an adult in their early twenties, who feels they are more sophisticated for serving overpriced coffee. When they applied for the job, they did not see an opportunity to make money; they saw how popular Coffee Bean is and wanted to be a part of the popular chain of coffee shops. They don't respect small businesses."

Working at desirable stores is an alternative way to consume the same brand and create a brand association. As they are consuming the brand by working there, many young people point to the intertwined relationship between work and consumption. For many young people, consuming the products of their workplaces is essential. Some admit to taking a job just to receive discounts because they enjoy the products so much. As Julie, a twenty-one-year-old political science major told me, "They [workers] get benefits out of working at a place they like. . . . [T]hey maybe can get some free food and drinks."

Opting for jobs with cool brands is not a simple decision of vanity. Many young people I interviewed told me that the part-time jobs *define* people. Jobs function as social markers that are more important than activities and school. Just as they differentiate between jocks and glee club kids, AV club and band kids, they differentiate on the basis of place of employment. Working, as such, is not simply a means to earn money but a marker of identity. Where they work defines them as people. Ashley, a nineteen-year-old female, noticed that people working at the coffee shop have a typical look and personality: "They are artsy, somewhat nerdy. The guys that work there usually play the guitar. Smart people usually work at Coffee Bean." Just by knowing that someone worked at the coffee shop, Ashley attributed many characteristics and interests to them. Although it might appear to be just a job to many adults, for many young people, a job is a social marker that helps define the worker's personality.

Amy, a twenty-one-year-old female, echoed Ashley's sentiment: "The typical Coffee Bean employee is someone who is hardworking and always polite. They tend to be artsy type[s] to make it easier to work in a coffee house environment, where people [who] are interested in arts tend to gravitate." By only knowing someone's place of employment, youth make assumptions about that person's interests (art), coolness (very), and intelligence (smart).

When asked to describe a Coffee Bean employee, here is what some college students said:

They are tree-hugging hippies. They enjoy playing their acoustic guitar or staring in amazement as others play their acoustic guitar. (Noah, twenty-one-year-old male)

Typical Coffee Bean employees are classy hippies who listen to the Grateful Dead and memorize the script to *Rent* and *Rocky Horror Picture Show*. (Eric, twenty-year-old male)

Liberal, artsy, upper to middle class, earring, tattoos, drives a green car, hates the war, and loves trees. (Mike, twenty-year-old male)

Someone who reads books for fun and [is] more on the nerdy side. (Francesca, twenty-year-old female)

They are mellow and not as outspoken. They are informed about different bands and interested in coffee and music. (Emma, eighteen-year-old female)

Most of these young people describe the same person: a worker who has interests in music and art, liberal politics, and intellectualism. The brand becomes inseparable from a type of person. Just by knowing where they work, youth make many assumptions about the workers. Their interests, social and political preferences, and other consumption habits are all deduced from the fact that they choose to work at a specific store. Perhaps more importantly, the workers are selecting these jobs because they believe that the identity of the store is in line with their own identities, a process abetted by the interviewers who are making blink decisions about hiring on the same basis.

In the same interviews, I asked participants in the study about the images presented by other employers. Fast-food chains, especially, came out badly. According to Sean, a twenty-year-old male, "A typical [fast-food] employee is a teenage student of an adult with problems and no education. Most [fast-food] employees are dumb." Instead of thinking that they work at a burger chain for the money, the respondents believed that the young people who work at these chains are inferior in their skills and intelligence. Julie, a nineteen-year-old undergraduate, thought it would be embarrassing to work at these places. I expected her to cite the low pay, the demeaning aspects of the job, or the working conditions, but she mentioned the brand: "They absolutely hate it there, and never admit they work at [a fast-food joint] because that is just embarrassing." For Julie, working at an undesirable brand overlooked structural inequalities of social class and race, but through the brand, she portrayed this inequality as a stylistic choice.

For these young people, the decision about where to work is not about the money but about projecting a certain image to others. Their supposed choice to work at undesirable chains leads other youth to make assumptions about their personalities, intelligence, skills, and social and political views. Being associated with an undesirable brand reflects badly on them, shadowing multiple layers of structural barriers under the disguise of images. The choice of workplace for young people is not about the money and working conditions but is all about the image. Workplace choice obscures multiple layers of inequality and often makes it look like it is a true *choice*. Rather than assume that young people working at such fast-food places do so because they lack other options, many young people assume that they are inferior in skills, intelligence, and qualifications.

End of the Interview: Barriers to Desirable Jobs

When we talk about common trends, it is important to acknowledge that there are inner differences in finding jobs. First, it is possible that there are differences between income groups in terms of the methods used for the job search. It is conceivable that youth from lower-income families, who are more likely to be looking for jobs for economic reasons, would be more likely to use methods neglected by the higher-income youth that have been the focus of this chapter. Getting jobs at the same place as their friends or by shopping for jobs also has implications for the meaning of work for the employed youth. Affluent youth may find work to be an enjoyable activity, like going to the movies, but working in the same job for youth from lower income brackets might be a different experience, leading them to employ different search methods. Instead of "shopping for jobs," getting jobs at the same places as friends, or contacting the employers directly, youth from lower income brackets might opt for methods that yield the highest-paying jobs, such as reviewing and answering job ads or contacting employment agencies or organizations that can aid their job search. Such direct methods would indicate a more monetary-oriented attitude, because getting a well-paying job would be more important than working with friends. It is important to note that despite these slight differences, there is an astonishing similarity in the ways in which youth from different income groups find jobs. Because affluent youth constitute the majority of the youth labor market and the economically disadvantaged find it exceedingly hard to get jobs, it seems that the rules of the labor market are dominated by the affluent workers. As a consequence of the dominance of aesthetic labor in these positions, many young people are unable find jobs. As Warhurst and Nickson (2007) suggest in the context of the United Kingdom, middle-class students are taking away jobs from others who need these jobs. In the United States, these effects are pronounced. Jen, who had worked as a manager at the coffee shop, told me that some people just do not "look right" or do not "fit in." In other words, young people who do not look or sound right, do not come from the right background, or do not wear the right clothes will never be hired or will have great difficulty finding the jobs they would like.

From the perspectives of employers, affluent young people offer a wonderful pool of potential employees. They are flexible workers who do not mind working nonstandard shifts, especially nights and weekends to accommodate their school schedules (Presser 2006). This, in particular, could make them preferable to older workers with families, who might need a predictable work schedule, or even just a predictable number of hours weekly. Many are satisfied with the limited number of hours they work. At the high-end clothing store where she worked, Jules did not get many hours. However, because she liked the environment so much and she did not depend on the money she earned from the store, she did not complain. If she depended on that income, the limited number of hours she received each week would have posed a problem. Affluent young people tend to have more fashionable self-presentations and offer more nuanced soft skills. Many affluent youth also have the economic ability to be consumers of the brand and therefore possess a higher knowledge of it. Furthermore, because they tend to come from more economically affluent backgrounds, they care less about the pay than do teenagers who need these jobs to survive. More economically disadvantaged youth, such as Mason, need to work more hours. Mason, a twenty-one-year-old social science major, resided in a predominantly African American, low-income town. He applied for jobs but had difficulty finding one. Affluent teenagers, on the other hand, use these jobs to see their friends and to align their identities with these brands. Many also admit to taking jobs for the discounts to further their brand consumption. Especially in workplaces that require employees to be dressed in the stores' current offerings, this discount really amounts to a tax on earnings that disadvantaged youth may not be able to afford.

From the perspective of the young people who constitute much of the labor force, we see that searching for a job is like shopping for a product. In finding jobs, working where their close friends work and the brand of the company they work for are more important concerns than pay, benefits, working conditions, and terms of employment. Even the methods by which they find the jobs suggest that they enjoy the brand association or get the jobs to be with their friends—but is that really true? Are American youth getting jobs as a form of recreation, like hanging out with their friends? Whereas this chapter has focused on finding jobs and the importance of being associated with cool brands, Chapter 3 discusses why American youth work and looks at the role of the workplace as a central social space in suburban America.

3

Fun or Exploitation?

The Lived Experience of Suburban Youth Work

People think I do this for the money. "Oh, you are a typical teenager they say: You need a car and a cell phone and clothes and stuff." But ... it's not like that. It's not just to buy stuff. ... I do have stuff, but I don't work here to pay for all that. It's fun, you know. This is where I hang out.

Jenny, a full-time college student, spoke these words to me as she emptied an overstuffed garbage bag at the end of her long shift. Like many young people, Jenny worked at the Coffee Bean after school. She commuted an hour and back every day to work, where she served endless lines of demanding customers, mopped floors, wiped tables, and carried out loads of garbage. In her typical shift, she was asked to follow a detailed script and perform every task according to the "manual." She did all this work for low pay and no benefits.

From the outside, many observers would interpret these working conditions as characteristic of "bad" jobs: Objectivist scholars would note that they are highly mechanized, with minimal skill requirements, low hourly pay, and long shifts. George Ritzer (2000) depicts such service work as "McJobs," boring and dehumanizing, in part because they involve deskilled, routinized labor that largely eliminates employee discretion and creativity. Such jobs are controlled by detailed rules and standardized techniques imposed from above: "From the employee's perspective, McJobs are irrational because they don't offer much in the way of either satisfaction or stability. Employees are seldom allowed to use anything approaching all their skills, are not allowed to be creative on the job. The result is a high level of resentment, job dissatisfaction, alienation, absenteeism, and turnover" (Ritzer 2000: 137).

In *Fast Food, Fast Talk,* Robin Leidner (1993) similarly depicts these jobs as detailed and scripted, leaving the workers with little autonomy or power. Chris Tilly, in his comprehensive study of part-time jobs, *Half a Job: Bad and Good Part-Time Jobs in a Changing Labor Market* (1995), differentiates within part-time jobs. He shows that some good—what he calls "retention"—part-time jobs are filled by skilled employees with higher wages and high productivity rates. However, those part-time jobs that are typically filled by young students are often bad or secondary part-time jobs. Tilly argues, "Secondary part-time workers have low skills and compensation compared to their full-time counterparts, and are immersed in a secondary part-time employment to attract workers, such as housewives and students, who will accept minimal compensation. Secondary part-time jobs are 'bad' part-time jobs" (1995: 48). Similarly, Arne Kalleberg's (2011) study of part-time jobs differentiates within part-time jobs and depicts some part-time jobs as "bad jobs." In either classification system, the jobs that are preferred by young people would be considered the bad ones: part-time jobs with low pay, nonstandard hours, few or no benefits, limited opportunities of growth and promotion, and limited creative input.

Because objectivist scholars assume that such jobs provide little intrinsic satisfaction, the reasons for working have been reduced to economic gratification. That is why many scholars often assume that these "bad" jobs are performed by the economically deprived: Young students working after school, especially under severe conditions, are traditionally thought to be working to supplement their incomes and put themselves through school. Why else would young people want to work under these conditions?

Jenny, like many other students working at the coffee shop I studied, deviated considerably from these preconceptions. Although such jobs have typically been associated with and taken up by the working classes, Jenny and her co-workers, with their fashionable hair styles, designer clothes, trendy accessories, brand-new cars, and smart phones, were far from working class. In fact, according to the U.S. Bureau of Labor Statistics's *Report on the Youth Labor Force* (Herman 2000), a majority of the current youth labor force comprises youth from higher socioeconomic backgrounds. According to the report, only 15 percent of teenagers in the lowest income quartile work, while employment increases substantially as the family income increases.

In both preconceptions and analyses of the youth labor market, the focus has been on the work experience of youth from lower socioeconomic backgrounds. Although the work experience of economically deprived youth is more visible to many researchers—and is a valid and important subject for research—such a perspective overlooks the lived experience of much of the current youth labor force. The perspective of these affluent young workers is also worthy of study: Their experience of what are referred to as "bad" jobs and their perception of this exploitation are often neglected.

Furthermore, bringing in this sometimes-ignored portion of the current labor force provides not only a more comprehensive understanding of the current youth labor force but also a unique opportunity to study motivations to work from the actors' perspective. If, in fact, these "bad jobs" provide *only* economic benefits (and meager ones at that), why would affluent youth take them? This analysis explains how "objective" inequalities are interpreted and justified in the everyday subjective experience of these workers' lives.

This chapter focuses on the lived experience of a large segment of the youth labor force—affluent young workers in suburban America—and looks at the everyday experiences of work from the perspective of the actors as they define and understand their seemingly exploitive occupations. In doing so, I try to show that inequality and exploitation are socially constructed interpretations (rather than inherent meanings) and that scholarly analyses of these concepts can be of benefit if they are based on the everyday perspectives of actors rather than outside observers (see also Gubrium and Holstein 1997; Harris 2000). The everyday perceptions and lived experiences often contribute to exploitation. Therefore, understanding the daily lives from the perspectives of the workers helps unravel why they tolerate potentially exploitative jobs. Such research is also important from an economic perspective, as it focuses on a substantial portion of the labor force filling service sector jobs in America today: affluent, suburban youth. As Tilly (1995) argues, youth constitute a substantial portion of the current labor force, performing an important number of all service sector jobs. Therefore, understanding their motives, aspirations, and everyday experiences will shed light on an important portion of our labor force.

The prevalence of youth labor in the United States is a result of a number of factors. First, the American economy has shifted to a predominantly service and retail-based economy. Between the 1940s and mid-1970s, the service and retail sectors combined created 15.8 million jobs: 9.3 million in the service sector and 6.6 million in retail (Ginzberg 1977). Today, more than two-thirds of our economy is dominated by service sector jobs (Cleveland 1999). Although the shift from production to service and retail created an unprecedented number of jobs, most of these jobs were "bad jobs." Ellen Greenberger and Laurence Steinberg (1986) characterize these jobs by low wages; odd hours; irregular shifts, including nighttime and weekend work; seasonality; high turnover; and absence of benefits and promotions. According to a recent U.S. Bureau of Labor Statistics press release (2012a), retail salespersons and cashiers, in particular, were the occupations with the highest employment numbers in 2011. Although these service jobs are among the largest occupations in terms of quantity, they are also some of the lowest-paying jobs (U.S. Bureau of Labor Statistics 2012a).

Because these jobs are assumed to be exploitive by nature—serving the interests of corporate elites and stockholders while providing few benefits to employees—analysts typically reduce work for these teenagers to economic need. That is why little research considers why young people would take such positions. The lived experience of youth employees from their perspective thus remains unexplored.

Although a rich sociological literature exists on youth employment, most of the existing research focuses on the effects rather than the causes of employment. The studies of these effects include analyses of youth's emotional and psychological development (Finch et al. 1991; Greenberger and Steinberg 1986; Mihalic and Elliot 1997; Paternoster et al. 2003), academic performance (Bills, Helms, and Ozcan 1995; D'Amico 1984; D'Amico and Baker 1984; Greenberger and Steinberg 1986; Marsh 1991; Mortimer and Finch 1986; Steinberg and Dornbusch 1991), acquisition of human capital and skills (Gardecki and Neumark 1998; McNeal 1997; Mihalic and Elliot 1997; Pabilonia 1997; Ruhm 1997; Smith and Rojewski 1993), and deviant behavior (McMorris and Uggen 2000; Mihalic and Elliot 1997; Paternoster et al. 2003). Although many sociologists have explored the effects of youth employment, its causes have been left to economists. Coming from an economic perspective, researchers have studied the causes of youth employment through macrolevel economic factors, such as governmental policies (Neumark and Wascher 1992), minimum-wage regulation (Card 1992; Gustman and Steinmeyer 1988; Neumark and Wascher 1992; Wellington 1991) and fluctuations in supply of and demand for youth labor (Card and Lemieux 2000; Pease and Martin 1997).

Although extensive work exists on youth employment, stemming both from the perspectives of sociology and economics, the most central actors of youth work—young people themselves—have been left out of the research.

Interestingly, along with the near exclusion of youth, the work experience has also received scant academic attention. Although youth employment has been studied extensively from the perspective of many individuals and institutions, such as parents, teachers, and employers, the perspective of the young people themselves has been largely neglected.

To bring this viewpoint into focus, this chapter looks at the lived experience of these "bad" jobs from the viewpoints of the young people who perform them (Wacquant 1995). It also identifies the mechanisms though which they define their work activities and studies what these seemingly exploitative jobs mean to the actors. Learning about their everyday experiences sheds light not only on how they view these jobs but also on why they work.

Many sociologists consider these jobs to be exploitive, highly automated, alienating, and unskilled (Greenberger and Steinberg 1986; Ritzer 2000; Tilly 1995), concluding that the only reason to take them is to make money. Although these jobs are not usually attractive for adults, and an objectivist perspective would consider them exploitative, they are considered acceptable and even desirable from the perspective of the young people. It is not surprising that corporations would want to employ young people, especially ones from affluent backgrounds. Unlike the adults who would otherwise fulfill these positions, affluent youth are not too concerned with receiving benefits or working unpredictable hours. Therefore, the low wages and lack of benefits that characterize exploitive jobs are not necessarily considered exploitive by youth who come from affluent backgrounds and have ample allowances and health benefits through their families.

This chapter looks at the everyday experience of these "bad" jobs and argues that, from the perspective of the actors, they are not simply jobs to be endured for economic reasons. Rather, my research shows that these jobs, ironically, provide opportunities for workers to have fun and to exercise their individuality, control, authority, and power.

Theory

For this work, I rely heavily on grounded theory (Glaser 1992; Strauss 1987). My observations and fieldwork construct a theory of youth labor. As Loïc Wacquant argues, "The best theory is that which is virtually inseparable from the object it brings to light" (1998: 6). As I construct a grounded theory of work from the perspectives of young people and attempt to understand *why* they do what they do, I start with *how*. Toni Morrison says, "There is really nothing more to say—except *why*. But since why is difficult to handle, one must take refuge in *how*" (1994: 8). By understanding how they work, we can move from how to why. A "thick description" of the work experience, a term borrowed from Clifford Geertz (1973), helps reconstruct the daily lives of young people to understand how work functions in their everyday lives. Only then can we move from how to why, in the formulation suggested by Jack Katz (2001). The everyday lived experience of work sheds light onto the meaning and value of work from the youth workers' perspective.

Setting and Appearance

To recapture how young people experience jobs, we must examine the setting. The setting, the decor, and the environment are crucial elements in understanding perceptions of work. Setting involves "furniture, decor, physical layout, [and] the other background items which supply the scenery and stage props for the spate of human action to played out before, within or upon it" (Goffman 1959: 22). The setting is important for the performance of work, because, as Erving Goffman argues, "a setting tends to stay put, geographically speaking, so that those who would use a particular setting as part of their performance cannot bring their act until they have brought themselves to the appropriate place and must terminate their performance when they leave it" (22).

The Coffee Bean is a vast rectangular open space with high ceilings and long spacious windows. The roomy shop consists of two main locations: the bar, where the counter, cash registers, and coffee-preparation sections are located; and the lounge, where overstuffed armchairs, a cozy couch, and scattered chairs and tables are located. The bar area is a long, low counter behind which all employees stand together. Unlike many workplaces, there is no functional—or physical—separation between workspaces and employees. Rather, employees shift between making coffee and working the cash registers easily. Even when they do not, they are not physically separated from the others working with them. The design of the counter allows for and accommodates interaction among all employees by physically concentrating them in the same place. Furthermore, the low counter allows free movement to either side and facilitates fluid boundaries between employees and customers. This particular layout enables young people to interact with customers and each other during a typical shift. Unlike a supermarket, for example, where the cashier works alone, removed from other workers, the design of the coffee shop makes it possible for workers to interact freely.

The bar is surrounded by large paintings and murals in vivid colors and oversize, bright prints, all illuminated by direct spotlights. Customers hang out at the bar, mostly holding coffee cups. From the perspectives of the teenagers, this environment is like a bar, although with legal stimulants. In contrast to the bar area, which is loud, hectic, and fast-paced, the lounge section has a serene feel, with its oversize cozy armchairs and couches surrounded by magazines and newspapers. Each side of the counter offers a different form of leisure: a fun Saturday evening or a lazy Sunday afternoon. Such a physical environment is conducive to leisure and sets the scene for the work experience of young people. How they relate to work becomes apparent in their appearance and gestures.

In this chapter, I highlight the central dimensions of workers' experiences with their jobs, comparing their interpretations with those of objectivist researchers and theorists.

Power and Control

Greenberger and Steinberg (1986) characterize typical teenage jobs as requiring no skills or creativity and highly mechanized with low pay. Ritzer (2000) argues that such jobs leave virtually no space for creativity. The coffee shops in which I carried out my research seemed to fit that description, at least at first glance: The young people who worked there were required to be at their shift on time and not leave the premises during their shift, save for a fifteen-minute break during which they were allowed one drink. Their tasks for each shift were strictly codified, described in detail in the employee handbook. Even what they were supposed to say to the customers was scripted. From an objectivist perspective, it would seem that the detailed scripts and organization of this occupation, like other service sector jobs, means that the individual workers hold little power. However, from the perspective of the youth, work at the Coffee Bean was "not like that." The meaning of these jobs, therefore, is not inherent, but differs according to the perspective of the viewer (Blumer 1969), including those situations that sociologists define as unequal or exploitive (Harris 2000). Amy, a nineteen year-old college student, described a typical shift in which she was in charge of the whole place. For her, getting to the coffee shop on the day of a blizzard despite her four-hour commute and decision to miss school was extremely important: She believed that if she did not show up, the shop could not function and serve coffee to customers on a cold day. "No one notices if I miss a class or two," she said, referring to the large university where she was a full-time student, "but it's different here—they need me." The fact that her tasks were specifically spelled out did not lead her to feel constricted, but rather gave her the feeling of being needed and in charge of that specific task. Sarah, a music student, said, "Not everyone can do what I do in the short time span that I do it in. . . . Many people would mess up, which is why I have to always be there, to make sure everything is under control and everyone is happy."

The sense of control over tasks comes not only from their strict definitions but also from the relative power the teenagers have over their work environments. Josh told me he felt "in control of everything" throughout a typical shift, because he got to make the "important decisions." Important decisions, according to Josh, did not concern the business of the shop—making coffee or operating the cash register. In fact, he was happy that those "unimportant" things were clearly defined so that he did not have to spend his time worrying about how to make coffee or what to say to the customers. Rather, he found freedom and control in the decisions concerning his clothing, appearance, and his work schedule. One of the reasons he chose to work at the coffee shop was that he could dress in almost the same way he normally did—in casual khakis and simple T-shirts. Monica, a fashion-conscious student, said that the uniforms were so fashionable, they were like a "GAP commercial." If she had to wear a polyester uniform like fast-food employees do, she would not want to work there at all. Unlike workers at some fast-food establishments who may not want to be seen in their uniforms, Monica said she sometimes wore her work clothes even after her shift was over. Besides, she added, "we can accessorize." One of the reasons that Monica wanted to work at the coffee shop was the freedom she had with her accessories: in her case, her signature Indian jewelry showcasing her ethnic identity. Neither of these traits was something she wanted to give up for a job. Josh agreed that work was a place where he felt accepted. In most places, his tattoos and numerous piercings—on his eyebrow, lip, and ears—were constant sources of conflict. "School, parents, friends," he said, were not too happy about his appearance. When he came into the coffee shop as a customer, however, he felt right at home: The female employee who served his coffee had a similar look. What was really surprising was that he covered his tattoos during his shift at the coffee shop, but he told me that knowing other employees had a similar aesthetic was important to him.

In addition to the freedom to express themselves through their appearance and clothing, many of the teenagers who worked at the coffee shop felt in control of their activities during their shifts. For Josh, as well as other workers I spoke with, the work aspect was secondary to hanging out with friends and listening to music. Many times, Josh said, he heard good music during his shift and decided to purchase it later. He often talked about the music selections with his friends at the coffee shop: The freedom to do that was what he called "the important stuff."

Many employees at the coffee shop also had freedom over their schedules. "We can also schedule the shifts however we like," said Kelly, an eighteen-year-old student who just started college. For Kelly, scheduling her shifts with her two best friends, Kirsten and Mel, was a paramount concern. Because of their hectic schedules, they often had trouble getting together, so working at the same time was their opportunity to socialize. "Sometimes," Kelly added, referring to her boyfriend who worked at the pizza place next door, "I schedule my shift to see Ben" (so that they could spend time with each other while she was at work). Sarah said, "I absolutely love the people I work with. It's fun."

Decisions about clothes, the accessories they use to express their personalities, music, and shifts were the issues that mattered to the youth who worked at the coffee shop. Thus, their lived experience of a work shift full of scripted responses and routinized button pushing was not perceived as one of rigid restrictions but as one where they made the decisions—or at least the ones that "mattered."

Lack of External Authority

Rigid rules and restrictions, repetitive work, and detailed, scripted interactions with customers are often presented as characteristics of service sector jobs (Tilly 1995). Implicit or explicit in such analyses is the idea that workers are subjected to external sources of authority and control, usually represented and enforced by on-site managers and quality-control inspectors. Contrary to these preconceptions, the teenagers at the coffee shop characterized their work experience as being absent of domination, control, or authority. Although a "supervisor" was scheduled to work during every shift, Josh told me that "she is not really like that." That is because the supervisor was Samantha, an eighteen-year-old college student who was also one of Josh's closest friends.

The "manager"—who was usually (but not always) an older and longer-term employee for whom the coffee shop position was a career—was present only during opening and closing shifts. The remainders of the shifts were supervised by Samantha and Anna, another nineteen-year-old college student. Because the supervisors were their peers and, in most cases, their friends, most of the teenagers who worked at the coffee shop did not feel as though a boss were on the premises. "It's more like hanging out with friends," Samantha said. "I'm technically the supervisor, but . . . they're my friends, you know."

Samantha told me that, among themselves, they did not feel as though there were a hierarchy: She said they all "hang out." "No one is assigned to one task," she said, and hence no one was singled out to be in a separate place. Rather, they all hung out behind the counter at what they referred to as the "bar" area. Because there was no physical separation and restriction, the teenagers felt free to move about the shop. The absence of formal occupational authority in the workplace was not the only form of freedom at the coffee shop: The workers saw the coffee shop as a safe haven insulated from other forms of authority as well. As Josh asserted, not only was it a great hangout place; his parents were okay with his decision to work. Like most young people who worked at the coffee shop, Josh said one of the advantages of working was that the workplace was insulated from parental restriction and authority. He complained that his parents "always tell him what to do," but when he worked at the Coffee Bean, they did not ask any questions. Chores and even homework became secondary considerations when Josh had a scheduled shift. "Even the teachers are nicer," Josh explained, referring to his professors. Like many of the other workers at the coffee shop, because Josh spent so much time at the coffee shop, he often missed classes and, on occasion, tests. However, he observed that his professors were much nicer to him when he had to miss class because of work. This type of work, therefore, offers a space absent of authority—employer, parent, and teacher—and provides the workers with a feeling of control over their activities.

Creativity

This feeling of control and authority also stems from the use of creative skills in these jobs. Traditional accounts characterize these service sector jobs as requiring minimal skills at best (Ritzer 2000), but this is not how the workers see them. Although the need for credentials, previous experience, and skill requirements are limited in these jobs, from the perspective of the teenagers, the jobs involve more than pushing buttons. Young people at the Coffee Bean did not perceive their work experience as one where they lacked skills but rather as a space where they could make use of their skills and their creativity. Samantha told me there was a lot more to coffee making than simply the button pressing described in the employee manuals. "It requires a lot of skill and concentration," she said, adding that the workers had informal foam-making competitions. Throughout the shift, they competed to see who could make the best foam: A good cup was a matter of pride, and they all agreed that Anna made the best foam. Anna, another eighteen-year-old college student, took this task very seriously: "Your milk has to be the perfect temperature and amount," she said as she elaborately described how she made ideal foam. Such tasks as topping coffee with foam may appear to require no skill to an objectivist analyst. However, these young people defined this task (along with other aspects of their job) as something that utilized their skills and concentration. "It's not just the foam," Anna asserted. Even the most straightforward tasks, such as making regular black coffee, required engagement and creativity: "Anybody can make coffee, but making good coffee requires a lot of skill."

Individuality

Working at the coffee shop gave these teenagers not only the feeling that they were engaged in creative activity but also a way to express their individuality. Although typical service sector jobs are portrayed as jobs where employees are expected to look uniform and standardized (Ritzer 2000), for many young people, work is a way to express their individuality. Monica said that she felt anonymous and alienated at her school, a large state school with big classes. At school, nobody knew who she was—she was just one of the students. However, working at the coffee shop distinguished her; among her friends from school, she was the girl who worked at the cool coffee shop. Her work not only provided her with a distinct identity but gave her and her friends something to talk about. Before she started working, Monica often felt left out of conversations, because her friends all worked and wanted to talk about their jobs. One of the reasons that she got a job was to give her something to talk about that was "hers."

Work provided these young people with a sense of identity not only at school and among their peers but also throughout their work shift. According to the young people who worked at the coffee shop, the uniforms they had to wear did not detract from their individuality. "This is what I normally wear anyway," said Josh, referring to the khakis and the casual T-shirt that served as his uniform. Moreover, employees' accessories and personalized items, such as Anna's long nails, Josh's piercings and tattoos, and Monica's ethnic jewelry, acted as important signifiers of the young people's identities. In displaying these symbols, the workers at the coffee shop informed customers and employees of their interests and hobbies. Dave, for instance, wore surfing accessories and T-shirts from his surfing trip to Costa Rica. Nick, similarly, wore skateboarding accessories to reflect his interest in the sport. These kinds of symbols indicated the young people's personalities and helped smooth social interactions by giving information about themselves to everyone who came into the store. Samantha told me that these personality markers helped workers meet people with similar interests. They also developed other ways to communicate their interests. "Sometimes, instead of carrying or wearing your symbols, you can write them on personalized coffee cups," Samantha said.

Fun and Friendships

Through these signs and symbols, workers defined and used the coffee shop as a place where they could meet new people. Although the work experience is traditionally portrayed as something to be endured rather than enjoyed (Adorno 1994), for these teenagers, work provided the opportunity to meet others in the area and socialize with friends (Besen 2004, 2005).

The people these young workers spent time with were not limited to the cool youth who worked there. The other people consisted of a heterogeneous group of new peers they met at the coffee shop, new friends they now worked with, and existing friends who stopped by to visit them during their shifts. Throughout a typical shift, young people were constantly stopping by to hang out with the friends who were scheduled to work. A hierarchy emerged among the friends who hung out at the coffee shop. Usually acquaintances who stopped by for a quick chat stayed by the side of the counter and enjoyed their drinks while they chatted with the working youth in a manner that resembled hanging out at a bar, a club, or a party. Closer friends not only hung out by the side of the counter but also sat down in the lounge area, where the workers on shift came by periodically to visit with them. Even among friends who hung out in the lounge, it is important to note that seating was not random but reflected the friends' closeness and importance. Closer friends, such as Dave, or boyfriends, such as Ben or Chris, sat adjacent to the bar so that throughout the shift, they were free to join in the conversation. Close friends also occasionally went behind the counter to help out; for instance, Dave helped Kristen lift a heavy box or make coffee, despite being (nominally at least) a customer rather than an employee.

Throughout a typical shift, these teenage employees, dressed in casual clothes, standing at the bar under spotlights, holding cups filled with legalized stimulants, laughed, giggled, and engaged in endless, loud talk about trivial matters. Unlike stereotypical jobs, shifts at the coffee shop were dominated by endless chatter accompanied by giggles and laughter. Sarah said her mother called her job a "waste of time" and "annoying," but Sarah saw it as a way to have fun and see her friends. She spent so much time there that she felt almost as though she lived there. She said she genuinely enjoyed being there:

She has many friends there, some co-workers and some customers, and she never got bored.

This excerpt from my field notes outlines the typical chatter that characterized the interactions between these young workers:

On Halloween 2001, Joy, in big fluffy slippers and oversized pajamas, and Jen, dressed in all black like a witch with red wig, hang out at the bar. They slowly sip their drinks as they sift through CDs and try to call Rachel on Jen's cell phone. As they try to choose music and anxiously anticipate Rachel's arrival, Rachel rushes in and joins the girls at the bar, accompanied by her boyfriend, who follows her behind the counter. The girls greet Rachel, accompanied by laughter and giggles. "C'mon show your costume," Jen says impatiently as Rachel takes off her jacket to reveal her butterfly costume. Her boyfriend adjusts her wings as Rachel takes out a pair of butterfly antennas from her bag as she exclaims, "Check these out." "Oh my God! Where did you get those antennas?" Jen shrieks excitedly. "These are the cutest antennas!" Joy exclaims. "There is a place off [a local highway, where] they have all sorts of antennas: butterfly antennas, giraffe antennas." "Really, what other antennas? Do butterflies have antennas?"

The endless chatter throughout the shift was not always substantial. They talked about school, work, and occasionally romance. The above excerpt is a typical example of the insubstantial and seemingly trivial chatter that occupied the young people and continued throughout the shift. The conversations in the shop tended to be centered on trivial matters and consumption; in general, talk in the coffee shop was loud and accompanied by endless laughter and giggles. The conversations were not only loud but also physically expressive: They involved waving at friends and hugging and kissing whenever the young people arrived or left.

Endless browsing and shopping accompanied the "antenna talk." The entire shift often consisted of regular visits to the stands where sale products were displayed. They browsed the mugs, stuffed animals, chocolates, new coffee beans, and new music. Many employees were also avid consumers of the products, so they talked about their favorite drinks. Monica told me that I just had to try the white chocolate mocha, her favorite drink at that time. The coffee shop also sold seasonal drinks, and Monica and her friends compared their favorites. Sometimes the conversation turned to the coffee beans: Which coffee bean, which type of coffee, and the country of origin all played roles in the discussion. The endless shopping not only accompanied the chatter but also constituted an important topic of conversation: They chatted about the products they wanted to purchase, compared their shopping lists, and engaged in endless discussions about which coffee beans they preferred.

The browsing and accompanying discussions of products usually reached its pinnacle around such holidays as Christmas, Easter, Halloween, and Valentine's Day or when new items were delivered. During a shift on Valentine's Day, Rachel and Kristen took turns going through the new products and then making lists of the items they wanted to purchase. They finalized their decisions by comparing the lists and going over each new item they wanted to purchase in detail. Both the conversations centered around trivia and consumption and were very loud, accompanied by laughter and giggles.

As they made their shopping lists, they shuffled through music with their friends who come into the shop as customers, discussing various bands.

The other young people who they hung out with at the coffee shop were a heterogeneous group consisting of the peers they met at the coffee shop, the friends they were scheduled to work with, and other friends who stopped by to visit with the workers. The coffee shop provided the social space for these teenagers in the suburbs to meet new people. John, a nineteen-year-old full-time student who moved to town for college, remembered when he started working at the coffee shop: "I'd just moved [here], and I didn't know anyone. So, I got a job." Like John, he remembered being intimidated and feeling lost in a large university and lonely in the suburbs. When John moved here from all the way across the country, he barely knew anyone. He moved away from all of his family and friends and found himself in the suburbs, where teenagers lacked space for social interaction. John did not know where to meet people and find friends, so he said this motivated him to work. He added that he believed that the young people who worked at the Coffee Bean would be "just like him." He not only made a lot of new friends there but also met his boyfriend, Chris.

Most people in the coffee shop were from the same age group and shared similar interests. Furthermore, the workplace gave them the opportunity to interact with each other in a small, personal space and get to know each other better. This was further facilitated by their clothing and accessories, which were geared toward introducing themselves and marketing themselves to their peers. John and Chris were working at the same shift, and like many other teenagers working at the coffee shop, used their accessories to display their interests.

Similarly, Josh said that he met most of his good friends, such as Rachel, Jen, and Joy, through his work at the coffee shop. These four were not just co-workers but close friends since they had worked at the shop. They made sure to schedule their shifts together and spent a lot of time together before and after the shifts. Josh said, "They're not just colleagues or something, you know: We hang out all the time." As John put it, "Where else can you meet people?" Customers who were neither existing nor potential friends still interacted

with the young employees in a friendly and casual manner. In a typical interaction, on Halloween, Jen, dressed as a witch, handed a disposable camera to a
middle-age woman who came in to grab some coffee. "Would you please?" Jen
smiled, asking for a photo of her, Joy, and Rachel in their Halloween costumes.
The customers seemed to appreciate the friendly environment. The middle-age
woman was not annoyed but took their photo and chatted with them about
the party, their costumes, and their makeup. Then she joined their conversation from the side of the counter where friends stood.

Donna Gaines has characterized the lives of youth in the suburbs as a
"teenage wasteland" (1998). Gaines justifies this label by referring to rumors of
Satanic cults, suicidal tendencies, and so-called troubled teenagers. However,
I found that for my respondents, suburbia was a "wasteland" because it was
unable to provide opportunities for socialization and meeting new people.
"You also get to meet other people," John said about his work at the shop. For
the teenagers working at the coffee shop, co-workers were not the only friends
to be made. A large group of pre-med students regularly stopped by the coffee shop around 2:00 in the afternoon and sat in the "lounge" section to study
and socialize. "That's how I met Dave," Kristen, a nineteen-year-old student,
told me. Kristen, with her endless chatter and jokes, had a very outgoing
personality. Despite these traits, she said that she did not have many chances
for meeting people before she began working at the Coffee Bean. She enjoyed
being surrounded by so many different people who constantly flowed into
the shop. Dave, a nineteen-year-old student, was a regular who spent almost
every afternoon at the coffee shop and became Kristen's best friend. He was a
full-time student at the nearby college, majoring in biology and planning to
go to medical school when he graduated. Every day after school, he came to
the Coffee Bean to study and hang out with his friends. He told me that many
medical students studied at this particular branch of the Coffee Bean; nursing
students hung out at another branch. He usually took a seat close to the bar,
where Kristen worked, and chatted with her throughout her shift. During her
breaks, they smoked outside together and often enjoyed pastries behind the
counter. They were also joined by their friend, Joe, who brought leftover pizza
at the end of the day from the pizza place where he worked after school. In
addition to their lack of opportunities to meet new people in the suburbs, the
suburbs were also defined by these workers as a social wasteland because of the
limited space they offered for social interaction. At the shop, however, a typical shift was characterized by a constant movement of friends stopping by to
hang out with the shop's employees. "It's such a convenient location, with my
boyfriend working upstairs at the bar," said Kristen, whose boyfriend worked
as a bartender, during shifts scheduled to coincide with hers. They saw each
other throughout their shifts and during breaks. With her boyfriend working
upstairs, her friends Joy and Jen working with her at the coffee shop, and her

best friend, Dave, visiting throughout the shift, the coffee shop was to Kristen a space for sociable interaction more than a space for monotonous, oppressive work.

"Sometimes, we go out afterwards," Dan told me, referring to Saturday night outings to clubs or parties, usually with Kristen, Joy, Rachel, and Jen. Right after their shifts ended, the teenagers sometimes went out together, so the coffee shop provided a great place for meeting and preparing beforehand. This was evident at the shop during Halloween 2001. Jen, Joy, and Rachel all dressed up in their Halloween costumes, and not just during their shift: Even those who were not working that night came to the shop to prepare, dress up, and plan a party after they all got off work. Their friends, who stopped by throughout the shift to get more information about the party, joined them. "Which party are we going to?" asked a teenage boy in a Radiohead shirt as he stopped by to get coffee. "The one at Gina's or Melissa's?" He hung out by the side of the counter, chatting with Jen and Joy for ten or fifteen minutes as he finished his coffee. "Gina's party is going to be better," Jen said. "Everyone's going to [Gina's] party, but Melissa's party has a band." After extended deliberation, a number of phone calls, input from a number of friends and acquaintances grouped around the bar, and a number of acquaintances stopping by to ask about the party, they collectively decided to go to Gina's party. "Great," the teenager in the Radiohead shirt said. He took out a pen, scribbled something on a napkin, and handed it to Jen. "Would you give this to Michelle?" he asked. "She'll stop by later to ask about the party. Just tell her I'll be at the party at 9. She is around five foot four—blonde with blue eyes."

As this example illustrated, the coffee shop was not only a social space for peer-to-peer interaction in the social wasteland, where space for meeting people and social interaction was limited, but also a center for distributing information and leaving messages. The employees at this low-wage service sector job were doing more than making lattes; they functioned as information brokers, making the shop a center in the centerless suburb. From my observations, it is no wonder that teenagers accept what objectivist analysts' view as bad jobs: In a very real way, these jobs place them at the center of their peer group's social universe.

"It's not just the parties," John told me in reference to the importance of the shop in coordinating social activities. Most of the time, friends did not host house parties, so being at the shop became a social activity itself. The suburb did not provide many places where they could all go and hang out, so, after the shift, the workers often stayed at the shop. There, they continued conversations with the employees coming on the next shift and with friends visiting the shop; they even occasionally performed odd jobs that would be part of their responsibilities if they were still "on the clock." For these young people, working in the coffee shop was not experienced as a negative or exploitive situation. Rather, it was one of the few ways for teens in the area to engage in social interaction, both employees and customers.

Consumption and Pay

For these young students, work was a more akin to a leisure activity, like going to the movies or to a club, than it was an economic activity. Work, traditionally viewed as production-oriented, is also a form of consumption in the context of suburban teenage labor. Although their jobs at the coffee shop facilitated consumption—the workers and visitors eagerly examined the merchandise for sale in the shop and compared notes on what they would buy—the work itself became an object of consumption. Few of the employees came to the shop looking for a job; they came, instead, for social interaction—the money and benefits were almost irrelevant. Rather than spend their money—although they did that as well—they spent their time to interact with their peers, the same way that their parents might have gone to clubs or lodges. Rather than work as a means to an economic end, they spent time at work as an end in and of itself. These types of jobs are consumed along with other products young people consume and allow them to be associated with brands they desire. Jenny told me she did not work just for money to "buy stuff." That statement did not mean that she did not "buy stuff," though: She told me that "of course" she had a car and the latest cell phone and fashionable clothes, but she said that the money she earned could not possibly pay for all her consumption; her parents, she said, paid or helped pay for all these items. It is one thing to purchase a branded item, but to be associated with a "cool brand" through employment is priceless.

Although objectivist analysts are correct in asserting that these jobs are typically associated with low pay and a lack of benefits, the low pay does not seem to be defined as an inequality or a problem for teenage workers. There are two main reasons for this. First, as noted before, any economic gains from their labor are almost superfluous, as the teenagers work more for social reasons than for money. Second, and parallel with this, many teenage employees come from affluent backgrounds. Jenna told me that she did not need the money—her parents were both professionals and quite wealthy—but she said that she would pay the company for the opportunity to work at the coffee shop and be associated with "such a cool brand." She added that she could never work in a place if she did not like the brand or enjoy its products. As she told me, she was going to get the products anyway, and "it's good to get the discounts." For Jenna, working was no different from consuming the products of the workplace. As she put it, "When you work somewhere, you are seen with the products," referring to the free coffee beans the store gave every week to the employees or the one drink they were each allowed per shift. For Jenna, she had to be proud to use and possibly show off the product.

Monica, a close friend of Jenna who had started at the coffee shop just a month before I spoke to her, was also into shopping—not just for clothes but for stuffed animals, mugs, and coffee as well. Whatever she bought came from the brands she enjoyed and sold to others. She told me that her first paycheck went straight to buying stuff from the shop.

I would argue that the consumption element of the job is also present in how positions are marketed to potential employees. Rather than focus on the benefits, pay, hours, or opportunities for advancement or experience, job ads ask customers whether they "want a job with their coffee." In these ads, and others like them, the job itself is marketed as a product, as an enjoyable experience to be consumed by the teenagers. Also, the marketing of these jobs is designed to reinforce the potential employees' consumption patterns. A job becomes a means to obtain the goods sold at the store. The discounts for the coffee beans, chocolates, coffee mugs, travel cups, and stuffed animals sold at the coffee shop became incentives for people to work there. The job is marketed as a way to consume and associate oneself with a shop's brand name, something these teenagers at Coffee Bean were happy to do.

Fluid Definition of Time

The social interaction that took place in the coffee shop depended on a very fluid definition of time that is a prerequisite for the fuzzy boundary between work and leisure. Unlike rigid definitions of work and leisure, in the lived experience of young people, these categories are not separated by such distinct boundaries but rather blend into each other. Unlike what might be expected, these young people did not leave the coffee shop immediately once their shifts w over. Rather, many arrived at the shop well before their scheduled shifts and hung out at the bar with their friends, where they sometimes helped make coffee even though they were not being paid. They also lingered after their shifts were over. Liz said she never went home immediately after her shift. Almost every time, unless she had something important to do, she took off her apron and blended right into the customers, enjoying her coffee in the lounge area.

Even when these young workers planned to leave quickly, they sometimes failed to do so. After their shifts were over, many stopped at the station where milk, sweeteners, stirrers, and napkins were located. Before Liz left, for example, she usually checked to make sure the supplies at the milk bar were full and fresh. As Goffman (1959) argues, the performance of actors is intensified when the definition of work activity is unclear. Because of the ambiguous definition of work, these teenagers did things like check and refresh the milk bar symbolically as they were leaving to make their work visible to themselves and to others.

Unlike traditional dichotomous definitions of work and leisure as two distinct categories (as in Adorno 2001), the young people's work experience was filled with elements of leisure, such as hanging out at the bar and relaxing in the lounge. And just as their work experience included many leisure elements, their leisure time was filled with work. During their breaks, many did not leave the coffee shop. The only reason that some teenagers left the shop was to smoke, and even smokers stood in front of the coffee shop, clustered together. Otherwise, they spent their breaks at the coffee shop and blended in easily with the customers as a result of their uniforms' looking like normal clothes. Throughout an average day, the young people shifted back and forth between their roles as employees and consumers, with the two roles often blending together.

Sometimes during the weekends, when they were not scheduled to work, young people visited the coffee shop as customers. Many of them stopped by after school to study and get a cup of coffee. Yet their roles as customers were not always separate from their roles as employees. One weekend, as John was hanging out with his friends at the lounge, a customer spilled coffee. Without saying a word, and even though he was not scheduled to work, he got up in the middle of his conversation with his friends, went behind the counter, and started mopping the floors. Even though he was not paid to do so, he helped his friends clean up. Such an anecdote shows that work is not an activity done solely for the purposes of pay. In this case, even though he was off the clock, he was happy to help his friends.

Working with Others: Older Workers

Joanne had been working at the coffee shop for some time. She was a single mother of a small boy. Usually, she was scheduled to work with Rachel and Jen. However, unlike those two, she really needed her paycheck to survive. Her motives for working were very different from those of the teenagers. However, working with affluent young people changed her daily experience of this job. On her shifts with the girls, she wrapped her cardigan around her waist and chatted with the girls. Rachel and Jen often asked Joanne for boyfriend advice and told her about their boyfriend troubles, school problems, and friend issues. Joanne was like a big sister for the girls: She gave advice, listened to the girls' troubles, and helped them. The girls, in turn, gave her fashion advice, and Rachel helped her with her makeup and brought her hair products. Her daily reality changed—even though she needed the job, her everyday experience was affected because she worked with young people. But this circumstance did not change the fact that her wages were low and she did not get enough hours.

Exceptions

Although my findings suggest a pattern of enjoyment and fun among the teenagers I studied at the coffee shop, there were some instances where workers complained. During periods when work obligations increased—such as when overtime or double shifts were required—some teenagers did grumble, especially if these requirements interrupted their social interaction. When the coffee shop had unusually long lines that interfered with chatting with friends, there was temporary uneasiness. However, as with other aspects of work, these obligations that hindered fun were reinterpreted to create a continuous meaning. For example, when I asked John how he handled his long shifts during one busy holiday season, he said they provided an excellent opportunity to spend more time with friends. Therefore, although I acknowledge that teenagers' daily work experiences are not devoid of what objectivist scholars refer to as "bad jobs," I would argue that even these "bad" qualities tend to be perceived in a positive light by the young workers, as they imbue even the most inconvenient qualities with positive, social meanings.

Another exception to the pattern of widespread contentment involved a less affluent worker who was not a student worker. Joanne was a slightly older employee from a relatively lower socioeconomic background compared to the other students working at the coffee shop. Especially after her mother became ill and quit her job, Joanne felt a greater need for money and started to be more concerned with getting benefits and working more hours. However, because the dominant culture of the coffee shop centered around fun (and related meanings), she defined her job there along the lines of the other teenagers and started working at another job to earn money, keeping the job at the coffee shop for social reasons.

Although these jobs are often portrayed from an objectivist perspective as exploitive, having no control and authority, limited opportunities to use skills or express individuality, and low pay and restrictive shifts, from the perspective of the teenagers, the lived experience of these jobs differs substantially. Teenagers who worked in the coffee shop defined their everyday work experience as one of a space free of adult supervision where they could socialize, make important decisions, and be creative. The teenagers enjoyed their jobs, in the interpretive sense of that word. They defined and treated their work as fun—as a situation of consumption rather than mere wage-earning production. Thus, the simple but larger point that I draw from my analysis is this: Situations that appear (to objectivist analysis) to be clearly unequal and exploitive may not necessarily experienced that way by the persons involved. Daily experience of work is socially constructed—that is, created through people's interactions and interpretations. Young people act on the basis of their perceptions of the job: In this case, these jobs were not perceived as "jobs," but rather as social spaces of interaction, devoid of external adult supervision, where they felt they had discretion and control. These findings regarding the suburban teenage workers of the coffee shop provide a necessary corrective to some of the taken-for-granted objectivist perceptions of work.

As Herbert Blumer (1969: 3–4, 11–12, 68–69) argues, meaning is not inherent: Nothing is inherently equal or unequal. Power, exploitation, inequality, and similar qualities are meanings that people must define into being if they are to exist for those people. Borrowing from Blumer, Scott R. Harris outlines a constructionist approach to studying inequality. He argues that a fundamental premise of this approach should be that "people act on the basis of their perceptions of inequality, if and when it is a relevant concern to them" (2001: 457). From an objectivist perspective, the jobs I studied lacked power, control, creativity, and individuality and were monotonous and dehumanizing. In short, conventional scholars would define these jobs as "no fun." However, a constructionist perspective alerts us to the fact that the very same occupations may not be interpreted or viewed as such by the teenagers filling them. The teenagers who worked at the coffee shop interpreted and defined their jobs as fun and social, with copious authority and freedom to express their individuality. Moreover, the coffee shop functioned as an important center for social interaction and was central to the flow of information between teenagers in their centerless suburbs. In addition to pushing buttons and making coffee, the employees of these shops distributed information, however trivial it may seem to an objectivist scholar, about which party would be better, which products and brands were in favor, and who was going to be where and when. In this function, and others, the teenagers at Coffee Bean found their work to be creative and engaging. The routinized button pushing was often extraneous to what they saw as their really "important" functions, as was the money they received for doing so.

My research shows that these jobs are not inherently "bad" or "exploitative," but that the actors transform these experiences into a different reality: one of social enjoyment, power, control, and creativity. From their view, the teenage coffee-shop workers did not feel exploited by the employers but ironically felt as though they were using these jobs for their own purposes. They were hired to push buttons and pour coffee but filled their time instead with social interaction. They were paid, essentially, to do something that they would have aspired to regardless: to serve as the center of an otherwise centerless suburb. As such, the young people's experience of these "bad jobs" differed considerably from the objectivist understandings of exploitive jobs.

The enjoyment of these "bad jobs" by young people, however, does not mean that fun is really what those jobs are, or that there is really no need to improve them. I am not using the idea that "meaning is not inherent" to imply that "everything is morally okay just as it is." Instead, I am using that constructionist premise to draw attention toward meaning making and toward how inequalities come (or not) to be defined, perceived, and experienced as such. I am arguing that in the study of work, too many scholars have imposed objectivist meanings, and more attention could be given to the lived experiences of these sorts of teenage workers. Thus, constructionist research like mine does not necessarily undermine or discount the contributions of conventional research and the proposals for reform that emerge from it. However, my work does complicate the sometimes "totalizing" narratives that objectivist scholars tell.

It is also important to acknowledge that not all employed teenagers come from backgrounds as privileged as those of my respondents. The employees of the coffee shop were predominantly white and identified themselves as middle to upper-middle class. The marked absence of race and working classes from the coffee shop obviously placed limits on my study. Young workers in the inner cities may be less likely to define their jobs as my respondents did. Moreover, the workers I studied were employed by a brand that is widely considered to be cool and desirable. Clearly, not all service sector occupations share this trait. Hence, even in affluent suburban settings, it is likely that many young workers do not experience their work as my respondents did. However, the marked absence of race and class points to the emergence of inequalities in access to workplaces, which is discussed in the upcoming chapters.

Representativeness and generalizability are important questions that can be raised about every ethnographic study: In the case of this project, I believe that Coffee Bean portrays a useful example of the kind of jobs that young people take in the suburbs. It may be possible to generalize from the coffee shop to some other service sector jobs in the suburbs, especially given the overall characteristics of the American youth labor force and the general movement of people and jobs from the cities to the suburbs. However, it is important to acknowledge that teenage workers in other kinds of businesses and in other areas (e.g., rural or urban) may or may not imbue their jobs with different meanings than what I found. It is an open empirical question. Unfortunately, my sense is that sociologists are not disposed to seeking out data that suggest that "workers may not experience their jobs to be as exploitive as we think they are." This is why studies such as mine can be helpful. It is necessary to round out the sociological portrayal of work by respecting and studying workers' lived experiences—even (or especially) those experiences that may be inconvenient to sociologists' accounts.

On the other hand, there is a way in which my study can be used to complement and buttress conventional accounts of inequality. My findings suggest another way in which "the poor get poorer." There can be important consequences when affluent youth consider work a fun activity and choose to spend their time after school hanging out in these "bad jobs": Their less-affluent counterparts find it more and more difficult to obtain these jobs.

This has important implications for the creation and reinforcement of existing inequalities, viewed from an objectivist perspective. Because "bad jobs" are enjoyed by youth who do not need money or benefits, employers may prefer them over their counterparts who are concerned with material benefits. Less-affluent youth are less privileged in finding jobs, as available jobs tend to be located in the more-affluent suburbs and not in the inner cities. However, even when they travel long distances, they are often not hired in favor of their more-affluent counterparts (Besen 2005; see also Newman 1999).

Thus, by understanding the work experience of these bad jobs from the perspective of the actors, we can provide a more comprehensive understanding of the perspective of the employers. By employing this particular group, they maintain a body of employees who do not mind the low pay and long shifts and truly enjoy the atmosphere and the products being sold. Understanding the work experience, therefore, increases our understanding of the creation and reinforcement of such inequalities and allows us to see the mechanisms through which employees consent to working under such conditions (see also Burawoy 1979).

Although constructionist analyses can be made to serve such conventional sociological ends, the constructionist perspective must be used carefully and not overly selectively. In the study of work, where work has been taken for granted as a set of activities performed for monetary gratifications, the constructionist perspective teaches us to be cautious of metanarratives of work. When objectivist scholars characterize entire employment sectors with broad generalizations, they risk obscuring and distorting the lived experiences of the people they write about. In contrast, a constructionist perspective encourages scholars to investigate putatively unequal experiences to discover what they mean to participants themselves. In the case of my study, the inequalities that sociologists decry were not experientially relevant features of participants' lives. This critique is possibly true of many other occupations and many other social situations. Therefore, a constructionist view can benefit the understanding of work as well as many other sociological arenas that have not yet fully been studied from the perspective of the actors.

4

Pay or Play?

*The Youth Labor Force in the United States
and Other Industrialized Countries*

The heart desires neither coffee nor coffee house: It desires
friendship, coffee is an excuse.
                                        —Turkish proverb

I n *When Teenagers Work* (1986), the pioneering work on youth employment
in the United States, Ellen Greenberger and Laurence Steinberg argue that
working while still in school is exclusively an American practice:

> The student worker per se is a distinctly American phenomenon. In
> many countries of the western world, it is virtually unheard of for
> youngsters to participate intensively in the labor force while still in
> school. The reasons why American teenagers are flocking to the work-
> place are embedded in events that have taken place in school, the fam-
> ily, and the economy—and in the motives, values, and aspirations of
> young people themselves. (1986: 4)

The view that working while still in school is a distinctly American phenomenon has been well established in the field. However, despite the unanimous
agreement on the unique nature of the American youth labor market, little
research has been done to compare the American youth labor force to those of
other industrialized countries. Often times, high rates of employment are cited
to justify the uniqueness of the American youth labor force. Greenberger and
Steinberg (1986) point to young people's motives and reasons for working in
understanding the unique nature of the American case; however, traditionally,
young people have been left out of the study of youth employment. Young
people's own motives for working and their aspirations and thoughts were
rarely included in typical studies of youth employment. Because young people
were typically left outside the study of employment, their reasons, motivations,
and aspirations were rarely examined. In recent years, however, an emerging

literature has called for the inclusion of the perspectives of the central actors into the study of youth work—young people themselves (Besen-Cassino 2008; Liebel 2004).

As Bernard Schlemmer notes:

> Even less than the labourer, the peasant, the immigrant, pauper or exploited person—already more often considered as the objects of social policies, development, integration, support and consciousness-raising rather than the subjects of their own history—the child is never perceived as an actor but always as the "target" (according to international institutions' current term, whose cruelty and cynicism one would believe to be unintended), the passive recipient of measures taken to protect him or her, i.e., to hold him/her "outside" the world he/she is going to have face on reaching adulthood. (2000: 4)

Because young people are typically considered to be passive subjects rather than active agents, their unique perspectives, motives, aspirations, and values have not been well documented. Although the effects of their employment, especially on academic progress, emotional development, future employment, and deviant behavior, have been widely discussed and debated, the young people themselves have rarely been included in the discussion. Because the central actors have been left outside the study of youth employment, their reasons for working have typically been reduced to an assumed economic need. That is why typical international studies of youth employment point to economic need and difficult conditions of work (Alvim 2000; Banpasirichote 2000; Fukui 2000; Gulrajani 2000; Lange 2000; Marguerat 2000; Mbaye and Fall 2000; Niuwenhuys 2000; Ramanathan 2000; Sastre and Meyer 2000; Schlemmer 2000; Suremain 2000; Tarancena and Tavera 2000; Verlet 2000). This has led scholars to study youth labor either as a historic artifact in industrialized countries or associate it with developing countries (Lavalette 2000). As Michael Lavalette argues:

> For many in Western Europe this is a phrase [child or youth labor] which applies to labour practices which have been abolished by "historical progress" or, alternatively, it is something which is pervasive in the NICs and UDCs and indicative of their economic "backwardness." In Britain it is generally assumed that when children work they do so in light, healthy jobs which are compatible with schooling and aid the transition into adulthood. (2000: 214)

This perspective is deeply entrenched in academic thinking on youth employment. Because youth labor in industrialized nations is seen as innocuous, youth labor exists as a social problem to be studied only in the context of newly industrializing countries. Even in such a context, the reasons for working are rarely explored. As Schlemmer observes, "Those not conforming to the ideal model are being seen solely as victims and, ultimately, objects: objects of pity, compassion and charity for well-to-do people turning their attention to their predicament; objects of shame and guilt for their parents, their families and communities" (2000: 4). Therefore, their perspectives, views, and reasons for working are rarely explored.

Particularly in industrialized countries, most research on youth employment focuses on the historic economic contributions of youth. Most of this literature comes from Britain and France, where, historically, children and youth made large contributions to the overall economy, often under terrible conditions. In recent years, emerging historic studies attempt to document the importance of youth employment throughout the history of many industrialized countries. Alessandro Stella observes, "Over the past two decades, labour history, which long used to be seen as the history of adult men, has made room for working women; the history of working children remains largely untold" (2000: 25). Yet this line of research separates contemporary youth labor from historical examples and assumes that the work experience of contemporary youth in industrialized countries remains outside the scope of study of youth labor. Many scholars consider the work of Western teenagers as "not out of necessity" and therefore not real examples of child/youth labor (Fyfe 1989; Whittaker 1986):

> Child labour is defined as work which does not take place in relatively idyllic conditions. It is assumed to have a degree of economic compulsion associated with it and, according to Fyfe, it involves a time and energy commitment which affects children's abilities to participate in leisure, play and educational activities. Finally, child labour is work which impairs the health and development of children. (Lavalette 2000: 215)

Because of this distinction, part-time work of many students has often been left outside the scope of inquiry in many industrialized countries. Beginning in the 1990s, research in many industrialized countries began to include students in the study of youth labor. According to Lavalette, "Research produced by a number of groups over the last ten years has emphasized that the exploitation of children at work is unfortunately alive and well in the British labour market and 'part-time out of school work' remains a significant feature of children's's lives" (2000: 216; see also Balding 1991; Finn 1987; Hobbs, Lavalette, and McKechnie 1992; Lavalette 1991; MacLennan, Fitz, and Sullivan

1985; McKechnie, Lindsay, and Hobbs 1994; Moorehead 1987; Pond and Searle 1991). Over the past twenty-five years, Walter R. Heinz (2000) in the context of Germany, and Katherine M. O'Regan and John M. Quigley (1996a, 1996b) have studied contemporary youth labor in industrialized countries. However, their work uniformly connects youth labor to poverty and economic need. Although O'Regan and Quigley (1996a, 1996b) identify availability of service sector jobs as a prerequisite, poverty and economic need are deemed the determining motivators of employment. Yet David Brady (2004) suggests that it is important to look at youth poverty and economic need as being relevant for only one portion of the labor market.

Although many industrialized countries have the same phenomenon of working students, the number of comparative studies on the topic is limited. In many cases, methodological difficulties have made international comparisons of employment difficult. Even though data collection is not a significant problem in industrialized countries, and almost every industrialized country collects data on youth employment at the national level, the comparability of the data across countries has been problematic, largely because of definitional problems. What is defined as "youth" or "labor" varies between countries, although the concepts do not substantively differ. However, these definitional differences are most problematic for studies including nonindustrialized countries, where youth labor often includes child labor. Among industrialized countries, this does not pose a problem, because child labor is rare and usually illegal. As such, the most important problem in finding comparable cross-national employment data for industrialized countries has been finding comparable data on the aspirations and motivations behind that labor. The focus of most youth-employment studies in industrialized countries has been economic factors, and, as the discussion of youth labor in the United States has made clear, they are not always appropriate. Thus, although typical data sets on youth employment offer country-level information on demand, supply, proportions of employed youth, number of available jobs, parental cash transfers, unemployment rates, and minimum wage, hardly any data have been collected regarding the motivation to enter the labor market. Beginning in early 1980s, however, data sets offering information on the labor-market entry decisions of youth started to emerge both in the United States and in other industrialized countries (see National Longitudinal Study of Youth and High School and Beyond). Although such data sets offer insight into the motivations behind youth's entering the labor market and have allowed researchers to address sociological questions about the youth labor market, they do not provide the opportunity for cross-national comparisons. Still, there has been an emerging interest in cross-national, comparative studies on the topic. Such studies have not only expanded the evidence from other countries but also highlighted nationally specific practices and characteristics that may be taken for granted within individual countries. This emerging interest in such studies has been paralleled by the emergence of large data sets that offer comparable and representative information on industrialized countries, such as the World Values Study. The emergence of such studies allows for the comparison of why youth in various countries choose to enter the labor market.

The previous chapters focused on the United States and provided in-depth, qualitative information to capture the everyday lived experience of work for young people. These rich stories, anecdotes, and observations described the process and the lived experience from the perspectives of young people. The aim of this chapter is twofold. First, I aim to generalize these in-depth findings by using large-scale surveys. Second, I aim to contextualize these findings by providing international comparisons. I compare the motivations behind working in the United States and other industrialized counties. I acknowledge that there are differences within industrialized countries, but the goal here is to put the findings about the U.S. case into context. Rather than emphasize the idiosyncrasies in each country, I aim to highlight broad patterns and commonalities to better compare them.

The main data source is the World Values Study, which contains representative survey data from forty-five countries, allowing us to compare responses to validated, translated questions across nations. For the present purpose, the sample has been split into two groups: respondents from the United States and respondents from other industrialized countries, including European Union states, Australia, and Canada (I have estimated the results using only European Union countries as well, and the results are similar). The selection of these countries is in line with the common practice in the literature (see Reubens 1983). To better compare and contrast the reasons for working in the United States and other industrialized countries, a logistic regression model has been used separately for both parts of the bifurcated sample. Within these subsamples—U.S. youth and youth in other industrialized countries—the samples are divided into student and nonstudent youth, and the labor-market entry decisions of youth are estimated for each using logistic regression techniques. First, I make use of the logistic regression to analyze the causes of youth labor for students in the United States and, separately, for other countries. Next, I compare the employment patterns of nonstudents within the United States with those of nonstudents outside the United States. Finally, I look at how student and nonstudent employment decisions differ in countries outside the United States. The details of my methodology are presented in the Appendix. Descriptive statistics for the variables evaluated are presented in Table 4.1.

TABLE 4.1 Descriptive Characteristics of the Current Youth Labor Force, by Nationality and Student Status

	Min	Max	U.S. Students		U.S. Nonstudents		Non-U.S. Students		Non-U.S. Nonstudents	
			Mean	SD	Mean	SD	Mean	SD	Mean	SD
Good pay	0	1	.83	.38	.83	.38	.73	.44	.74	.44
Pleasant people	0	1	.77	.42	.77	.42	.73	.44	.72	.45
No pressure	0	1	.34	.47	.37	.48	.37	.48	.35	.48
Security	0	1	.71	.46	.71	.46	.58	.49	.63	.48
Promotions	0	1	.63	.48	.61	.49	.50	.50	.45	.50
Respected	0	1	.50	.50	.41	.49	.40	.49	.36	.48
Good hours	0	1	.61	.49	.64	.48	.45	.50	.52	.50
Initiative	0	1	.51	.50	.40	.49	.54	.50	.44	.50
Useful	0	1	.48	.50	.32	.47	.47	.50	.36	.48
Good holidays	0	1	.24	.43	.34	.48	.31	.46	.35	.48
Meet people	0	1	.63	.48	.60	.49	.50	.50	.48	.50
Achievement	0	1	.80	.40	.70	.46	.60	.49	.54	.50
Responsibility	0	1	.68	.47	.57	.50	.45	.50	.41	.49
Interesting	0	1	.81	.39	.75	.43	.65	.48	.60	.49
Meets abilities	0	1	.64	.48	.54	.50	.62	.49	.49	.50
Confidence in education system	1	4	2.00	.81	2.14	.92	2.30	.84	2.33	.83
Live with parents	1	2	1.16	.37	1.28	.45	1.10	.40	1.18	.38
Socioeconomic status	1	4	2.54	1.25	2.86	1.12	2.44	.94	2.92	.87
Decision to work	0	1	.55	.50	.72	.45	.18	.38	.71	.46

Source: Data analyzed are from the World Values Study (Abramson and Inglehart 1995, 2000).
Note: The non-U.S. nations represented in the table are the European Union states, Australia, and Canada. Min, minimum; Max, maximum; SD, standard deviation.

American Youth Are More Likely to Work

The logistic regression analysis confirms the hypothesis that the U.S. student youth labor market is, indeed, a unique case (Table 4.2). First, both students and nonstudents are more likely to work in the United States than in other industrialized countries (Table 4.3). For student youth in the United States, the overall likelihood of working (56 percent) is considerably higher than for student youth in other industrialized countries (17 percent). Even nonstudents in the same age cohort in the United States are somewhat more likely to work than their counterparts in other industrialized countries: 81 percent of nonstudents in the United States work, while 71 percent of nonstudents work in other industrialized countries. Yet although both students and nonstudents in the United States are more likely to work than their counterparts in other industrialized countries, the difference is clearly more pronounced among students (39 points). Working, therefore, is much more prevalent for American youth, particularly American student youth.

TABLE 4.2 Logistic Regression Coefficients for Youth Labor-Market Entry Decisions on Selected Variables, by Nationality and Student Status

	U.S. Students		U.S. Nonstudents		Non-U.S. Students		Non-U.S. Nonstudents	
	Coeff	SE	Coeff	SE	Coeff	SE	Coeff	SE
Good pay	.045	.451	−.215	.649	−.160	.135	−.091	.143
Pleasant people	−.412	.433	.522	.594	.572*	.148	.259	.136
No pressure	−.550	.390	−.219	.547	.067	.127	−.200	.135
Security	.086	.403	−.627	.586	.139	.128	−.002	.129
Promotions	.021	.397	1.000**	.547	−.098	.132	−.045	.135
Respected	.151	.367	−1.279*	.661	−.061	.129	−.119	.146
Good hours	.060	.387	−.289	.647	.030	.131	.032	.135
Initiative	−.005	.419	.449	.665	−.142	.13	.304*	.140
Useful	.230	.378	1.276**	.723	−.095	.127	−.220	.142
Good holidays	−.127	.409	−.794	.577	.094	.134	−.068	.143
Meet people	.906*	.388	.482	.572	.050	.125	.026	.134
Achievement	.084	.447	.576	.595	.043	.132	−.031	.135
Responsibility	.514	.407	−.091	.583	.021	.133	.194	.141
Interesting	.345	.464	.353	.613	.032	.129	.153	.133
Meets abilities	.328	.399	−.537	.649	−.097	.129	−.069	.136
Confidence in education system	−.581*	.223	.095	.258	−.013	.065	.007	.070
Live with parents	.374	.457	.465	.526	−.319*	.119	.109	.146
Socioeconomic status	.480*	.141	.889*	.287	−.143*	.058	.258*	.067
Intercept	−1.446	.988	4.263*	1.505	−2.59*	.293	1.640*	.334
Log likelihood	−116.757		−64.552		−1,114.870		−934.777	
N	199		145		2,444		1,579	
LR chi²(18)	40.540		41.710		40.980		39.310	
Prob > chi²	.002		.001		.002		.003	

Source: Data analyzed are from the World Values Study (Abramson and Inglehart 1995, 2000).

Note: Coeff, logistic regression coefficient; SE, standard error; LR chi²(18), likelihood ratio chi-square (18 degrees of freedom).

$*p < .05$; $**p < .01$.

Unique Composition

Higher labor-force participation certainly sets American youth apart. However, this is not the only difference: The socioeconomic characteristics of American youth laborers are also markedly different from those of comparable workers elsewhere. As might be expected, the socioeconomic status of the students has a significant effect on their labor-market entry decisions. However, for students in the United States, the likelihood of labor-market entry increases as the socioeconomic status increases. Mirroring the findings of the U.S. Bureau of Labor Statistics studies (Herman 2000), students from higher socioeconomic backgrounds are more likely to work. Although logistic

TABLE 4.3 Monte Carlo Simulations of the Effect of Selected Variables on the Likelihood of Entering the Youth Labor Market, by Nationality and Student Status

U.S. Students	
Overall mean likelihood of working	.555
Effect of Socioeconomic status	.337
Effect of Meet people	.219
Effect of Confidence in education system	.374

U.S. Nonstudents	
Overall mean likelihood of working	.809
Effect of Socioeconomic status	.349
Effect of Promotions	.160
Effect of Respected	.208
Effect of Useful	.164

Non-U.S. Students	
Overall mean likelihood of working	.174
Effect of Socioeconomic status	.055
Effect of Pleasant people	.074
Effect of Live with parents	.511

Non-U.S. Nonstudents	
Overall mean likelihood of working	.715
Effect of Socioeconomic status	.153
Effect of Initiative	.063

Source: Data analyzed are from the World Values Study (Abramson and Inglehart 1995, 2000).

regression estimation identifies the significant predictors of entering the labor market, logistic regression coefficients are difficult to interpret directly: We can identify the significant effects and the direction of the relation, but we are unable to measure the magnitude of the effects. For this purpose, Monte Carlo simulations have been employed. Monte Carlo simulations for a coefficient measure the magnitude and the direction of the effect that variable has on the likelihood of working, controlling for all other variables in the model. Each number shows how much the likelihood of working increases or decreases depending on the sign of the coefficient, moving from the minimum value of the independent variable to the maximum value. For students in the United States, the overall likelihood of working is 56 percent, controlling for all the factors in the data set. Moving from the lowest socioeconomic status group of students to the highest increases the overall likelihood of working by 30 percent. Although students from the lowest socioeconomic status have around a 40 percent chance of working, students from the highest socioeconomic status can be expected to work nearly 70 percent of the time. Overall, the American youth labor force is dominated by the higher socioeconomic students and nonstudents, a finding that supports the qualitative conclusion that coming from a higher socioeconomic background provides a marked advantage in the job market.

Reasons for Working

In addition to labor-force participation rates and demographic differences, the reasons for working are also substantially different in the United States than in other countries. The World Values Study asks respondents about their reasons for working, giving them a list of options to choose from. In the logistic regression model, saying "yes" to these possible options is used as a predictor of entering the labor market. For students in the United States, the decision to enter the labor market is not explained by the options representing economic values, or factors that may help enhance future employment, such as good pay, job security, chances for promotion, good hours, or opportunities to use initiative. Rather, the decision is strongly predicted by the options representing social values. An American student who values meeting people on the job, holding all other variables at their means, has a 63.4 percent chance of working—an increase of 22 percent over an American student who does not value meeting people (of whom 41.5 percent are expected to work). In addition to the significant effect of meeting people, the other significant social predictor of youth work is confidence in the education system. American students' lack of confidence in the education system makes a student in the United States 37 percent more likely to work, raising the predicted probability of working from 41.5 percent to 78.8 percent. The social implications of the complex relationship between work and education are discussed in depth in Chapter 5. The data here support the findings of the qualitative research: that social considerations are dominant in the decision of young Americans to enter the labor market.

Student versus Nonstudent

To put these findings more deeply in context, we can examine how the same variables predict the labor-market entry decisions of nonstudents in the same age bracket in the United States. Although all youth in the same age bracket are treated uniformly, within the United States, there are marked differences between students and nonstudents. Nonstudents display a fundamentally different pattern than their student counterparts: Almost 80 percent of all youth who do not go to school work. They are more likely to work than their student counterparts, and their labor-market entry decisions follow a different pattern. As with students, socioeconomic status is a significant predictor of labor-market entry decisions. The effect of socioeconomic background not only is significant but also follows the same path, with nonstudents from higher socioeconomic groups being more likely to work. Moving from the lowest socioeconomic status group to the highest, for American nonstudents, the overall likelihood of working increases from 60.5 percent to the near certainty of 95.1 percent. Even for dropouts, similar aesthetic-labor considerations are in effect, and we see a bias against dropouts of lower socioeconomic status.

However, except for the similar effect of socioeconomic status, the predictors of labor-market entry decisions among nonstudents in the United States show a different pattern. None of the social factors measured significantly predicts the labor-market entry decisions of nonstudents in the United States. However, the decision to work is significantly predicted by usefulness of the job, respect commanded by the job, and possibility of promotion. Nonstudents in the United States who value the respectability of the job are substantially less likely to work, and those who value the possibility of promotions as well as those who value the usefulness of the job to society are more likely to work. Both of these variables have z-values slightly outside conventional levels of statistical acceptability ($p = .06$ and $.053$, respectively), but given the relatively small sample size for logit estimation, the results are not wholly uninterpretable: Both of these are relatively more work-related concerns than those voiced by U.S. students.

The negative coefficient on the respect value could be explained by the presence or absence of "respectable" jobs available for nonstudents between ages sixteen and nineteen. Among nonstudent youth with limited skills and education, valuing respectable jobs makes an individual less likely to work. Overall, social factors do not help predict labor-market entry decisions among nonstudents. For nonstudents, the significant predictors are all economic, or at least work-related, in nature. Unlike students, whose labor-market entry decisions are largely explained by social factors, the nonstudents' labor-market entry decisions are predicted by factors at least relating to the job. This unique set of factors can be explained through the lack of social space for and alienation of students in the United States.

Other Industrialized Countries

Although the American student population emerges as a unique group much different from the nonstudent Americans in the same age group, its members also show important differences from students in other advanced economies. Student youth in other industrialized countries are less likely to work than their American counterparts, and they work for economic, as opposed to social, reasons. In other industrialized countries, the student youth labor force is dominated by lower socioeconomic status youth. This difference in socioeconomic composition of the labor forces is important because it not only illuminates the differences in characteristics of two labor markets but also has important implications for why students work in these two different settings. Because the student youth labor market is dominated by lower socioeconomic groups, one would expect students in those countries to work out of economic need. In line with this prediction, the decision to enter the workforce for students in industrialized nations outside the United States is dominated by economic factors. One of the most important predictors of their work decisions is whether they live with their parents: Students who live with their parents are far less likely to work than those who do not, compared with an insignificant effect of living with parents for students in the United States. Living with parents seems to provide an economic safety net. Thus, in industrialized countries other than the United States, student workers are more likely to come from lower socioeconomic backgrounds, and their likelihood of working increases substantially if they do not live with their parents. In sum, student youth employment is a widespread activity in the United States that is predominantly performed by youth from higher socioeconomic backgrounds for social reasons, such as meeting new people. In contrast, student labor in other industrialized nations is relatively rare and more likely to be undertaken by students from lower socioeconomic backgrounds, especially if they do not live with their parents.

The nonstudent workers in the United States and in other industrialized countries, on the other hand, appear to be very similar in terms of their composition as well as the reasons that they work. For nonstudent workers in the United States and in other industrialized countries, low socioeconomic status is a significant and an important predictor of the decision to enter the labor market. Furthermore, for nonstudents in the United States and in other industrialized countries, economic reasons dominate the decisions to work. In the United States, the workforce entry decisions of nonstudent youth are explained by the possibility of promotions and the respectfulness and usefulness of the job. In other words, nonstudents in the United States are more likely to work for economic benefits. If the job is respected by others, or if it is useful to them in terms of providing needed skills, nonstudents are more likely to work. Similarly, in other industrialized countries, youth are more likely to work if the job includes taking initiative.

The similarity between nonstudents in the United States and in other industrialized countries is not surprising. Because young people from lower socioeconomic backgrounds are less likely to continue in school than their peers, their economic situation is a very important predictor of labor-market entry. The decisions of nonstudent youth in both settings are explained by economic and job-related concerns; they are unlikely to work for social reasons.

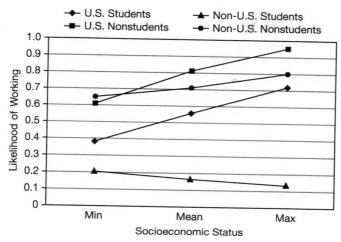

FIGURE 4.1 Effects of Socioeconomic Status on Likelihood of Working

On the other hand, students in other industrialized countries show similarities to their nonstudent counterparts, despite being very unlikely to work. Their decisions to enter the labor market are predominantly explained by their socioeconomic background, with the lower socioeconomic background student youth more likely to enter the labor market. However, in contrast to their nonstudent peers, students who live with their parents decrease their likelihood of working. For students in other industrialized countries, therefore, labor-market entry is most likely among students who come from lower socioeconomic backgrounds and do not live with their parents.

First, as Figure 4.1 shows, for students in the United States, high socioeconomic status increases the likelihood of working. The most pronounced difference in the effect of socioeconomic status on workforce participation is between the student youth from the United States and those from other countries. Among students in the United States, higher socioeconomic status leads to an increased propensity to work, while having the opposite effect among students in other industrialized nations.

Second, for only students in the United States, social reasons, such as meeting people, predict the likelihood of working. As Figure 4.2 demonstrates, for both students and nonstudents in other industrialized countries and for nonstudents in the United States, meeting new people is not an important factor in predicting the likelihood of entering the labor market: In other words, none of these subsamples works just to meet new people. Students in the United States, however, generally do work to meet new people, as detailed in Chapter 3.

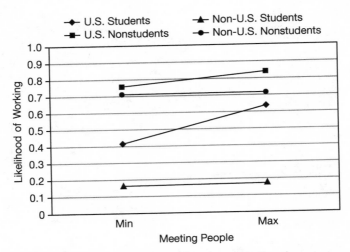

FIGURE 4.2 Effects of Meeting People on Likelihood of Working

Finally, for student youth in the United States, lack of confidence in the education system increases the likelihood of working. As Figure 4.3 shows, the lower their confidence in the education system, the more likely these individuals are to enter the labor market. This, too, is in line with the qualitative findings that young people are working to supplement the social experiences that

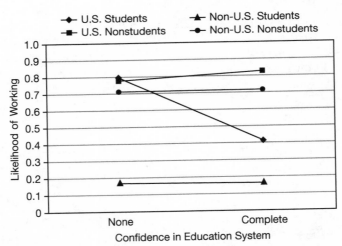

FIGURE 4.3 Effects of Confidence in the Education System on Likelihood of Working

they are not finding in their schools: If the schools were doing what the students expected of them, the students would not be working in the first place.

What Does It Mean?

These unique motives for working can be explained through the lack of social space and alienation of students in the United States. Many scholars have noted the alienation of young people, especially in the suburbs (Gaines 1998). In the past, the social needs of young people were met by schools or other social organizations. For today's students, work is replacing clubs, organizations, and other social groupings. Among a similar population, research has shown that workplaces function as gathering places for youth, message centers, and, generally, arenas in which youth can meet new friends and socialize with their peers (Besen 2004).We can argue that for students in the United States, work is a medium through which new acquaintances are made. U.S. students are the only group for whom the chance to meet people is a significant predictor of working. American students could potentially fulfill this need at school, but they may be prevented from doing so by their lack of confidence in the education system. As a result of the perceived inability of schools to create social cohesion, educational institutions may have lost their role in creating an environment that allows students to meet others. Work, therefore, provides an alternative to school in creating the social environment in which to meet peers.

In addition, there has been a decline in the perceived ability of schools to provide a common meaning and narrative for young people. Students today are much less likely to be involved in campus activities, such as intramural sports or clubs; less likely to attend campus sporting events; and even less likely to live on campus. Work, therefore, provides an alternative social environment in which to meet peers. Work provides not only the opportunity and the space to meet new people but also a common narrative and a common language for that interaction. This phenomenon is discussed in further detail in Chapter 5. In short, we see that the students are working to fulfill unmet social needs.

It is important to note, however, the student labor force consists predominantly of higher socioeconomic status students. Of course, for some youth, especially those in inner cities and impoverished rural areas, the work decision might be entirely economic. However, to focus on these young people is to miss the overall trends in youth employment for students in the United States. The marginal effect of these young people can be seen in the relationship of socioeconomic status and likelihood of working in the United States. Overall, in the United States, youth from higher socioeconomic backgrounds are more likely to work. Recent findings show that disadvantaged youth have difficulty finding work even when they want it, as the jobs are primarily filled by higher socioeconomic status youth (Newman 1999). This serves to reinforce the notion that work is primarily a social decision for students: It is as if youth employment is a commodity that only the affluent can afford.

Work as Social and Personal Space

The need for a place to hang out in the suburbs goes beyond the basic need to socialize and meet new people. Young people achieve a sense of independence when they get away from adult surveillance and adult supervision. International research confirms that privacy and psychological space are very important in developing a sense of self and independence for many young people (Abbott-Chapman and Robertson 2009; Robertson and Williams 2004). Many young people cite "hanging out with friends" and "thinking about things" as leisure activities that are central in their identity formation and independence (Tarrant et al. 2001). Joan Abbott-Chapman and Margaret Robertson (2009) identify places in nature, the countryside, sporting venues, public parks, the seashore, and even the bedroom as spaces away from surveillance, where young people are not bothered by adults. Unfortunately, many teenagers are unable to find such spaces so easily in the United States. In the area where I conducted my research, access to nature, countryside, or the seaside was limited, if not impossible. Public parks and spaces were not available, were limited in scope, or even had specific restrictions on use by teens. Many teenagers complain about the lack of available space in the suburbs when it comes to socializing. Even their leisure time is controlled and dominated by adults. Many extracurricular activities or sports events are organized or chaperoned by their parents or other adults. Therefore, such organized and behaviorally controlled leisure activities do not offer young people the unsupervised, private space that they need to develop their individual personalities, interests, and identities (Frank and Stevens 2007). With such limited space allocated for social interaction, many young people have turned to malls and shopping centers. In previous years, it was not uncommon to see teenagers flocking to malls, hanging out in front of stores, and congregating in mall parking lots. However, the past few decades have witnessed the emergence of what we can refer to as anti-teenage policies. In 1996, Mall of America in Minnesota, the biggest mall in the United States, banned unattended teenagers and implemented a "parental escort policy" for all teenagers. According to this policy, teenagers under age eighteen have to be accompanied by a parent or a guardian over age twenty-one. Following this example, many malls developed their own anti-teenage policies.

Some malls have implemented other policies to discourage teenagers from congregating. Crossgates Mall in Albany, New York, for example, opted for a teen curfew. Teenagers are not allowed on the premises after 4:00 P.M. on Saturday. After this strictly enforced curfew, teenagers who are found in the mall are escorted out by security.

Some malls and shopping centers are less worried about individual teenagers shopping at the mall but have restrictions regarding teenagers' congregating and using the mall as a social venue to see friends. The Atlantic Terminal Mall in Brooklyn, New York, bans groups of four or more unsupervised youth under age twenty-one. When five or more shoppers under age twenty-one are found to be congregating, they are asked to either break up into smaller groups or leave the premises.

Some businesses, such as movie theaters, have banned teenagers altogether. As a result of such anti-teenage policies, young people in the suburbs suffer from a lack of social space to congregate and hang out. In centerless suburbs, teenagers already had difficulty finding common spaces to socialize and meet new people. The widely spread-out landscape, large distances, and lack of public transportation already made it challenging for young people to socialize with their friends. Young people had been hanging out at shopping malls, stores, and movie theaters to fulfill that social need. However, young people hanging out together in public places have been characterized as a "counter-productive activity" (Abbott-Chapman and Robertson 2009). Instead of seeing such gatherings as a social activity, many adults simply characterize them as a "waste of time," taking time away from more organized leisure activities or school work.

In addition to being unproductive, the idleness of young people hanging out has been characterized as "dangerous." As Donna Gaines observes, "Even if young people are talking about serious things, working out plans for the future, discussing life, jobs, adults just assume they are getting wasted" (1998: 97). Young people hanging out or congregating are seen as suspicious, and few public spaces are available to young people to socialize as a result. After implementing anti-teenage policies and restrictions, many malls reported experiencing a substantial boost in their businesses from adults. Adult consumers who previously perceived the malls as being dominated by teenagers felt less threatened by the marked absence of teenagers and more confident in patronizing the businesses.

Jamie, a nineteen-year-old full-time student and employee in the coffee shop, reminded me, "[Work] is not something you do for money or experience, you know. It's where I hang out. And my parents are okay with it." Many young people tell me that getting a job was a decision that their parents were supportive of and even encouraged. Josh agreed that his parents supported his decision to work. Work offered an environment that provided a central space to socialize and see friends without adult supervision, and parents like Jamie's and Josh's not only allowed it but also highly encouraged it. Even though their children might really be there to hang out and see friends, parents did not see the work as an idle activity. Work, even in relatively menial jobs, is perceived as providing skills that may be useful later on, such as time management, work ethic, and budgeting. These factors mean that work has become the ideal way for young people to escape the watchful eyes of parents and other adults; Jamie admitted to using work as an excuse to get out of family obligations and house chores.

Not all parents are oblivious to the motives. Sarah's mother, for example, knew she was at the coffee shop to see her friends. Wiping dirty tables, washing dishes, carrying trash bags, and dealing with needy and annoying customers were not ways she thought her daughter would develop her skills and utilize her knowledge. In fact, she characterized her daughter's time at the shop as a "waste of time" and "annoying." However, this job still kept her "out of trouble" and "busy."

Parents are not the only ones to feel the effects of such anti-teenager policies. Many young people complain about the lack of common spaces. Despite the working conditions, Sarah said she loved the people she worked with and found the job "fun." She scheduled her shifts with her friends, and many acquaintances would trickle in as customers to see friends. She spent so much time at Coffee Bean, where she worked, that she felt as though she lived there. In reality, where else could she go where she could have the opportunity to see her friends and would also be welcome?

For Sarah, being free from adult supervision was an important part of her decision to work. Even though she had a manager during her shift, he was a young college student. He was tough when he had to be and was fair, but generally he was calm, laid-back, and cool. Overall, working at the coffee shop offered a refuge from adult supervision and parental authority and provided the opportunity to see friends and socialize, especially in an environment where young people are surrounded by their peers away from the judgmental eyes of mall security and disapproving strangers. At the coffee shop, they were not viewed as idle, aimless, or criminals.

This is not to say that the job did not include real demands. Although the job offered a wide range of social benefits, the pay was still dismal and the hours were long and cumbersome, although the affluent teenagers did not care so much. Sarah would sometimes be at the coffee shop from 7:00 A.M. to 11:30 P.M. During her shift, she was expected to know the recipe for each drink, and she made drinks and sandwiches, arranged sliced cakes, cleaned, and washed dishes throughout her long shift. On busy days, she would rarely get more than a few ten-minute breaks, and her shifts would typically be spent on her feet for hours. To add to this long shift, she had a substantial commute just to get to this particular branch of the coffee shop. During the busy holiday season, she would not get a day off. She worked under these conditions for nearly five years for low pay and no benefits. The ample social benefits she enjoyed did not obscure or legitimize the working conditions. In her words, she simply did not care. Just like Josh, who said he felt in charge of something when he worked, Sarah felt powerful, important, and needed.

The social and emotional benefits are important in the way young people talk about their jobs. But the important question is, why work? Why do the workplaces fulfill the function of providing social spaces and individual identities rather than schools? Why are places of education not the central social spaces in young people's lives?

5

"They Need Me Here"

Work as a Perceived Alternative to School

John had been studying at the local state university for some time. Even though he kept changing his mind about his major, he was sure about his workplace. The Coffee Bean had been the constant in his life through changing majors, partners, and roommates. On the day of a blizzard, I ask him whether his school was in session. "Oh, yes," he told me. In fact, he had a class that afternoon, but instead of going to class, he chose to come to the coffee shop. He even stayed longer to help his friends in the later shifts and missed a later class as well. When I asked him why he chose the Coffee Bean over his academic work, he had a simple answer: "They need me here." He was not alone. Amy, a nineteen-year-old college student, made a similar choice, picking work over school. She agreed that she was needed.

At the large state university where John was a full-time student, most of his classes took place in large lecture halls. If he did not show up for class, John told me that nobody noticed. His professors did not know his name; many of his classes were taught by teaching assistants anyway. Because the classes were so big, he did not know any of the other students. Many students would come to class and leave immediately afterward, so John never had the chance to meet most of them. If he missed a shift or did not hang out as usual at the coffee shop, however, his absence *was* noticed: His co-workers would text or call him.

Sarah agreed that she was noticed at the coffee shop. In five years, Sarah had not missed a single shift. Neither weather conditions nor sickness ever stopped her from showing up for her scheduled hours. Once she was on the schedule, she felt as though she had an obligation to work, not because she was afraid of her manager, but because she felt a sense of loyalty and did not want to let down her co-workers. Because she was in charge of specific tasks, she believed that if she missed a shift, the coffee shop would not operate properly. She was an integral part of the operation, and other people depended on her. If she did not show up, both the customers and her co-workers would suffer.

For both John and Sarah, the commitments they made to their jobs were very important. Unlike the commitments they made to their schools and classes, the commitment to their jobs was strong. They shared a sense of loyalty toward the workplace, and they took pride in the work they accomplished at the coffee shop. Whether it was the way they made foam or made coffee, they felt as though they were good at something. This sense of loyalty and responsibility was so strong that they prioritized their workplace over their school commitments.

In this chapter, I explore the complex relationship between work and school. I aim to answer the following questions: Why do many young people feel such a strong sense of loyalty toward work and prioritize it over school? And why do many young people utilize workplaces to fulfill social functions when many go to school every day? Why have workplaces emerged as alternatives to school in creating social bonds? Why are schools unable to fulfill that function?

What about Schools?

The relationship between work and school is indeed complex and intertwined. Education and work are not only basic institutions but also two of the most important institutions for young people in our society. William Richard Scott observes that institutions "consist of cognitive, normative and regulation structures and activities that provide stability and meaning to social behavior" (1995: 33). Therefore, these particular institutions, work and school, are not just useful entities for educating our students and training our workforce but also social sites to define central values of our society. They are instrumental in socializing young people into our society and providing structure for them to live by those learned values (Bills 2004). It is very important to study school and work to understand the social values and norms they reflect and reinforce. Although the structure and the institutions help shape and reinforce the values of youth, young people in turn influence the values of these institutions.

This chapter explores these key institutions: work and school. Studying these institutions from the perspectives of young people sheds light on their values and their attitudes as well the attitudes of society regarding education and work.

The relationship between work and school has been a central object of inquiry in academic research, especially over the past few decades. Prior research has focused primarily on the *effects* of working on education, particularly on dropout rates, school attendance, academic performance, and acquisition of industry-related skills to find future jobs.

First, scholars have looked at the effects of working on dropout rates. Ronald D'Amico and Paula Baker (1984) show that working while still in school substantially lowers dropout rates. Especially among non–college bound youth, working helps keep students in school longer and reduces dropout levels (McNeal 1997). International studies confirm that by providing the means to cover school expenses, working helps keep students in school longer. However, many scholars have established that such benefits are limited to non–college bound youth (D'Amico and Baker 1984).

A second strand of research has explored the effects of working on school attendance. An International Labour Organization (ILO) study using surveys from thirty-four countries between 1998 and 2006 shows that working negatively affects school attendance (Allais and Hagemann 2008), although some contrary findings have suggested that working does not have such detrimental effects on school attendance (Edmonds 2008; Guarchello et al. 2005; Krishna 1996). Typically, studies examining the academic effects of employment take the number of hours worked into consideration. Although working fewer hours each week does not interfere with academic progress, working long hours or full-time is associated with poor school attendance (Edmonds 2008). Jeylan T. Mortimer (2003) shows that working has negative effects on school attendance only when students work more than twenty hours per week. A Scottish study shows that even when working students miss some days, the number of days they miss is not substantial (Howieson, McKechnie, and Semple 2006).

A third wave of research has focused on the effects of working on homework time and academic preparation. Many international findings point out that working lowers school preparation and results in lower academic performance (Nambissan 2003). However, in the United States, recent studies, such as the Youth Development Study, show that working is not in direct competition with homework time. Work time usually comes out of passive hanging out time, television time, or time for other leisure activities (Mortimer 2007). Therefore, working does not take away time from academic preparation. This finding correlates with the idea of seeing work as a form of leisure.

Another wave of research has focused on the effects of working on academic performance. Today, many reputable scholars argue that work hinders academic success (Entwisle, Alexander, and Olson 2000; Greenberger and Steinberg 1986; Marsh 1991; Mortimer and Finch 1986; Steinberg and Dornbusch 1991). If work intensity is considered, working few hours, especially fewer than ten hours per week, has no significant effect on school performance (D'Amico and Baker 1984; Post and Pong 2009; Stack and McKechnie 2002).

However, working too many hours interferes with academic success. Although the negative effects of intense hours exist, the extent of the academic damage is not clear. Some studies have shown that working more than 19.5 hours a week reduces the time young people have for homework and studying, resulting in detrimental academic effects. Studies from Turkey, Tanzania, Venezuela, and Bolivia show that working students are more likely to fail in school (Akabayashi and Psacharopoulos 1999; Guarchello et al. 2005, 2007; Psacharopoulos 1997).

The final wave of studies has explored whether working while still in school helps secure better jobs in the future. Many scholars have argued that working teaches important job-related skills that help young people find jobs more easily once they graduate. For non–college bound students, early labor-market experience results in better employment (D'Amico and Baker 1984; Meyer and Wise 1982; Stern and Nakata 1989). Non–college bound students who work while in school secure employment more easily once they graduate and perform better in their future jobs compared to their nonworking counterparts. However, these benefits are limited to these non–college bound youth.

Although the effects of working have been studied from the perspectives of many parties, including educators, administrators, and parents, the central actors have been left out of the discussion. As historian Barbara Finkelstein (1991) aptly observes, politicians, academics, journalists, and labor leaders have discussed the role of education, while young people have been left out of this debate. That is, even though the *effects* of their work decisions have been studied extensively, their views on education and work have been left out. As a result, how they feel about education and work remains largely unexplored.

In this chapter, I explore the complex relationship of work and school from the perspective of young people. During economically challenging times, when education has become central in securing future employment, why do young people work if they do not need to?

Although other people's views have been explored in great detail, the lived experience of young people has been largely left out. How *they* see school and work is a very important factor that needs to be addressed. The social meaning of school and jobs illuminates their work and school decisions and provides an in-depth understanding of young people's work experiences and lives. By understanding their perspectives, we can shed light on their work and their education-related decisions.

In this chapter, I rely on two sources of information. First, I use in-depth interviews and stories to understand how young people see school and work. Second, I use large-scale survey data to generalize these findings and provide comparisons.

Case of the United States:
Work and Confidence in the Education System

According to the World Values Study, approximately 54 percent of the students in the United States work while still in school, whereas only 16 percent of their non-American counterparts do so (Table 5.1). On the basis of the results of the logistic regression explaining youth's labor-market entry decisions, confidence in the education system is a significant and substantial predictor of student youth's market-entry decisions in the United States (Table 5.2). For these students, the lower the confidence in the education system, the higher the likelihood of entering the labor market. For nonstudents in the United States and both students and nonstudents outside the United States, on the other hand, confidence in the education system has little impact on their labor-market entry decisions.

Among students in the United States, however, Monte Carlo simulations (Table 5.1) predict that moving from the lowest level of confidence in the education system to the highest level of confidence decreases the likelihood of working on average by 37 percent: The less confident American students are in the education system, the more likely they are to decide to work (see also Figure 4.3). The Monte Carlo simulations show that this effect of confidence in education on the likelihood of working applies only to students in the United States. On average, approximately 81 percent of nonstudents in the United States work. Yet moving from the lowest level of confidence in the education system to the highest level of confidence decreases the likelihood of working by approximately 5 percent, an effect too small to be statistically significant. For students outside the United States, the overall average likelihood of working is 17 percent, and moving from the lowest level of confidence in the education system to the highest level of confidence makes practically no difference at all. Similarly, for nonstudents outside the United States, the overall average likelihood of working is approximately 72 percent, and confidence in the education system again has virtually no effect on the likelihood of working. The effect of confidence in education in explaining youth's labor-market entry decisions is significant only for students in the

TABLE 5.1 Monte Carlo Simulations of the Effect of Selected Variables on the Likelihood of Entering the Youth Labor Market, by Nationality and Student Status

	U.S. Students	U.S. Nonstudents	Non-U.S. Students	Non-U.S. Nonstudents
Overall mean likelihood of working	.536	.779	.155	.716
Effect of Socioeconomic status	.357	.400	.201	.500
Effect of Confidence in education system	.374	.055	.025	.032
Effect of Meet people	.212	.052	.046	.107

Source: Data analyzed are from the World Values Study (Abramson and Inglehart 1995, 2000).

TABLE 5.2 Logistic Regression Coefficients for Youth Labor-Market Entry Decisions on Selected Variables

	U.S. Students		U.S. Nonstudents		Non-U.S. Students		Non-U.S. Nonstudents	
	Coeff	SE	Coeff	SE	Coeff	SE	Coeff	SE
Confidence in education system	−.571*	.216	.088	.258	.054	.067	.063	.063
Socioeconomic status	.506*	.134	.958*	.262	−.145*	.056	−.068*	.068
Meet people	.874*	.351	.332	.514	.196	.117	.119	.119
Race	.087	.347	.529	.464	.898*	.190	.163*	.163
Gender	.144	.325	−.788	.473	−.16	.113	.118*	.118
Good pay	.185	.440	−.101	.627	−.086	.131	.140	.140
Good holidays	.037	.377	−.494	.494	.126	.127	.130	.130
Live with parents	.566	.444	−.258	.469	.331*	.118	.137	.140
Intercept	−1.355	.952	5.461*	1.627	−2.865*	.369	.383*	.383
Log likelihood	−113.314		−63.64		−1,038.6		−890.655	
N	184		130		2,393		1,526	
LR chi²(18)	27.67		26.13		44		62.62	
Prob > chi²	.0005		.001		0		0	

Source: Data analyzed are from the World Values Study (Abramson and Inglehart 1995, 2000).
Note: Coeff, logistic regression coefficient; SE, standard error; LR chi²(18), likelihood ratio chi-square (18 degrees of freedom).
*$p < 0.05$.

United States, and it is not only statistically significant but also substantial: Even controlling for all the other factors in the model, a lack of confidence in the education system leads students to be much more likely to work.

It is also important to note that confidence in education shows very low correlation with other confidence variables (Table 5.3). Traditional approaches associate confidence in the education system, or lack thereof, with confidence in other institutions in society and often allude to confounding effects. However, as the correlation matrix shows, similar effects (i.e., low correlation) are detected between confidence in the education system and confidence in the church, the armed forces, the legal system, the press, unions, the police, parliament, companies, civil service, Social Security, television, the media, and NATO. Furthermore, the lack of confidence in the education system is present regardless of socioeconomic status and gender.

Overall, on the basis of the logistic regression results explaining the likelihood that students in the United States will work and Monte Carlo simulations on the World Values Study data, we can conclude that only for the students in the United States, confidence in education, or the lack thereof, is a significant and substantive predictor of likelihood of working. For students from all socioeconomic levels, genders, and racial groups, the likelihood of working increases as confidence in the education system decreases (see Figure 5.1). So,

TABLE 5.3 Pearson's R for Selected Confidence Variables

	Church	Army	Education System	Legal System	Press	Unions	Police	Parliament	Civil Service	Companies	Social Security	TV	NATO
Church	1.000	.289	.266	.188	.173	.148	.164	.203	.249	.206	.170	.046	.104
Army		1.000	.277	.293	.176	.183	.380	.284	.323	.298	.283	.139	.303
Education system			1.000	.466	.240	.262	.289	.303	.326	.253	.368	.157	.142
Legal system				1.000	.287	.277	.437	.406	.383	.307	.376	.227	.216
Press					1.000	.361	.208	.325	.308	.302	.206	.221	.172
Unions						1.000	.285	.315	.347	.292	.281	.226	.208
Police							1.000	.405	.407	.328	.365	.289	.295
Parliament								1.000	.544	.381	.362	.262	.262
Civil service									1.000	.453	.432	.244	.258
Companies										1.000	.355	.357	.316
Social Security											1.000	.287	.274
TV												1.000	.528
NATO													1.000

Source: Data analyzed are from the World Values Study (Abramson and Inglehart 1995, 2000).

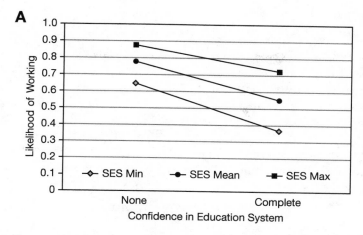

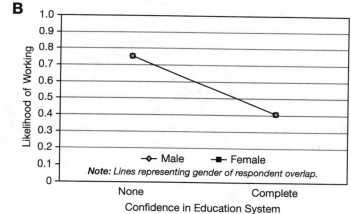

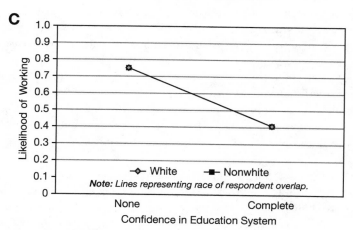

FIGURE 5.1 Effects of Confidence in the Education System on Likelihood of Working among Students in the United States, by **(A)** Socioeconomic Status, **(B)** Gender, and **(C)** Race

what is it about American students' lack of confidence in the education system that makes them work?

Large-scale survey data point to the lack of confidence in the education system as an important predictor of working, but qualitative interviews guide us through the process of how students arrive at their work decisions. In these in-depth interviews, I asked students questions specifically designed to elicit their understanding of the social meaning of school and jobs. Why do so many teenagers report having little confidence in the education system?

"I Have to Be There!"

In the week prior to our interview, the average student had worked for twenty-two hours. However, averages might not make much sense, because 53 percent of the students I talked with had worked more than twenty hours, and many had worked more than forty hours. Compared to how many hours they worked, the average number of hours they spent doing homework weekly was 6.8 hours. Even though many did not think their work interfered with their studies, in terms of how much time they invested, we see an imbalance. The problem is not just working long hours: In addition to working many hours, 82 percent of the young people I interviewed said they worked after 5:00 P.M., and 75 percent said they worked on weekends. Many remembered having to juggle work and school. Eighteen-year-old Abby had worked forty-five hours in the previous week, including the weekends and some nights. When I interviewed her during the 2011 holiday season, she told me things were "crazy" at work. The high-end department store where she worked was having holiday sales in her department. Her week was full of night shifts, weekend shifts, long lines of customers inquiring about holiday sales, coupons, and promotions. Because of her "crazy" schedule, she got to see her parents, who lived nearby, for only two hours. She did not even have a chance to see her grandparents, who lived around the corner. In her words, outside work, she barely had time to see her friends. During the week we spoke, she had studied for fifteen hours. This amount of time was not typical for her, because she was working toward her finals and term papers. Unfortunately, the holiday shopping season coincided with her university's finals schedule. As a result, she ended up missing some classes.

Lucy agreed that her month had been busy. Even though she had worked only fourteen hours in the week before our interview, she had been on call for many more. For these work hours, she was on a rotating schedule of nights and afternoons. She also had to give up her weekends. Because of her schedule, she had no time to see her family or to participate in extracurricular activities or volunteering. Her long commute to the desirable retail store, where she enjoyed the store discounts, took time out of her day as well, especially with the holiday traffic. Even though she was paid for fourteen hours, her job included many more unpaid hours. During the holiday shopping season, she was also asked to come in during high-traffic hours, which often coincided with final exams or study groups for them. Because of the job requirements, she ended up missing some classes and had had only two hours in the prior week to study for her classes.

Brianna, a nineteen-year-old student, had a similar experience. She had worked twenty-six hours the week of the interview, including night and weekends. These hours were the only times she had the chance to see her friends. Other than that, she had no time to see her parents or extended family or to be involved in any extracurricular activities. She even had cut back on her volunteer work: Normally, she worked with animals at a local shelter for one to two hours each week. She had spent only ten hours on her school work, even though she said she needed much more time.

When asked whether they felt as though school and work were in conflict, many study participants said no, yet all of them remembered at least one specific incident where they had to choose between work and school. Josh remembered many occasions when school and work were in conflict and he chose to be at the workplace. So did Sarah, who worried that if she did not show up, the whole Coffee Bean would fall apart. Work or school: which one to choose? Interestingly, many chose work over school. Why would these students choose work over school? What makes work more important?

First, the respondents cited material repercussions for not showing up at work. Lucy and Brianna said they might not be given hours or desirable shifts and could even be fired, especially if they did not take certain shifts during the holiday season. They agreed that such considerations were important in their decisions to skip class, although there were also other considerations. Many young people pointed to their pronounced social visibility in the workplace as a core factor in deciding whether to show up. Like John said, if he did not show up for work, his co-workers would text him immediately.

Many times, the concrete repercussions (i.e., losing a shift or losing money) are less important than concerns about letting colleagues and friends down. As Sarah put it, she did not want to be seen as lazy or untrustworthy. If she ditched school, nobody would think she was untrustworthy, but being labeled as lazy in the work environment was unacceptable for her.

For John, not showing up meant letting his friends down, especially on a snowy day. If he did not show up, his friends would be completely on their own. Unlike in class, where he did not feel integral, at the workplace, he felt useful and in charge. If he did not show up for class, according to John, it was just one person missing: The class still went on. However, if he was not at work, it mattered. He was needed and in charge of something: Co-workers and cus-tomers depended on him.

John confessed that in smaller classes, where the professors knew him, he was less likely to skip class. However, he believed that his decision to prioritize work over school was supported by his professors. When he told his professors that he had to miss a class because of work, his professors typically were more understanding than they were with other excuses. Josh agreed.

Not only the professors but the parents were more understanding and showed great respect for work. Many young people said that their parents even strongly encouraged their working. In fact, some young people said they exploited this attitude to get out of chores they did not want to do and events they did not wish to attend. Work was very important to his parents, accord-ing to John. Many times, to get out of things, he scheduled a work shift. If he had to go work, his parents respected that. Mortimer explains this encourage-ment of work through parents' attitudes toward it:

> Most American parents believe that working will teach their children to be self-reliant and to obtain general knowledge about the workplace (how to act at work, what to wear, the need to be on time, etc.), per-tinent skills (especially people skills fostering smooth interpersonal relations), and positive work orientations (a positive work ethic and recognizing the importance of being able to take responsibility when others depend on you) that will enable them to participate effectively in this sphere in the future. (2007: ii)

According to many parents, work is an inherently valuable experience. At work, young people can learn things that they cannot learn elsewhere. Because they believe that work will teach their children personal or professional skills or simply keep them out of trouble, many parents encourage and praise work. Of course, not all parents are wholeheartedly encouraging toward it. Sarah's mother, for example, was well aware of the fact that her daughter went to work to hang out with her friends. Therefore, she did not have any illusions about how working at the coffee shop would prepare her daughter for her future career in the fine arts or help her in her application to graduate school. She also was skeptical of her daughter's obsession with her work. However, she allowed it, because the workplace kept her out of trouble. From her perspec-tive, the coffee shop was a safe space, where Sarah could interact with her peers without getting into trouble. Even though she herself may not have been con-vinced of the educational benefits of this particular job, she still believed that work provided structure in her daughter's life and offered some social benefits that her school did not.

Social Role of Schools

In explaining their lack of confidence in the education system, many young people point to the decline in the social role of schools. Although many educators would interpret a decline in the confidence in the education system as a reflection of a decline in the academic component of schools, many young people point to schools' lack of social interaction. Schools, after all, are places where young people spend large periods of time every day. For them, schools are not just about classes, lectures, and papers but about a large social component. Schools, therefore, should provide the opportunity to meet new people, offer the space to socialize with friends, and provide a common vocabulary to communicate with others. However, the common sentiment is that schools do not adequately fulfill these functions. Many young people told me that they felt *lost* at school but needed at work. Like John, who said that people noticed his absence if he did not show up for a shift, these young people felt important at work. School did not offer opportunities for hanging out or socializing. After attending the school for some time, John said that he still did not have the chance to meet many new people. The local state university, where he was a full-time student, was often filled with students at all hours. For an outsider, the sight of the student union, brimming with students at all hours, and the long lines at the school cafeteria could be misleading. The busy campus was filled with students, true, but they were there for specific reasons: a class, an activity, office hours, or exams. Once the activities were done, many drove away, leaving little opportunity to socialize.

The lack of confidence in the education system is only partially due to social reasons. Many young people also mentioned their distrust in schools' ability to prepare them for the job market. Many scholars have debated the function and role of education for young people: Should educational institutions prepare the students for future jobs, or should education be separate from future job requirements? A large body of literature explores and discusses the role of education in our society. Many scholars argue that it should not the role of the educational institutions to teach applied and marketable skills that will be useful in the workforce. In the past few decades, even politicians have debated the role of education. A February 23, 1994, *New York Times* headline read, "Clinton Tells Educators Youths Are Not Getting Practical Skills for Jobs." In the article, President Bill Clinton is quoted as saying, "In the nineteenth century, at most, young Americans needed a high school education to make their way. . . . In the twenty-first century, our people will have to keep learning their whole lives." Especially with the recent recession, many debate the role of education in preparing American youth for the future. Some argue that more applied skills and credentials are essentials in the current job market and insist that schools should be teaching more market-oriented knowledge with economic utility.

Others, on the other hand, argue that the role of education is to provide general and more theoretical education. Scholars may be focused on the importance of teaching abstract notions, such as critical thinking, but it seems that students—and many of their parents—link the concept of a good education with the acquisition of concrete skills that will help the students get jobs (Postman 1996). Especially with the elevated unemployment levels and uncertainty for young people, these students, perhaps rightly, feel ill-equipped for the real job market. If students in the United States define education through the acquisition of economically useful skills and practical knowledge with economic utility, the lack of such benefits in school could potentially deteriorate their confidence in the education system. This, in turn, could result in their decision to enter the labor market while they are still in school to obtain skills with economic utility. Traditional explanations of youth's labor-market entry decisions have concluded that youth's early work experiences provide human capital and result in the acquisition of skills useful for future employment (Entwisle et al. 2000; Tienda and Stier 1996). These benefits, such as human capital and skill acquisition, are closely related to institutions of education. As Finkelstein asks, "How has it come to pass that American politicians, academics, journalists, and labor leaders turn to schools to solve economic problems? What possible construction of thought about education and work could integrate economic problems and calls for school reform in this manner?" (Bills 2004). Many different agencies, institutions, and individuals are turning to schools to solve economic problems and expect them to provide more preparation for the workplace as finding and keeping jobs becomes more unpredictable. With rising anti-intellectualism among young people in the United States, many young people and parents see work as an important venue for education. Work, they think, can teach things that schools cannot. This anti-intellectual sentiment is prevalent among many young people: 83 percent of the young people I talked with in my study agreed that work was more valuable than school in teaching new skills; 92 percent of the students I interviewed said they believed that working would help their careers in the future. For college-bound youth, these benefits are unclear. Work might help less-affluent youth pay for school, stay in school, or even translate into skills for a career, benefits that have been demonstrated by a number of scholars in the past. D'Amico and Baker (1984), for instance, find that for young people who do not intend to go to college, these early job experiences can help them find long-term jobs, prepare them for these jobs, and provide them with early training. This study does not tell us anything, though, about what middle-class youth get out of the work experience. Typically, youth jobs have been characterized as "dull and repetitive and offer[ing] little opportunity for learning, . . . [and as doing] nothing to encourage a positive orientation toward work as [young people] gain in experience" (Bourdillon et al. 2010; see also Greenberger and Steinberg 1986). In her Youth Development Study, Mortimer follows the same youth for twenty years and tracks the types of jobs they choose throughout their early adult life. She shows that students take simple jobs initially. However, as they gain more experience, they move into more complex jobs. However, even when the tasks become slightly more complex and the youth are given more responsibility, the tasks remain unrelated to most of their future careers. According to Jyotsna Tiwari, "For the most part, the jobs held by U.S. teens are not conceived as stepping stones on a life career path. Other developed countries, such as Germany, Denmark and, Switzerland, have long included adolescent employment as a part of formal apprenticeship, school-to-work, and work experience and career exploration programs that are closely linked to the educational process and lead to specific adult jobs" (2004: 20). For American youth, though, these early jobs have no resemblance their future career jobs. In addition to the content, even structurally these early jobs are very different than future career jobs. Although these jobs have been praised for teaching discipline and stability, recent research documents that the youth labor market is actually volatile. Young people bounce between jobs, often experiencing bouts of unemployment. In contrast to popular views, it is often a time of instability and is referred to as "churning" or "floundering" (Cooksey and Rindfuss 2001; Namboodiri 1987; Ostermann and Ianozzi 1993; Veum and Weiss 1993).

"I Make a Difference"

Whether we objectively find them simple or complex, however, the students themselves report finding these jobs intrinsically rewarding. Most students report having positive attitudes toward work: Many believe that they learn something from their part-time jobs and gain rewards from them, such as opportunities to express themselves and feel useful (Mortimer 2007). John felt useful at the Coffee Bean, because he believed he made a difference in the workplace. He also felt as though he were in charge of something. In that realm, nobody told him how to perform a task: He was its master. Although such tasks as making cappuccino or getting the right temperature for milk or the right foam consistency may not seem substantial or important to outside observers, they were important to him.

Young people and their parents place great importance on working, believing that the work experience teaches young people in ways that schools cannot. As Barbara Schneider and David Stevenson (1999) show, what students (and their parents) "know" or "believe" about work and the role of school in preparing them for work does not often reflect the reality. Surprising numbers of students view the opportunities provided by work, in terms of career training and advancement, to be much greater than they actually are and believe that part-time work might fulfill the function of preparing them for their future jobs. Unfortunately, as Mortimer suggests, "Educators argue that extensive formal schooling is more important today than ever before: the changes in the society, and especially in the economy, place a growing premium on knowledge that is gained most effectively in school. In order to obtain sufficient knowledge and credentials to equip them for the work of the twenty-first century, young adults need to be protected from the demands of adulthood for an even longer period. Early participation in activities and adult-like roles that diminish involvement in education, whether in the labor force or in the family, must be discouraged" (2003: 11).

Many of the students I talked with agreed that they needed to be better equipped for the job market, especially given the current economic climate. When I asked about the role of education in their lives, many told me that working was very important. Only six students of my entire sample thought of work as an equivalent replacement for education: For the overwhelming majority of them, education was also important in helping them get better careers. However, many separated their educational credentials from practical skills. Although universities provide the credentials necessary to find jobs, in the perceptions of many young people, they do not create the skills needed for these jobs. Young people are not entirely ignorant of the realities of adult work: Work is a central part of American culture. Recent findings show that even elementary school students show an in-depth knowledge of adult jobs and occupations and have detailed mental maps of the adult world of work (Bills 2004). This illustrates how central work is in young people's lives and how they are socialized to prioritize and respect work. But despite learning about work from a young age, many young people view it incorrectly. Schneider and Stevenson (1999), for example, show that high school students' knowledge and beliefs about work are largely incorrect. An overwhelming number of high school students massively overestimate the available work opportunities offered and show unrealistic expectations from the world of work. Similarly, Kathryn Wilson (2001) confirms that even though many young people are intimately familiar with the youth labor market, their views of the adult workforce are often limited and much different than the reality (see also Bills 2004). Even though many students see work as a beneficial activity, the effects of teenage work on future careers are limited. For some non-college-bound youth, working in high school increases the likelihood of finding jobs, but these effects do not necessarily translate to college-bound youth; especially heavy doses of work help some youth secure jobs yet diminish their likelihood of attending college. In terms of wages, however, working in school has no effects on future earnings (Bills 2004). Furthermore, not all young people benefit equally from these jobs. Minority students, for instance, benefit much less than white students do, perhaps because of the different kinds of jobs they are funneled into. In the case of many African American students, future employers do not consider their work experience a sign of productivity or trainability because of prejudicial attitudes (Steele 1992). Interestingly, students of both high and low socioeconomic status hold similar views of work.

A small group of students say they need education to achieve their often unrealistic goals and dreams in the workforce (Schneider and Stevenson 1999), but many students see their academic performance as irrelevant to their future employment prospects. According to David B. Bills (2004), many students find few linkages between their academic performance and future success in their careers. Hard work at school, for many of them, does not translate into success in the workplace (see also Bishop 1999). The responses of schools to students' lack of motivation and hard work exacerbate the problem. As Bills argues, "Because students are on the hunt for grades and credentials rather than learning itself, schools and students collaborate on developing norms against hard work, pushing students toward taking easy courses, and the dumbing down of the courses. The fact that college selection decisions are based so heavily on such indicators as SAT, ACT, and GPA, and class rank makes the situation even worse" (2004: 159). As more and more students see little relevance of school learning to future jobs and place little importance on hard work in the classroom, they may rationally be interested in only the diploma and not the actual learning. After all, if they are going to school only to get a degree rather than to learn, they should take the easiest courses they can. As education becomes a universal experience for many young people, American society has seen a substantial decline in the economic value of a high school diploma; in recent years, the value of a bachelor's degree has declined as well. They might have been tickets to security in the past, but these diplomas today may fail to secure middle-class or even working-class jobs.

As Arthur G. Powell, Eleanor Farrar, and David K. Cohen find, schools contribute to this trend, offering students a wide array of courses that resembles a shopping mall. Students are offered what they refer to as boutique and fast-food courses with a confusing assortment of options and possibilities with limited guidance. Despite the availability and broad selection, many classes provide only shallow and superficial knowledge. Because the choices are many and broad, students, parents, and schools remain confused, failing to transform the process of course taking into viable career paths (Bills 2004).

Preparation for work is only one part of the picture. Robert Dreeben's classic work *On What Is Learned in School* ([1968] 2002) argues that school is not only about the formal curriculum; it is central to the social education of students. The organization of school—discipline, the division of labor, patterns of authority, rules, norms, and relationships—prepare the students just as much as the formal curriculum. These skills are important and central for young people's transition into adulthood. The goal, as Bills paraphrases, "is to teach children the norms of independence, achievement, and universalism and specificity. That is, schools teach children to understand when and how they need to act in self-sufficient ways, that they need to display some level of mastery, that they can expect to be treated as individuals rather than representatives of categories, and that different aspects of their selves are open for inspection in different settings" (2004: 148). By accumulating these skills, children are prepared for life in the adult world. As such, young people are not entirely wrong when they argue that the failure of schools to provide social opportunities represents a general failure of education. If students recognize that these skills are necessary, they have to get them somewhere, and these school functions seem to have been taken over by part-time jobs. In recent years, schools have been responding to this trend by creating career academies—high school programs geared toward the world of work. In such programs, a relatively small cohort of students stay together, educated by the same teachers for a couple of years in a predominantly academic curriculum with a work orientation (Bills 2004; Maxwell and Rubin 2000; Urquiola et al. 1997). This approach came out of the need to integrate more applied, work-related skills with academic knowledge, but there has been little consensus on the effectiveness of such programs. Nan L. Maxwell and Victor Rubin (2000) find them to be successful in integrating academic knowledge and more applied skills, but some find that such programs have little effects on the labor-force outcomes in early adulthood (Kemple and Snipes 2001; Linnehan 1996).

In addition to the education system's absence of economically useful skills (Collins 1979), the lack of confidence in the education system could be explained by the inability of the education system to provide an identity. Identity creation, of course, is not limited to the youth labor force. Today, work is a source of identity for many adult Americans as well. As Richard Sennett (1998) demonstrates, work's day-to-day experience, predictability, and accumulation of skills offer the basis of a unified identity for many workers. Therefore, for many adults, work is not just work (Muirhead 2004) but an integral part of their identities. It is not surprising that many young people follow the example of adults in our society to define themselves through work. If many adults think their work is central in shaping who they are, we should expect the same for young people as they transition to adulthood. Alan Kerckhoff

(2000: 457) argues that one of the reasons for this is the low degree of stratification in the American education system: "A distinctive feature of the American education system, in contrast with almost all Europe, is its low degree of stratification into different curricular and status streams." Because schools do not provide social hierarchy and stratification, affluent youth are using jobs to create such distinctions. As Richard Robinson and David Hurst (1999) show, the creation of a status hierarchy is central to youth's lives, but with the declining role of schools in creating status, work becomes the source of identity. In fact, not only does work provide an identity—an adult identity—it also provides a *branded* identity, which schools cannot do.

Many scholars have argued about the decreasing ability of institutions of education to create a meaningful community (Fischel 2002). As a result of this inability to create social cohesion, institutions of education lose their role in creating the environment that allows students to meet people. This, too, may contribute to the decline in confidence in education. When students lose confidence in the educational institutions' ability to foster social connections and help youth meet new people, their likelihood of working increases. When we talk about a declining confidence in the education system, a typical interpretation is a lack of confidence in the academic function of the school. However, what is prevalent in the in-depth interviews is a lack of confidence in schools' social function. Many young people use workplaces as social centers in the suburbs to meet new people and see their existing friends. As Bills argues (2004: 162), "High school prepares (or fails to prepare) people for work by providing skills and dispositions relevant to the workplace, but it also does so by serving as the foil of students' lives. In many cases, it is work, rather than school that secures the primary commitment of high school students. U.S. students work in high numbers (much higher than comparable countries), they start young and they work a lot of hours." In addition, when the two responsibilities are in conflict, as we have seen in John's case, work takes precedent.

In addition to the perceived decreased ability of educational institutions to offer economically relevant and marketable skills and provide the opportunity and social space to meet people, there has been a decline in schools' ability to provide a common meaning and narrative in youth's lives (Postman 1996; Powell, Farrar, and Cohen 1985), which has increasingly led disenchanted students to the decision to work. Work, as an alternative to school, is perceived to provide both economically viable skills and create the opportunity to meet peers as well as offer a common culture and social cohesion within the workplace for youth (Besen 2004).

This chapter has explored the effect of the declining confidence in the education system in the United States on the most central actors of education: students. The findings show that for students in the United States, confidence in the education system strongly predicts their decision to enter the labor market while still in school. For students in the United States, the likelihood of working increases substantially with their lack of confidence in the education system. This could be interpreted as youth's attempt at creating an alternative to school that provides economically relevant skills, opportunities to meet people, and a socially cohesive environment. The mechanisms through which these perceptions translate into decisions to enter the labor market are ripe for future examination.

6

"White, Young, Middle Class"

Aesthetic Labor, Race, and Class in the Youth Labor Force

A typical Coffee Bean employee is usually a stuck-up Caucasian teenager who was spoiled by their parents.
— Aaron, twenty-two-year-old male

People in the long line of customers who visited the Coffee Bean daily often noticed the young and vibrant composition of the workforce at the coffee shop. Linda, a middle-age regular customer, told me she really enjoyed the cool, hip, and young atmosphere of the coffee shop. Despite patronizing the coffee shop on a daily basis, many customers failed to also recognize the racial and ethnic composition of the contemporary workforce. Yet the majority of the young people I spoke with were well-aware of the racial and economic inequalities that plague the youth labor force. Bobby, a twenty-year-old male liberal arts major, described the current composition of the Coffee Bean's staff as predominantly affluent and white. He believed that "a typical Coffee Bean employee would probably be Caucasian. He or she would probably be a high school or college student working part-time from middle to upper class." Similarly, Brianna, a nineteen-year-old fellow female student, described the current composition of the coffee shop as "white, young, middle class." Such racial and socioeconomic inequalities are not limited to the coffee shop, but are typical of many desirable jobs. To outside observers, these youth jobs may all appear to be identical. Like objectivist researchers, all people see is that these youth jobs offer low pay, no benefits, and odd hours, rendering them all about the same. However, as we have seen in the previous chapters, the lived experience of these jobs from the perspectives of the young actors is vastly different. Where young people choose to work does not just reflect taste or choice but becomes an important social marker. As Pierre Bourdieu (1984) argues in *Distinction*, consumption habits, tastes, and lifestyle choices often reflect socioeconomic and class inequality. Similarly, in the context of youth jobs, we see a similar reflection of racial and socioeconomic inequality in choice of jobs. Jules remembered that at the popular high-end clothing store where she worked part-time while still in school, all her co-workers were from the "same background, they came from a very high socioeconomic class, no one was considered poor." Working at this particular clothing store was considered a prestigious job in her peer group, and being from a higher socioeconomic class gave her an advantage in getting the job. She perceived that the employees had a certain look: The majority of her co-workers looked very fit and athletic, with straight teeth and fashionable clothes. Working there was an important marker of social status, confirming the outward appearance of affluence. Many times, after the store closed, Jules would hang out with her co-workers and go to parties. After the store closed for the day, she remembered turning the music on, getting some free pretzels from other friends working at the pretzel place, and just hanging out. Working at the store gave her social cachet, and so long as she was at the mall, she retained it; once she went home, she was no different from anyone else. The hierarchy of jobs and stores creates layers of inequality surrounding workplace choice. In this chapter, I explore the socioeconomic and racial inequalities that surround youth jobs. In particular, I focus on socioeconomic and racial inequality's influence on getting jobs, showing that less-affluent and minority youth have difficulty entering the labor force. Furthermore, many who do find jobs find them in undesirable locations or in stores with less social appeal. Because part-time jobs create opportunities for socializing and confer social status upon young people, I show that youth from lower socioeconomic backgrounds and minority youth have difficulty finding desirable jobs. Later in the chapter, I show that such inequalities are justified and perpetuated by employers through notions of aesthetic labor. As Jules remembered, all the workers at her clothing store conformed to the look of the store: athletic builds, fit bodies, shiny hair, and gleaming straight teeth. Such physical attributes are covert markers of socioeconomic status and social class. Therefore, more-affluent youth have an advantage in getting these more desirable jobs. Furthermore, class inequality is reflected in the ability to purchase goods sold in the store. Every week at the clothing store, Jules told me, the staff were required to wear a different color polo shirt, and only the affluent youth—those who were able to afford spending their whole paycheck on high-end clothing—were able to keep up with the requirements. Jules later regretted having worked at the clothing store because of the amount of money she spent on the clothes. Even though the pay was low and the hours were limited, the opportunity to use her employee discount and keep up with her peers resulted in a great financial burden. Using similar in-depth interviews, I discuss the costs and social implications of such inequalities in the labor force.

The Affluent Youth: Socioeconomic Inequality in the Youth Labor Force

Many of the young people who worked at the Coffee Bean admitted that they did not do it for the money. For them, the prestige of working for a desirable brand was one of the attractions. This is not to say that they did not understand that other people working there may have needed the money, but the workers I interviewed held that these disadvantaged youth were in the minority. A number of interviewees said that disadvantaged young people could not get jobs in better places and were stuck in less desirable positions, such as fast-food jobs. The hierarchy among jobs is one that is known to many. Amy, a twenty-one-year-old student, differentiated among youth jobs and observed how lower-income youth got stuck in fast-food jobs: "The typical [fast-food] employee tends to be someone of lower educational background, who works there out of necessity. [These individuals] . . . also tend to come from a family of lower socioeconomic status."

The sorting of teens into jobs was evident to almost everyone I spoke with. Greg, a nineteen-year-old male, similarly identified the young workers of the coffee shop as middle- and upper-class youth who did not have to work: "A Coffee Bean employee is generally a young and spirited person from the middle to upper class of society. . . . They have a good future ahead of them and are just doing this as a part-time job."

What was really striking was that these affluent young people were happy to work and monetary gratifications seemed secondary. Work fulfilled a specific, current function for these young people, but they were not there for the long term: They were "just doing this as a part-time job," and they would move onto bigger and better things in the future. However, as a result of the fun environments and the social benefits, the more prestigious and better jobs are often taken up by more affluent youth. Even if less affluent youth were to apply for these more desirable jobs, the young people I spoke with agreed that it would be very difficult for them to be hired. As we see by the way corporations market these jobs, more affluent youth are preferred.

Also surprising in young people's description of the typical Coffee Bean employee and fast-food-chain employees was the immediate association of work with personality, social and political affiliation, and lifestyle choices: "A typical Coffee Bean employee would be stuck up. They would probably be more Republican than a fast-food employee. Because of the difference in price of the product and the income of the customers, Coffee Bean branches are located in richer areas than fast-food chains are" (Charlene, eighteen-year-old female).

Even though many of them acknowledged the central role that economic background played in finding desirable jobs, the choice of workplace still

resulted in inferences about personal, social, and political choices and personality traits. Instead of seeing this economic inequality as a structural issue,
many young workers reduced economic, social, and racial barriers to differences in personality: It was not that the less affluent youth could not find work
at certain stores, but that they were not the kind of people who would work
there. These youth who worked for less desirable brands were just different,
socially, politically, and personally. Like lifestyle branding, where consuming
a product signifies a particular lifestyle, working for certain corporations has
a similar effect. Because a student works for a less desirable fast-food fran-
chise, he or she is considered personally inferior rather than a person who
is funneled into a work choice as a result of structural barriers. Such a view
was prevalent in the interviews I conducted. As twenty-one-year-old Stephanie observed, "[Coffee Bean employees] are preppy people. They sit huddled
around as they wait to make coffee and . . . they make jokes. . . . [At fast-food
chains] they are young people that are not usually too happy about the fact
that they are working in a place that is not too friendly, and the people are
usually of a different quality."

The social element of the job—hanging out with their friends and meeting new people—is central to young people. Work provides not only a central
space for young people to socialize but also a common vocabulary for that
socialization. Because the products are geared toward a higher SES audience,
young people take these jobs to be associated with the cool brands. Mostly, it
is about the atmosphere that the workplace creates. The atmosphere of the coffee chain might have been designed to attract customers, but it also attracted
employees. As Jules remembered, the high-end clothing store was like a party
full of cool people. She wanted to work there because it was the most fashionable place and the place to be seen. Because less affluent youth do not have the
right look, it would be very difficult for them to find these jobs; just as they
would not be invited to that party, they would not fit in at the store.

This is not to say that wages play no role in work decisions. However, the
young people I interviewed agreed that "it's different." According to Dylan, a
nineteen-year-old male student, workers at the Coffee Bean did not use their
earnings for necessities or immediate needs. Their earnings went to what he
called "elite expenses": "The typical Coffee Bean employee is probably a college
student trying to pay off [elite] expenses like car notes or phone bills. . . . The
typical fast-food employee is probably a high school student or a high school
dropout. The student is probably just trying to pay off his or her expenses . . . or
just trying to make ends meet." Others who were not so lucky as to find these
desirable jobs were the ones paying for school or helping their families. Sean,
a twenty-year-old college student, said that employees of the Coffee Bean were
not supporting families or using their earnings for necessities, whereas typical
fast-food workers needed their paychecks for more immediate financial needs.

Overall, in the discourse of young people, we can see how seemingly similar jobs actually hide enormous inequalities. The desirable jobs are reserved for more affluent youth, who have the right look and image. The more economically disadvantaged youth, who need these jobs to survive, are often left with the less desirable fast-food jobs. Such inequalities are typically normalized through looks, appearance, and aesthetic labor. The mechanisms through which such inequalities are normalized and sustained are discussed later in the chapter.

Racial Differences in the Workforce

In addition to more attractive jobs being dominated by more affluent youth, we also see a racial component in the descriptions of youth who take those jobs. Many young people I spoke with described these desirable jobs as "white jobs." Just as economically disadvantaged youth find it more difficult to get jobs, nonwhite youth, especially African American youth, also find it much harder to get these jobs. Mason was an African American full-time college student at a state university. During his college education, he had been working part-time. He told me about the difficulties he had had finding a job. Because he lived in a predominantly African American, working-class town, he believed that his place of residence was associated with crime and poverty. He said that once he put his address down on applications, he reduced his chances of getting a callback. In his experience, high-end malls in particular did not like applicants from his neighborhood, because potential employers feared their brands would become associated with low-income consumers. He also remembered being asked whether his friends from the neighborhood would be coming to the store to hang out or ask for discounts and free merchandise. Often times, he provided the address of his grandmother—who is in a more acceptable area—or his school address when applying for jobs. Many times, the higher-status and better employers turned him down, telling him he just did not have the right look or that his look did not fit the image of the brand. Carter, another African American college senior, worked at a high-end clothing store and told me that he noticed that many African American youth were utilized in stock-room positions rather than at the front of the store. According to Carter, it was not clear whether this was due to their race or socioeconomic status, both of which were highly correlated. Many African American youth, according to Carter's observations, had ended up in the less visible back of the store because they did not have the means to keep up with the business's appearance requirements. Mason and Carter agreed that, although the inequality inside the store in terms of positions and job requirements was important, a bigger form of inequality lay in the barriers against entry into the jobs to begin with.

The stories these young people told are reflected in the larger data. Typically, there are marked racial and ethnic differences in the youth labor force. Before the economic recession, 64 percent of white youth between ages fourteen and fifteen were employed while still in school. However, the labor-force participation rates of African American and Hispanic youth remained at 43 and 41 percent, respectively. As teenagers get older, their labor-force participation rates increase for every racial and ethnic category, but the racial differences remain consistent. Even among youth employed in freelance jobs, we see a marked racial difference: 48.3 percent of white fourteen- to fifteen-year-olds are employed in freelance jobs, whereas freelance labor-force participation rates for African American and Hispanic youth are only 33.1 percent and 30.1 percent, respectively (Herman 2000). With older youth, we still see the persistence of racial inequality. According to the U.S. Bureau of Labor Statistics (Herman 2000), among white youth between ages sixteen and nineteen, the employment rate in 2010 was 36.8 percent, while it was only 24.9 percent among African American youth. Especially when we compare unemployment rates, we see markedly higher unemployment rates for African American youth, which tells us that they are actively looking for jobs but are unable to find them. Even as young people age, we see that the racial and ethnic differences are sustained. Among fifteen- to seventeen-year-olds, the unemployment rate—the number of people looking for work who cannot find it—is 35 percent for African American youth and 30 percent for Hispanic youth, but it is only 17 percent for white youth (Herman 2000). Unemployment inequality still persists among older youth. The U.S. Bureau of Labor Statistics (Herman 2000) finds that among white sixteen- to nineteen-year-olds, the unemployment rate is only 21.7 percent, while among African American youth in the same age bracket, the unemployment rate is 41.3 percent.

Since the recession, youth labor-force participation has declined considerably. According to the U.S. Bureau of Labor Statistics (Herman 2000), approximately one-third of all youth are employed while still in school. A limited number of jobs means that when affluent youth take positions to secure social benefits, there are real consequences for others—youth who really need the money, or adults forced into these less desirable jobs—who are not able to get the jobs the affluent youth are taking. This increased competition also means that employers can be more selective about whom they hire and can afford to reject candidates who do not perfectly match the stores' preferred images. Mason remembered preparing for one interview by shopping at the store and wearing the most recent clothes from the store to the interview; even so, in some high-end clothing stores, he and his friends were told they did not have the right look. Racial inequality within jobs, such as African American workers' being assigned to different tasks, has received ample attention in the literature, but here we are seeing a different kind of inequality, one in which

African American youth are left out of the labor market entirely or are pushed into lower-status workplaces. Moreover, just as we shall see with the role of gender in youth employment, many of the reasons often given for the different statuses of African Americans and whites in the labor force simply do not apply to the youth labor market. It is difficult for employers to argue that there are differences in positions based on race because of qualifications or experience when almost none of the prospective employees, African American or white, has any experience at all.

Race and the Adult Workforce

In the adult workforce, it has been documented that African American and Hispanic workers show significant differences in employment and unemployment rates compared to their white counterparts. Such differences are significant not just because of the inequalities they create in the youth labor force but because such early differences in employment result in significant differences in the adult workforce. Research suggests that early differences in employment and unemployment influence future employment opportunities and wage outcomes (Becker and Hills 1983; Ellwood 1982; Meyer and Wise 1982; Ruhm 1997; Gardecki 2001). Typical research on the racial differences in the labor force has focused on wage differences between white and African American youth. However, it seems that employment rates are a bigger and more important source of inequality than the relatively small differences in wages. In southern states, for example, according to the Current Population Survey (2010), white teenagers earn 6.5 percent more than their African American counterparts. Such differences are important, but whether the teenagers get hired in the first place creates a greater inequality than the differences in wages (Ahn et al. 2010). White teenagers may earn 6.5 percent more than African American teens, but they are 72 percent more likely to be hired than their African American counterparts (Ahn et al. 2010). This difference holds up even when we control for how likely teens of various racial groups are to look for work. Even though white and African American youth are just as likely to look for jobs, job holding is much lower among African American and Hispanic youth (Gardecki 2001).

These racial differences persist throughout the teenage years (Michael and Tuma 1984). Richard Freeman (1987) argues that work is an important trade-off for criminal activity. On the basis of self-reports, he argues that young people who reported committing a crime in the previous month were less likely to be employed. John Bound, Richard B. Freeman, and Jeff Grogger (1992) attribute these differences to differences in criminal records, where the potential employers are reluctant to hire youth who have been arrested; although these differences may account for some of the hiring gap, they cannot account for all of it.

Racial and ethnic inequality in hiring is also strongly correlated with income. Recent research finds that many African American and Hispanic youth are less likely to be employed, as they come from lower socioeconomic backgrounds. Especially those families who come from poverty are less likely to work. Mary Corcoran and colleagues (1992) show that, among teens, families' and communities' welfare-recipient status decreases the likelihood of working.

Neighborhood factors are central in understanding the underemployment of African American and Hispanic youth. A number of studies have shown the importance of geographic location in young people's employment. Bound and Freeman (1987) show that geographic location accounts for an important part of the racial gap in unemployment. Freeman (1982), in a different study exclusively on youth employment, finds similar results, determining that economic activity in the immediate area of young people determines the jobs available to them and significantly affects their employment. Proximity to a rich area and commute times determine employment rates: Longer commutes, especially, have a detrimental effect on minority youth's employment (Ihlanfeldt and Sjoquist 1990; O'Regan and Quigley 1996a, 1996b). Many service sector and retail jobs that young people living in less wealthy areas might wish to take are simply not available in the areas where they reside: They would need to commute even to find these jobs, meaning that transportation to and from work becomes an important part of the work search (Arnott 1998). Especially among early teenagers, the inability to drive naturally restricts the job search to the immediate area (Gardecki 2001). Even among much older youth (ages sixteen to twenty-four), we find similar results. Residence constraints, nonownership of a car, long commutes, and high travel costs result in lower employment rates and limited job searches for minority youth (Gardecki 2001).

The jobs that are available in these neighborhoods, which often include heavy industry, might lead to fewer opportunities for employment because of environmental regulation. In fact, Katherine M. O'Regan and John M. Quigley's analysis of census data shows that employment opportunities for minority youth in white and lower-poverty areas are considerably better (1996a, 1996b).

Neighborhood characteristics are also important because of job networks. High unemployment among youth in a given area results in reduced networking opportunities, because young people in the neighborhood are not able to relay job-opening information to friends and acquaintances (Weinberg, Reagan, and Yankow 1999). Remember, many affluent youth I spoke with reported hearing about jobs from their friends or applying at places where their friends already worked. If their friends were unable to find jobs, they would also have greater difficulty.

Young people's employment has important and systematic effects. Obviously, not being employed puts economically disadvantaged youth at a further disadvantage economically and socially. Such effects are not limited to the young people themselves. Albert Rees and Wayne Gray (1982) show that although parents' work status and characteristics have no effect on youth's employment, siblings' work status has positive effects on youth's work behavior. Therefore, as these young people are shut out of the labor force, the negative effects trickle down to their siblings. Bruce Weinberg, Patricia Reagan, and Jeffrey J. Yankow (1999) also argue that large numbers of youth being unemployed in the same geographic area result in demoralization and the normalization of unemployment.

Young people I spoke with made frequent references to the association between race and placement of desirable jobs: Desirable jobs were seen as white jobs, whereas most fast-food jobs were described as predominantly nonwhite. Bobby told me there was a vast difference among youth jobs. A worker at a more desirable job, such as a Coffee Bean employee, was described as "probably Caucasian. He or she would probably be a high school or college student working part-time, from a middle- to upper-class family." A fast-food worker, on the other hand, was not be as privileged. He described these workers as probable minorities or young immigrants, who needed to work part-time to support themselves and their education. Because of the low wages, he predicted that many dropped out of school to work multiple jobs. Greg agreed with Bobby's perception of the differences within youth jobs: "A Coffee Bean employee is generally a young and spirited person from the middle to upper class of society. They have a good future ahead of them and are just doing this as a part-time job. . . . [A] fast-food employee usually represents someone who is from the lower class part of society. They have low wages and usually do not come from the best living conditions. Usually these employees are from ethnic backgrounds and are people who have low education." From the outside, nearly all service and retail jobs that employ young people appear similar and have comparable wages, hours, and benefits. However, young people's own accounts showed that they saw these jobs differently. In their own discussions of how they saw brands, they pointed to important racial and ethnic differences in occupations; more affluent youth had an advantage in getting the more desirable jobs, while minority youth were stuck at fast-food jobs.

Untucked Shirt, Baggy Pants, and Crooked Hat: Mechanisms of Inequality

Inequalities of socioeconomic status and race, which are intertwined in the youth labor force, are often normalized and perpetuated through what Dennis Nickson and Chris Warhurst (2007) refer to as aesthetic labor. Although in theory young people may resent the existence of racial and socioeconomic inequalities in the workforce, they explain these differences through variations in dress, appearance, behavior, and social skills. Such aesthetic- and social-labor requirements function as mechanisms through which inequalities are created and reinforced in the youth labor force. Corinne, a nineteen-year-old college student, pointed to aesthetic labor in explaining such inequality. In describing fast-food workers, she said they "usually aren't well-groomed and appear to be not so clean." How young people look and present themselves play an important role in getting desirable jobs. Young people I interviewed argued that the failure of some youth to find better jobs was explained by the fact that the individual workers did not possess more sophisticated and fash-ionable self-presentations. Their personal hygiene and grooming habits, in their reasoning, explained their job placement. Nineteen-year-old Matt agreed with Corinne. Referring to fast-food establishments, he said, "There are the kids or young adults who look like they work there because they have no other choice. . . . They don't present themselves in the way that they are probably supposed to. I would not be surprised to see their shirts untucked or baggy pants or a hat that is not straight, whereas . . . the other type of worker [one from the coffee shop] is in perfect order."

On the one hand, Matt acknowledged the lack of choice these young people were faced with. Why else would one work at a fast-food place? On the other hand, he blamed their lack of choice on self-presentation: untucked shirt, baggy pants, and crooked hat. Such aesthetic concerns normalize and justify the existing status quo. If only these workers had been better groomed, according to Matt, they would have been employed in a better place. However, such a view obscures the role of income in creating and maintaining a well-groomed self-presentation.

As a result of different self-presentations, Matt saw the coffee-shop work-ers as inherently different. He said, "A typical Coffee Bean employee is usually a person who seems experienced and wants to be there and is definitely not a little kid or someone who is incompetent. They tend to be nice and want to make the experience a convenient one. They are normally knowledgeable and very presentable, because they are always in uniform and always looking per-fectly groomed. They act like they are classier and upper class . . . because they kind of are."

He pointed to differences in grooming and clothes in explaining the dif-ferences between the workers themselves. The workers at the coffee shop had better self-presentations and cleaner and tidier clothes. On the one hand, these aesthetic differences were boiled down to socioeconomic status. On the other hand, such aesthetic differences obscured larger structural inequalities in the market and put the responsibility on the shoulders of the individual workers. If only they had had the right look, they might even have worked at the Coffee Bean.

Aesthetic differences in these jobs are not limited to the clothes. Many young people pointed to physical differences. Julie, a twenty-one-year-old female college student, described a typical fast-food worker as "overweight and pimply." Similarly, David, a twenty-one-year-old college student, said fast-food workers were usually "overweight." Such differences in appearance and presentation of selves, as Bourdieu (1984) argues, are highly correlated with material resources. As Jules remembered, at the high-end clothing store where she worked, all the employees looked uniformly fit and athletic. White and affluent youth fit the look, while low-income minority youth did not have the monetary resources to get the right look.

These types of differences in appearance might also be exacerbated because of what Erving Goffman refers to as "role distance" (1961). Role distance is an individual's ability to distance him- or herself from the role the individual has been assigned. Young people assigned to low-status positions and jobs, for example, might exhibit role distance and perform their jobs in a less enthusiastic way to signal to their audience that they deserve better. Therefore, the disinterested, unenthusiastic manners and more disheveled self-presentations of many fast-food employees could be an example of role distance. Mason, for example, remembered that he had to take a fast-food job for some time. He remembered disliking the experience and thinking that he deserved a better job. During his shifts, he remembered not caring about how he looked, how untidy his outfits were, and how unfriendly his general demeanor was. However, these traits were a way to distance himself from an undesirable job.

In addition to self-presentations, many study participants referred to differences in consumption patterns. Joel, a twenty-one-year-old college student, said, "A typical [coffee-shop] employee is someone who can make your coffee without having to know what it is that you ordered, because they have a system down of how to order coffee . . . as [if] it was another language." Because these young people were avid consumers, they already were familiar with the products. Such an intimate knowledge of the products gave the white affluent youth an advantage. According to Julie, young people who worked at the coffee shop were such dedicated consumers that the prospect of getting free drinks, products, and discounts was just as important as working at the brand they liked. Consumption, just like appearance, was highly correlated with income. As Mike, a twenty-year-old student, said, young people who worked at the Coffee Bean were "white, upper to upper-middle class," while fast-food establishment workers were "black . . . lower-class to poverty."

Partly, the availability of jobs was to blame, something that many of the respondents I spoke with noted. Charlene, an eighteen-year-old female, observed, "Because of the difference in price of the product and the income of the customers, Coffee Bean branches are located in richer areas than fast-food

establishments are." Because desirable places tend to be located in more affluent neighborhoods, minority students are left with limited options.

Because better-quality jobs are taken up by more affluent youth with
more upper-class self-presentations and product knowledge, those who really
financially need these jobs cannot find them. Dylan, a nineteen-year-old male,
described young fast-food employees as "high-school students or dropouts. . . .
The student is probably trying to pay for his or her expenses, while the dropout is just trying to make ends meet, whereas a Coffee Bean employee is after
the experience." Therefore, even if the money that affluent youth earns is used
for consumption, it pays not for necessary items but for elite consumption,
and in many cases to fund the consumption habit at the place of employment.

Nickson and colleagues (2011) show in their survey of employers that
product knowledge, dress sense and style, overall physical appearance, voice
and accent, weight, and height are important characteristics in performing
frontline work. As such appearance and consumption-related characteristics
become central in hiring decisions, Warhurst and Nickson (2007) point to the
emergence of a "labour aristocracy" in the context of retail and service workers. In the case of youth employment, the trend is remarkably similar: Working
for more affluent, desirable, glamorous brands is associated with more affluent
and glamorous youth. Although the so-called soft skills preferred in these
jobs appear to be just that—skills that employers might reasonably take into
account when making hiring decisions—such skills function as proxies for
socioeconomic status, race, and ethnicity. Philip Moss and Chris Tilly define
"soft skills" as "skills, abilities and traits that pertain to personality, attitude
and behavior rather than formal or technical knowledge" (1996: 253). In their
study, they show that many employers discriminate against African American
candidates on the basis of soft skills. Most of the racial bias is exhibited at the
interview stage, and these researchers show that it is justified by the concept
of soft skills: common understandings and shared knowledge that allow for
effective communication. At the interview stage, Joleen Kirschenman and
Kathryn Neckerman (1991) show that employers associate African Americans workers with lower levels of soft skills. On the basis of their study of
Chicago employers, Zamudio and Lichter (2008) show that employers view
African American workers as "having a bad attitude and poor work ethic,
prone to conflict, and being unreliable and lazy." Kirchenman and Neckerman (1991) also show that physical addresses associated with "the projects"
are linked to dysfunctional behavior in the workplace, so potential employees
from such neighborhoods experience "address discrimination." Young people
I spoke with discussed the same issue: Carter, like Mason, remembered using
his school address or extended family's addresses on job applications because
the predominantly African American town in which he resided was associated
with poverty and crime.

Regardless of the mechanisms, African American candidates face racial bias in the interview process, seemingly owing to perceived differences in soft skills and home-address discrimination. According to Moss and Tilly (1996), soft skills are important for two reasons: interaction and motivation. Interaction "involves ability to interact with customers, coworkers and supervisors," which is an essential component of service sector jobs. Motivation, on the other hand, "takes in characteristics such as enthusiasm, positive work attitude, commitment, dependability, integrity and willingness to learn" (Moss and Tilly 2001: 44). Part of the motivation, or lack thereof, is due to role distance, as previously discussed. These skills are becoming more and more central in the service sector, and many scholars find that employers in different settings perceive African American workers to possess worse or fewer soft skills. It is important to note that employers' assessment of soft skills is "inherently subjective" (Moss and Tilly 2001; Zamudio and Lichter 2008). Moss and Tilly argue that "in a work world characterized by increasing levels of interaction, racially biased attitudes held by customers or co-workers of other racial groups can themselves lead to lower measured productivity—that is, productivity differences can be the direct result of discrimination" (1996: 270). William Julius Wilson (1978) similarly notes that the growing importance of soft skills and interaction in the workplace results in a mismatch between the soft-skill requirements of the available jobs and inner-city blacks, who are segregated from mainstream culture. With the shift to a predominantly service economy, we see an economy characterized as a "game between persons" (Bell 1973: 148–149) rather than a "game against nature" or a "game against fabricated nature" (Bell 1973: 147). Unlike manufacturing jobs, where specific production skills are emphasized, the service sector has emphasized soft skills (Braddock and McPartland 1987; Zamudio and Lichter 2008). The most typical way to assess soft skills, unlike standardized tests, grades, credentials, skills, or prior work experience, is through an informal interview. Unfortunately, judging interpersonal skills through interviews is a highly subjective measurement (Adler 2001: 251). Unlike standardized measures of abilities, such subjective measures often result in increased racial bias in hiring. Prior research has already documented that at the lower end of the job spectrum, employers show higher racial bias in hiring (Moss and Tilly 1996). Therefore, in service sector jobs, which normally are at the lower end of the spectrum, we expect to find more racial discrimination. In addition to this, we would expect increased racial bias in service sector jobs with increased soft skill expectations. As Margaret M. Zamudio and Michael I. Lichter observe, "The unintended consequence of categorizing these attributes as skills is to supply a veneer of legitimacy to the discriminatory strategies of employers. Because these attributes have been accepted as skills, employers can provide a 'legitimate' reason for excluding low-skilled, native blacks from the labor market. They simply lack the skills to do the job" (2008: 577).

Within the context of fashion retail, for example, the work is dominated by the middle class (Leslie 2002; Nickson et al. 2011; Walls 2007). In this context, being middle class and white (and, in the case of the coffee shop, affluent) is a skill. Students' service and retail work in the United Kingdom involves mainly middle-class students taking jobs away from not only students from lower socioeconomic backgrounds but also other types of workers, such as the long-term unemployed or older working-class individuals (Nickson et al. 2011). We observe a similar trend in the United States and its youth labor force. What is particularly problematic about this phenomenon is what Witz, Warhurst, and Nickson (2003) refer to as "embodied dispositions": aesthetic attributes, social and physical capacities, and soft skills that are required or preferred by employers in many interactive retail and service sector jobs. However, such soft skills are often correlated with social class, race, and ethnicity. Deborah Leslie (2002) notes that the soft skills required and preferred for retail and interactive service jobs align with being white (see also Moss and Tilly 1996; Nickson et al. 2011).

In recent years, this situation has been publicized via a lawsuit against Abercrombie and Fitch, in which African American, Latino, and Asian American plaintiffs claimed they were excluded from sales positions located on the shop floor or were eliminated as job candidates because of their appearances. In 2005, *Gonzalez v. Abercrombie and Fitch* argued that the company discriminated in hiring on the basis of race and gender. The corporation's "natural classic American style," according to the plaintiffs, excluded many nonwhite applicants. They claimed the look of the company was "virtually all white" and "the attractive look the employer was seeking was not just pretty, but pretty and *white*" (Corbett 2007: 155). This case was settled in 2005 for approximately $50 million, and Abercrombie and Fitch agreed to implement new programs to increase diversity. What is really important and interesting about this case is the definition of a corporation's "look." One of the important debates raised by the lawsuit focuses on the strong correlation of race and ethnicity with a company's image.

Costs and Social Consequences

Being left out of the labor force has important consequences. First, there are economic repercussions. Youth, especially ones from more economically disadvantaged backgrounds, often need the income they would have derived from working. This lost income will inevitably have adverse effects on their lives, ranging from inability to contribute to the family's pooled income to inability to cover school-related expenses. However, the negative effects of unemployment are not limited to economic repercussions. Working while still in school, especially fewer hours of employment in nonintensive sectors, can be beneficial in other ways, such as emotional development or work habit formation.

All told, better jobs are dominated by association with a more affluent white look, while lower-income and minority youth are left with less desirable jobs or are often left out of the workforce. What is more troubling is the fact that such decisions are normalized and perpetuated with considerations of aesthetic labor: Nonwhite and nonaffluent youth simply do not have the right look.

7

Origins of the Gender Wage Gap

Gender Inequality in the Youth Labor Force

[Coffee Bean employees are] clad in way too much jewelry, be it excessive piercing or body parts, or millions of necklaces and arm bands. They are uni-gender.

—Ryan, twenty-year-old male

Jules remembered that the sales crew of the high-end clothing store where she worked was dominated by women, while immigrant men cleaned up after store hours. Today, young people's part-time jobs are practically synonymous with women. Parallel with the wider economy, retail and service sector positions are typically occupied by women (Mason and Osborne 2008; Roberts 2011; Skillsmart 2007). In fact, the youth labor market often appears as a democratic arena, offering abundant positions for women. Many young men who look for such retail and service positions are seen as the "lost boys" (Roberts 2011).

Despite the widespread racial and socioeconomic inequality, the young people I interviewed assured me that gender was equally distributed at the Coffee Bean. In Ryan's view, the Coffee Bean had a distinctive look and image, but it was uni-gender look. To these young people, jobs like these were equally distributed between young men and women, and the gender of the worker was largely irrelevant. Most young people in this study agreed with Ryan that gender was equally split at the Coffee Bean and other youth jobs. According to Mike, another twenty-year-old student, "The typical Coffee Bean worker is going to be a liberal college student. It's an even split between male or female. They will be part of the trendy crowd." The important part was that the worker was a part of the trendy group: Gender did not seem to matter. In this chapter, I explore the role of gender in youth jobs. These youth jobs often appear to promote gender equality, but is that really the case?

Equal Labor-Force Participation

Young people are right about one thing: Males and females are equally likely to participate in the youth labor force. According to the U.S. Bureau of Labor Statistics (Morisi 2008), sixteen- to nineteen-year-old females are slightly more likely to work than their male counterparts, although males in the same age group are more likely to hold employee-type jobs. From summer 1948 to summer 2000, young women's labor-force participation was in an upward trend, while the ration for young men was at a downward trend. In 2000, young women overtook young men in employment rates, with both genders' employment rates slightly declining in the recent years. By summer 2009, females between ages sixteen and nineteen became slightly more likely to work than their male counterparts. In 2009, 33.8 percent of females in this age group worked, as opposed to 32.1 percent of males. Both females and males in this age group experienced substantial losses in employment during the recession: The employment rate for females declined by 16.9 points between 2000 and 2009 (Morisi 2010), while the employment rate for males declined by 20.5 points over the same period. Despite the decline in labor-force participation due to the recession that hit in 2008, the gender gap between young males and females in labor-force participation has eroded and today, despite lower overall labor-force participation, young females are equally likely (if not slightly more likely) to work. Because unequal labor-force participation between men and women in this age group has been a traditional form of gender inequality, with the current equal labor-force participation rates, the youth labor force is often characterized as gender utopia, a sanctuary from the gendered workplaces that dominate later life. Although gender inequality may exist in many areas of the labor force, youth labor does not seem to be one of them. Especially in recent years with the shift to a service economy, female workers have become valuable resources for retail and service jobs. Young female workers have become sought after in the youth labor force. Traditionally, women have been closely associated with people skills and soft skills, so with the growing need for employees to perform service and retail jobs, young women have been characterized as benefiting from this shift.

Drawing on quantitative findings from the National Longitudinal Study of Youth and a rich body of quantitative interviews, this chapter explores the gender differences in the youth labor force. Here, I argue that the gender differences move beyond simple labor-force participation statistics. All youth jobs appear identical, but I show that there are marked differences in pay. First, I focus on some of the inequalities that early job experiences create. In particular, I focus on one of the most important forms of gender inequality in the workplace: the gender wage gap. I show that early labor-force participation is also the source and origin of the gender wage gap, which widens with time. Although early labor-force participation has early repercussions for gender inequality, it also has some positive effects. Later in the chapter, I explore the positive aspects of gender in the youth workforce, and I focus on the role of early workplaces in creating alternative masculine identities.

Pay Gap in the Adult Labor Force

The gender wage gap is among the most persistent and durable facts about labor markets and women's lives in the United States. Because of widespread social and academic interest in the topic, much progress has been made in explaining the gender wage gap, although a substantial portion remains unexplained. Many social scientists have approached the problem of pay discrepancy between men and women from different perspectives, ranging from economics to psychology to sociology. However, despite the differences in approach, almost every study on the gender wage gap focuses on *adult* employment. Whether it is part-time or full-time, as Paula England summarizes (1997; see also Blau, Ferber, and Winkler 2006), most studies on the topic focus on the adult labor market. However, in the United States, many teenagers work while still in school (Entwisle, Alexander, and Olson 2000; Manning 1990). Therefore, employment—and hence, possibly, the gender wage gap—actually begins well before adulthood.

Prior research on the topic considers a wide selection of potential explanations of the pay differential, although in all explanations, the gender wage gap is typically measured by annual earnings of full-time workers (England 1997) or part-time employees (Corcoran and Duncan 1979; see also Polacheck 1981). Despite the variance in measurement, this sort of analysis can fully explain the gender wage gap only if we agree that the experience of work begins with the onset of adult employment. On the contrary, men and women in the United States rarely enter the labor market for the first time after the completion of their education. According to the U.S. Bureau of Labor Statistics's *Report on the Youth Labor Force* (Herman 2000), almost every American high school student works sometime during school years (Herman 2000; see also Finch et al. 1991; Greenberger and Steinberg 1986; Mortimer and Finch 1986; Paternoster et al. 2003; Schoenhals, Tienda, and Schneider 1998).

Thus, in the United States, the labor market experience of both men and women begins well before the adult employment that previous studies have focused on. Explanations of the gender wage gap cannot be complete if only adult employment is considered; rather, an understanding of the gap requires that we also examine the pay patterns of teenagers in the labor market. Furthermore, as Barbara Reskin and Irene Padavic demonstrate, "the younger the workers are, the more equal women's and men's pay" (1994: 107). Therefore, a study focusing on early employment patterns provides not only a more comprehensive understanding of the gender-based wage differentials by including a previously excluded—yet substantial—portion of the labor force but also the opportunity to trace the origins of the gender wage gap and account for a number of variables that have proven confounding in previous studies.

A substantial body of research attempts to explain the difference in pay for men and women. Prior inquiries operate under two distinct strands. The human capital/productivity approach focuses predominantly on the individual differences between men and women and attempts to explain gender wage gap through individual differences that might result in lower productivity (Becker 1985, 1993; Bielby and Bielby 1988; Mincer 1962; Schultz 1960). In such explanations, the lower earnings of women are argued to be the result of lower productivity among women and are often associated with their domestic duties and child care responsibilities or with interruptions in employment due to these duties (Berk and Berk 1979; Hersch and Stratton 1997; Hochschild 1989; Mincer and Ofek 1982; Ross 1987; Waldfogel 1998).

Other attempts to explain the gender wage gap in this vein have come from proposed differences in education and experience between men and women. Earlier studies have argued that differential levels of formal education between men and women account for the gender wage gap, but this explanation has failed to fully provide for gender-based differences in earnings (England 1997; Tomaskovic-Devey 1993; Treiman and Hartmann 1981). However, many similar studies have shown that years of experience on the job account for a substantial portion of the gender wage gap. Because of women's traditional domestic duties, such as child rearing and housekeeping, the average woman on the labor market has fewer years of experience in the workforce than the average man, which contributes to the difference in pay between men and women (Light and Ureta 1995; Mincer and Polachek 1974; Polachek 1975; Reskin and Padavic 1994; Sandell and Shapiro 1978).

Some scholars have also focused on differential preferences of men and women. Randall K. Filer (1983) argues that different tastes and personality characteristics predict differential earnings for men and women. However, the hypothesized effect is an indirect one, where values and preferences predict different types of jobs, which result in unequal pay; the mechanisms through which these values lead to a wage disparity remain unaddressed. A more direct association between values and the wage gap can be observed in a number of studies that examine the relative importance men and women place on earnings and other occupational characteristics. These findings indicate that men place more importance on earning than women do and therefore end up in higher-paying jobs (Brenner and Tomkiewicz 1979; Herzog 1982; Lueptow 1980; Major and Konar 1984; Peng, Fetters, and Kolstad 1981), although some studies fail to find such a difference (Walker, Tausky, and Oliver 1982). More recently, however, the field has accepted as conclusive Jerry A. Jacobs and

Ronnie J. Steinberg's (1990) research showing that men and women value different things at work and rejected a line of reasoning based on differential preferences and values.

Instead of focusing on the characteristics of the employees, a second set of explanations focuses on structural and occupational differences and characteristics between men and women. The most prominent position of this strand of research argues that the difference in pay between men and women is due to their employment in different industries (Bayard et al. 2003; Blau 1977; Daymont and Andrisani 1984; Groshen 1991). Earlier studies show that women are more likely than men to be employed in traditionally feminine occupations that require nurturing social skills and are generally associated with lower pay (Jacobs and Steinberg 1990; Kanter 1977; Kilbourne et al. 1994; Steinberg 1990; Steinberg and Silverberg 1986). In addition to sex segregation by occupation, there is also sex segregation by firm. The disproportional employment of women in lower-wage firms only adds to the gap created by occupational sex segregation (Aldrich and Buchele 1989; Beck, Horan, and Tolbert 1980; Blau 1977; Coverdill 1988; Ferber and Spaeth 1984; Hodson and England 1986). Most importantly, for men and women, there is a difference in the types of jobs they are employed in. Men tend to be employed in employee-type jobs, characterized by set duties that are completed on a regular basis, set rates of pay, regular paychecks, and some level of governmental regulation, while women on average tend to be concentrated in freelance jobs, which typically lack repeated duties, government oversight, and regular, predictable paychecks. The unequal concentration of women in freelance jobs, which on average pay less than employee-type jobs, is identified as a factor contributing to the gender wage gap. Furthermore, even in similar settings, men tend to be concentrated in managerial positions, whereas women typically occupy non-managerial jobs (Blau, Ferber, and Winkler 2006).

In addition to the above explanations, the gender wage gap has been explored on the basis of such female characteristics as race, ethnicity, and age that exacerbate the gender wage gap, showing that women of different racial and ethnic backgrounds experience the gender wage gap differently (Goldin 1990; Jones 1985; Kessler-Harris 1986). Finally, instead of explaining pay discrepancy in terms of demand and supply, many feminist scholars have explored the organizational setting and argued that the gendered nature of the workplace has resulted in the gender wage gap (Acker 1990; Feldberg and Glenn 1979; Ferguson 1984; Kanter 1977; MacKinnon 1979; D. Smith 1979).

All these explanations focus on different aspects of employment that contribute to the gender wage gap, but even when they are taken into account, a substantial part of the gender wage gap remains unexplained. Given that the majority of the labor force experience the labor market before the time of adult employment, it is possible that the gender wage gap originates from early employment periods. Hence, this analysis of early employment patterns not only complements the current literature on the gender wage gap by focusing on a substantial portion of the youth labor force but also provides the opportunity to trace the origins of the gender wage gap. For the first time, we are able to see how early labor-market experiences contribute to the gender wage gap.

In the youth employment literature, extensive research has reviewed youth wages. Prior research on youth wages has operated within two major strands. The first, and more dominant, wave of studies focuses on structural factors in determining youth wages, such as governmental policies and restrictions, parental cash transfers (Pabilonia 2001), training programs (Andrews, Bradley, and Upward 1999; Grossberg and Sicilian 1999; Lynch 1992; Schiller 1994; Sweet 1995; Umana 1992), minimum hour requirements (Chen 1991), labor unions (Oklah 1987), neighborhood characteristics (Vartanian 1999), and, most importantly, changes in the minimum wage (Abowd et al. 1997; Currie and Fallick 1996; Mangan and Johnston 1999; Meyer and Wise 1983; Neumark 1995; Neumark and Wascher 1992; Welch and Cunningham 1978).

The literature on youth's wages is dominated by such structural explanations, but the inner variance among young workers has received relatively scant attention. This was partially because of data limitations and partially because all youth were assumed to make approximately the same amount of money—minimum wage. Recent years, however, have witnessed the burgeoning literature on the individual factors in determining youth's wages. Because all youth were assumed to make similar wages, the most dominant wave of research in this new literature focuses on "deviant" youth and attempts to identify factors that result in lower wages for some teenagers. Extensive inquiries explore the effects of smoking (Levine, Gustafson, and Velenchik 1997), alcohol consumption (Kenkel and Ribar 1994), drug use (Gill and Michaels 1992; Kaestner 1991), arrests (Grogger 1995), teenage pregnancies (Klepinger, Lundberg, and Plotnick 1999), obesity (Register and Williams 1990), and interrupted schooling (Light 1995) on youth's wages. In addition to deviant behavior, more recent studies have also explored the effects of nondeviant activities, such as extracurricular activities (Ewing 1995) and academic majors (Weinberger 1999), on wages. Finally, demographic factors have been included in the study of youth wages, the most important demographic factor being race (Weinberger 1998). However, the youth employment literature includes almost no work on the effects of gender on youth earnings. Typical studies of the gender wage gap often portray the youth labor market as gender utopia. A limited number of studies point to differential earnings of boys and girls, the most definitive one being Ellen Greenberger and Laurence Steinberg's (1983) work entitled "Sex Differences in Early Work Experience: A Harbinger of Things to Come." However, such analyses have various shortcomings. First, the gender wage differential is noted on only the descriptive level—the discrepancies in pay are not explained. Second, these youth employment patterns are not linked to the adult labor market. Finally, because of data restrictions, an accurate difference from a nationally representative sample has not been offered.

With the exception of these few works, the youth labor market has traditionally been considered an area of near gender equality. The aim of this chapter, therefore, is to focus on this understudied part of youth employment—youth wages and differential pay by gender—to determine whether the youth labor market is in fact a "gender utopia."

The "Gender Utopia" of Youth Work

My first source of data in this line of enquiry is the National Longitudinal Study of Youth 1997 (NLSY97). NLSY97 was funded by the U.S. government and consists of a representative sample of the noninstitutionalized U.S. population born between 1980 and 1984. The 8,984 youth respondents (including an oversample of black and Hispanic youth, requiring the use of sample weighting) interviewed in the five waves of this longitudinal study were between ages twelve and sixteen as of December 31, 1996. Comparable data on older youth, ages sixteen to nineteen, were supplemented by data from the Current Population Survey, which were also collected by the U.S. Department of Labor using the same definitions and questions.

NLSY97 provides ample data on income and employment variables along with demographic information on youth. For my purposes, the data set was aggregated by age to enable analysis and allow exploration over time of changes among three cohorts: twelve- and thirteen-year-olds, fourteen- and fifteen-year-olds, and sixteen- to nineteen-year-olds. This data set is particularly valuable in terms of not only the detailed, nationally representative data it provides on the employment characteristics of youth but also its inclusion of twelve- to fifteen-year-olds, who are traditionally omitted from youth labor analysis.

When solely focused on labor-force participation rates, I found no significant differences between genders in any of the three age cohorts (see Figure 7.1). Among the twelve- and thirteen-year-olds, 36 percent of girls and 37 percent of boys work; among the fourteen- and fifteen-year-olds, 47 percent of girls and 51 percent of boys work; and among the sixteen- to nineteen-year-olds, 65 percent of girls and 66 percent of boys work. Such marginal differences mean that we can treat the labor participation rates, at least, as being approximately equal. This well-known finding, perhaps, contributes to the perception of the youth labor market as a place of gender equality.

However, a lack of differences in young people's likelihood of working does not imply equality in all aspects of youth employment. Even though boys and

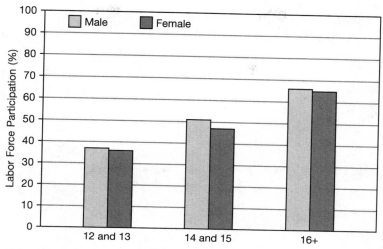

FIGURE 7.1 Labor-Force Participation, by Age and Gender

girls of a certain age are equally likely to work, it is possible that they receive differential pay for their work or are segregated into different types of jobs.

The Emergence of the Wage Gap

In terms of earnings, we observe approximately equal annual median earnings for both genders during their early employment years on the basis of median annual earnings of dependent youth (see Figure 7.2). Among twelve- and thirteen-year-olds, boys, on average, make $120 annually, while girls make only slightly more: $125. As further analysis shows, by the time the youth in the study enter the second age cohort, boys' earnings outstrip girls' substantially, with boys earning an average of $400 a year, and girls earning only $266. Thus, we first observe a sizable gender wage gap among fourteen- and fifteen-year-olds, and it only grows with older cohorts. Sixteen- to nineteen-year-old boys, on average, make $950, grossing $200 more than their female counterparts.

Although yearly wages are the conventional and more reliable method of measurement because of the low hourly pay at earlier ages and relatively lower number of work hours, it is important to also review the hourly pay rate. Interestingly, parallel with the above findings, we observe that fourteen- to fifteen-year-old boys have higher hourly wages than girls of the same age. However, at these early ages, most working youth are engaged in freelance work. As freelance work is often paid on the basis of a completed task rather than on an hourly rate, calculating hourly rates of pay leads to high standard deviations in the estimates of hourly earnings. Thus, annual earnings are a more reliable

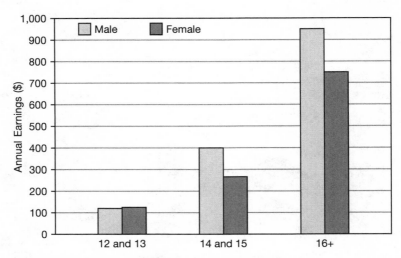

FIGURE 7.2   Median Annual Earnings, by Age and Gender

measure of earning power, but it is important to note that an analysis of hourly wages yields results similar to those for the median annual wages.

Figure 7.2 shows that when youth are twelve or thirteen, there is no real difference in pay, but when they reach age fourteen or fifteen, the gender wage gap begins to emerge, and it continues to widen with age. The mechanism behind this increasing gap is not immediately clear.

Most of the traditional explanations of the gender wage gap fail when brought to bear on youth employment. Explanations of the gender wage gap based on individual differences in productivity or years of education are not applicable to the case of youth employment. Girls in that age group almost certainly are not less productive as a result of having children; similarly, explanations based on differences in human capital between boys and girls are not applicable. For youth in the specified age bracket, differences in education, skills, credentials, or experience are not relevant factors leading to differential pay. All of them have the same education (less than high school) and the same experience (none).

Despite the fact that almost all individual explanations fail to account for the gender wage gap, the only applicable individual difference is the number of hours each youth works per week. It is important to note that boys might be working more hours than girls, resulting in the gender wage gap. But contrary to these common perceptions, when we look at the aggregate data, girls and boys on average work almost equal numbers of hours, with girls working slightly more than boys. According to the NLSY97 data, girls on average work 7.9 hours per week, with a standard deviation of 9.9, while boys work

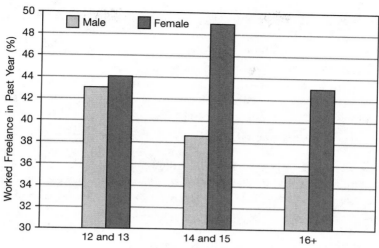

FIGURE 7.3 Participation in Freelance Work, by Age and Gender

7.2 hours per week, with a standard deviation of 9.9. Therefore, with similar standard deviations, girls work slightly more hours than boys do; as a result, there is no reason to suspect that differential hours of employment contribute to the gender wage gap.

Because the gender wage gap in youth jobs cannot be explained by individual differences, such as disparity in productivity, education, and experience, especially due to domestic and maternal duties, we must look for alternative explanations. The second set of explanations in the literature focuses on structural factors, such as the type of job. One potential explanation is that boys and girls have equal labor-force participation rates but may work in different types of jobs.

The types of jobs that employ youth do seem to differ by gender (see Figure 7.3). Among fourteen- and fifteen-year-olds, girls are more likely to be employed in freelance jobs, such as babysitting, while boys tend to be employed in employee-type positions, working more regular hours at an organization, for set rates of pay. Here, the U.S. Department of Labor defines freelance jobs as self-employment; typical examples of this type of work are babysitting and yard work. Employee-type jobs, however, are defined as work for an organization, such as a fast-food restaurant or a retail store.

Even though we observe a gendering of jobs within employee-type and freelance jobs, which are discussed at length later, the gendering seems to be present at ages twelve and thirteen, and the change over time seems to be slow. However, the largest effect is in the concentration of boys and girls in freelance and employee-type jobs, respectively. It seems that teenagers adopt traditional gender roles quickly upon entering the workforce, with the freelance versus employee-type job distinction as the major difference.

The overall analysis of the data shows a difference in the types of jobs, especially a marked concentration of girls in freelance jobs and boys in employee-type jobs, but we have yet to show that these concentrations are the cause of the gender wage gap. The data do show a disproportionate concentration of girls in freelance jobs and points to the gendered nature of the jobs taken in both broad categories. However, we cannot be immediately certain that the gender wage gap arises from these differences. First, no evidence suggests differential pay for different types of jobs among the youth. The vast majority of youth employed in employee-type jobs receive minimum wage, and there is no reason to believe that freelance jobs pay more to one gender than the other.

Second, the disproportionate employment of girls in freelance jobs cannot alone be the cause of the gender wage gap, as child-labor restrictions restrict youth under sixteen from employment. Therefore, the twelve- to thirteen-year-old and fourteen- to fifteen-year-old samples are predominantly employed in freelance jobs. If the disproportionate employment of girls in freelance-type jobs explained the gender wage gap, there would not be the degree of differential pay for the fourteen- to fifteen-year-old cohort that is observed, as relatively few of these teenagers work in employee-type jobs. In fact, the wage gap is significant even among this group. Moreover, while the concentration of girls and boys in traditionally gendered jobs increases, this does not map onto the earliest signs of the gender wage gap. Even among the twelve- to thirteen-year-old cohort, where girls actually earn slightly more than their male counterparts, there is a concentration of girls and boys in traditionally gendered jobs. The extent to which job choice results in the discrepancy in pay needs to be tested.

The purpose of this analysis is to account for the effect of gender on income by controlling for all the possible confounding factors. Even though the number of hours does not differ for boys and girls, it is important to control for it as a confounding variable. In addition to the average number of hours worked per week, the regression analysis includes several variables representing structural explanations for the wage gap applicable to youth, such as the type of job (freelance versus employee-type) and demographic control variables traditionally included in similar analyses, such as race (white or Asian vs. nonwhite or Asian), age (as youth typically earn more as they become older), socioeconomic status of the household (measured through household income, as a percentage of the local poverty level), and, of course, the gender of the respondent. I use all these factors to explain the income of the respondent, logged to minimize the impact of outliers. Simply put, the existence of a difference in wages based on gender rather than on hours worked or any other explanation is evident from a significant coefficient attached to the variable representing

TABLE 7.1 Descriptive Characteristics of Selected Variables from the National Longitudinal Study of Youth 1997

	Min	Max	Overall		Female		Male	
			Mean	SD	Mean	SD	Mean	SD
Hours worked	0	90	16.34	11.54	16.43	10.59	16.26	12.29
Age	12	18	14.31	1.48	14.32	1.48	14.29	1.47
White?	0	1	.52	.50	.51	.50	.52	.50
Freelance?	0	1	.36	.48	.39	.49	.32	.47
Employee-type?	0	1	.25	.43	.22	.42	.28	.45
Grades	1	13	5.74	1.76	6.05	1.67	5.41	1.79
Household income*	0	1,627	283.26	270.15	280.04	266.84	286.33	273.27
Logged income	0	11	5.57	1.55	5.49	1.53	5.65	1.57

Source: U.S. Department of Labor, National Longitudinal Study of Youth 1997.

Note: Min, minimum; Max, maximum; SD, standard deviation.

*Household income is expressed as a percentage of the local poverty level.

the gender of the respondent. The descriptive characteristics of the variables used are presented in Table 7.1.

However, a simple linear regression is insufficient to sort out these effects because of the expectation of a great deal of heteroskedasticity in the model. As the youth in the study get older, there are simply more work opportunities available to them, leading us to expect that the variance around the dependent variable should increase substantially with age. Also, as is almost always the case with income measures, the measurement becomes less precise as the dollar values grow larger. That is, an individual making several thousand dollars a year is likely to err by a few hundred in reporting income, while an individual who makes several hundred is likely to make errors on a much smaller scale. A battery of heteroskedasticity tests on the model bears out this expectation. The results of the Breusch-Pagan test identifying the presence of heteroskedesticity in the model are presented in Table 7.2.

Of course, there are several ways in which one could potentially account for this heteroskedasticity. The most common way of doing so is simply to make use of White-Huber estimation procedures to generate robust standard errors, inflated to account for the problems inherent in estimating a heteroskedastic dependent variable. However, my purposes are better served by using a maximum likelihood procedure to directly model the heteroskedasticity. Using this approach allows me not only to achieve consistent parameter estimates while avoiding artificially inflated standard errors but also to test hypotheses regarding the nature of the variance. As I have noted, for reasons inherent in the data, one would expect the variance to increase with both the age of the respondent and the amount of money that they make. However, my theoretical argument also holds that as youth age, their work patterns necessarily converge on those that they will hold as adults, moving more and more

TABLE 7.2 Maximum Likelihood Regression of Logged Income, with Modeled Heteroskedasticity

	Coeff	SE	z	p > z	Dollar Value
Gender	−.134*	.042	−3.14	.002	$93.05
Age	.426*	.018	24.19	.000	$295.67/year
Hours worked weekly	.17*	.002	7.60	.000	$117.99/weekly hour
Freelance?	−.353*	.057	−6.15	.000	$245.01
Family socioeconomic status	.0015*	.001	2.10	.036	$104.11/multiple of poverty line
White/Asian?	.092*	.047	1.97	.049	$63.85
Constant	−.691	.272	−2.54	.011	
Sigma					
Age	.027	.011	2.64	.014	
Income	.002	.000	7.92	.000	
Age × Income	−.001	.000	−7.42	.000	
Constant	.551	.159	3.47	.001	

Wald chi^2	908.68
Prob > chi^2	.00
N	2,564
OLS Breusch-Pagan test for heteroskedasticity chi^2	197.45
p	<.001

Source: U.S. Department of Labor, National Longitudinal Study of Youth 1997.
Note: Coeff, logistic regression coefficient; SE, standard error; OLS, ordinary least squares.
*$p < .05$.

into employee-type jobs with standardized rates of pay and the gender wage gap that has been repeatedly shown to exist in adult employment. Thus, the variance that should increase with both age and income should decrease as a function of the interaction of the two. As youth become older and earn more, one would expect that the variance of the dependent variable should decrease as they converge into adult work habits.

As shown in the first section of Table 7.2, all the predictor variables in the model have statistically significant effects on youth income. When interpreting the table coefficients, it is important to note that all reflect changes in logged, rather than actual, income.

The most important finding of this regression is in the coefficient attached to the gender of the respondent. Accounting for all the explanations applicable to the youth in my sample, including the number of hours worked and the nature of the job, girls can expect to earn about $93 less per year solely by virtue of their gender. Although this may not seem like a great deal, it is very large relative to the average earnings of a girl in the sample, which come to only $606.76 per year. Thus, at these young ages, girls are making almost 13 percent less than boys solely because of their gender.

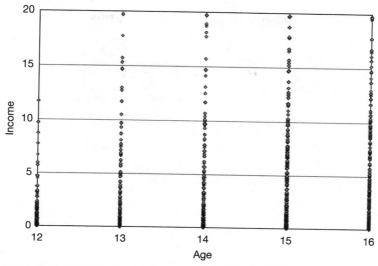

FIGURE 7.4 Income by Age: Modeled Heteroskedasticity

Other factors in the model are used solely for control purposes to identify the pure effect of gender but also provide interesting comparisons to illuminate the magnitude of the effects of gender on income. It is interesting to see that the effects of race results in an average of $63, while the pure effect of gender is $93.

The heteroskedastic maximum likelihood regression also allows me to substantively interpret the causes of the variance in my model. As predicted, the variance in the model increases with age and income—the latter bolstering our assertion of depressed model fit due to reporting error in the dependent variable—but decreases with the interaction of the two, a striking result, especially given the relative strengths of the coefficients. I can interpret this result to mean that as youth become more like adults—older and earning more money—the relationship of their demographic characteristics to their earnings becomes more predictable. It may be only this variance that allows for the equality of pay in the youngest cohorts, and it fades away rapidly with increases in age and earnings. But interestingly, a further analysis of the heteroskedasticity patterns shows an interesting clustering of higher age/higher income youth, most of which are boys, with the marked omission of girls. (See Figure 7.4.)

So far, I have identified the pure effect of gender on the earning of youth, controlling for all possible explanations and demographic characteristics. However, it is important to show how these factors translate into the gender wage gap. Although the maximum likelihood estimation identifies the direct effect of gender, we can also see that gender results in unequal earnings through the

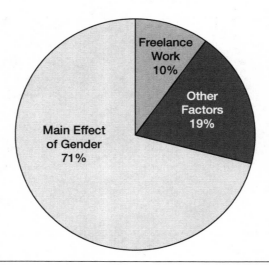

Total Gender Wage Gap = Average Wage of Boys ($737.57) – Average Wage of Girls ($606.76) = $130.81

Portion Explained by Main Effect of Gender = Dollar Value Attached to the Coefficient for Gender = $93.01

Portion Explained by Freelance Work = Expected Value of Freelance for Girls (.4775) – Expected Value of Freelance for Boys (.4244), Multiplied by the Dollar Value Attached to the Coefficient for Freelance ($245.01) = $13.01

Portion Explained by Other Factors = Total Gender Wage Gap ($130.81) – Portion Explained by Main Effect of Gender ($93.01) – Portion Explained by Difference in Likelihood of Freelance Work ($13.01) = $24.79

FIGURE 7.5   Proportion of the Gender Wage Gap Explained

concentration of girls in freelance jobs. As shown in Figure 7.5, the total average gender wage gap in the youth sample is about $131, 71 percent of which is accounted for by the main effect of gender. In addition to this, 10 percent of the difference is accounted for by the differential concentration of girls in freelance jobs. Therefore, I can say that overall, the model accounts for 81 percent of the gender wage gap.

In my attempt to unravel the factors that contribute to the making of the gender wage gap, I have reviewed the three major approaches in explaining the pay differential between men and women. The first set of explanations, or the individualist approach, is not applicable to the youth labor market. Girls in that age group do not show any differences in education, skills, experience, and the number of hours they work. Furthermore, typically they neither are married nor have maternal or domestic duties.

The final set of explanations, which explain the pay differential through the characteristics of the job, however, provide an interesting partial answer to why girls make more than boys. When youth approach ages fourteen and fifteen, girls tend to be concentrated in freelance jobs, while boys are employed in employee-type jobs. This polarization explains an important portion of the gender wage gap but offers only a partial explanation. Although only 10 percent of the gender wage gap is explained by the difference in type of jobs, the most important portion of the gender wage gap is explained purely by gender. More than 80 percent of the gender pay discrepancy is "the cost of being a girl."

My model explains a substantial portion of the gender wage gap, but there is still a minor unexplained portion of the gender wage gap. Although this difference cannot be accounted for by individual differences or value differences, it is possible to consider further inner differences in the types of jobs boys and girls are employed in. It is important to note that, in my sample, the main and the most pronounced difference is between the types of jobs: freelance or employee-type. Despite the small magnitude of such effects and the limitations of the data, it is important to acknowledge the inner differences within all categories. Such differences in the minor job assignments often are obscured through the data-collection process, but it is important to test for such effects for future research, especially after more detailed data collections enable us to observe the nuances in job selection.

A Final Possibility—Values

I have so far considered several sets of explanations for the wage gap among youth and successfully accounted for an overwhelming majority of the gender wage gap. Some of the explanations, which have been applied to the adult wage gap, are simply inapplicable to youth; other explanations are dispelled in the maximum likelihood model. But a pay differential of 19 percent has yet to be accounted for. So far, the first two set of explanations have been tested for, but the third set of explanations remains unknown. Could the reasons that boys and girls make different amounts of money be because they work for different reasons? To ensure that my findings are accurate, I now examine a final set of explanations: the differential values of boys and girls regarding the job market. I have yet to account for the possibility that boys and girls might be working for different reasons and value different aspects of work, which might then contribute to the gender wage gap. Even though extensive research refutes this argument for the adult labor markets (see Jacobs and Steinberg 1990), it is important to test whether differential values of youth might account for their differential earnings. First, I test to see which values, if any, are important to the work decisions of youth, and, second, I consider whether these values differ substantially between boys and girls.

This analysis is based on the replication of similar studies measuring the differences in values in predicting labor-force market entry decisions in the adult labor market. The data employed for this analysis come from the World Values Study (Abramson and Inglehart 1995), which provides reliable data on economic- and social work–related factors on the population of interest. For the age group of interest, ages sixteen to nineteen, I focus on the differential reasons for working among boys and girls. In Chapter 6, I estimated a logistic regression model predicting the labor-market entry decisions of youth. In this chapter, the same model is replicated for boys and girls to capture the differential reasons for working.

Overall, I see the domination of the work decisions of youth in the United States in the specified age group by social factors. However, when controlling for gender and replicating the same logistic regression model for boys and girls separately, we observe no differential reasons that boys and girls work. Traditional explanations associate women's work with social and noneconomic reasons and men's work with economic reasons and try to link these differential values in working with the gender wage gap. However, no statistical evidence suggests that such a differential exists in the reasons that boys and girls work. Based on the 95 percent confidence intervals presented in Figure 7.6, the coefficients attached to these variables in predicting the work decision can be safely said to be indistinguishable at any standard level of statistical significance. In short, no evidence supports the existence of differential reasons for working for boys and girls.

Furthermore, I also find that when I replicate the same study of values and estimate a logistic regression with gender interactions of each category, the gender interactions are not statistically significant, as shown below, indicating that boys and girls do not work for different reasons or value different aspects of work (see Table 7.3).

Mechanisms of the Youth Gender Wage Gap

While I capture the emergence of the first gender inequality in the workplace, the analysis so far does not explain the mechanisms through which gender inequality emerges and is transmitted. The majority of the gender wage gap in the youth labor force emanates from the gendering of sectors, but even in the same types of jobs, tasks are gendered. Research on the adult gender wage gap points to the everyday experience of the jobs leading to the pay gap. Yasemin Besen and Michael S. Kimmel (2006) argue, in the case of the recent Walmart lawsuit, that pay discrimination is not necessarily a result of one big individual act but a combination of small, everyday, seemingly harmless acts that result in discrimination. I have adapted the model proposed by Nijole V. Benokraitis and Joe R. Feagin (1986) that describes the mechanisms by which men

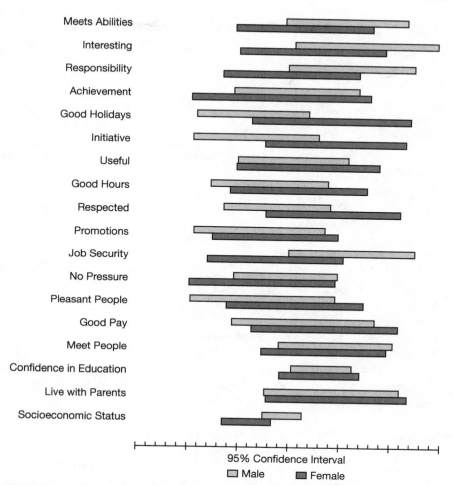

FIGURE 7.6 95% Confidence Intervals around Logit Coefficient Estimates, by Gender

undermine women. Benokraitis and Feagin enumerate nine such mechanisms: condescending chivalry, supportive discouragement, friendly harassment, subjective objectification, radiant devaluation, liberated sexism, benevolent exploitation, considerate domination, and collegial exclusion.

Because Benokraitis and Feagin are referring to the adult workforce, it is important to determine whether the youth labor force experiences similar mechanisms. In the Walmart sex discrimination case, all mechanisms were present, resulting in the pay gap. In the youth labor force, though, the majority of these mechanisms are not at play. First, as many prior studies confirm, the

TABLE 7.3 Logistic Regression Estimates of Interactions of Variables with Gender of the Respondent

	Coeff	SE	z	$p > z$
Respected	−1.275	.801	−1.59	.111
Achievement	.576	1.200	.48	.631
Initiative	.825	1.220	.68	.499
Promotions	−.929	.868	−1.07	.285
Good holidays	−.032	.959	−.03	.973
Good hours	−.781	.868	−.90	.368
Security	1.355	.909	1.49	.136
Meets abilities	1.670	1.187	1.41	.159
Meet people	.573	1.152	.50	.619
No pressure	1.273	.946	1.35	.178
Pleasant people	−1.290	1.223	−1.06	.291
Responsibility	.056	1.182	.05	.963
Useful	.314	1.155	.27	.786
Socioeconomic status	−.322	.508	−.63	.526
Confidence in education system	.333	.466	.71	.475

Source: U.S. Department of Labor, National Longitudinal Study of Youth 1997.
Note: Coeff, logistic regression coefficient; SE, standard error.

gender composition of the workforce is essential in determining the lived experience of gender inequality in the workplace. As Rosabeth Moss Kanter's landmark book on gender inequality shows, when women are in the minority in the workplace, the situation is often detrimental for them and sometimes creates a hostile work environment. Unlike these workplaces, many teenage workplaces, including the coffee shop, offer a more gender-balanced composition.

However, we observe the widespread practice of condescending chivalry and benevolent exploitation. Condescending chivalry refers to the polite, helpful acts of men in the workplace. Many young women I interviewed remembered incidents that could be categorized as condescending chivalry. Often at the coffee shop, Billy volunteered to take out the large trash bags because they might be heavy for Monica. Similarly, Brianna remembered that at her workplace, they always waited for the manager to replace the water cooler. Even though it was not in his job description, because of the gender composition, he always took on this duty. Men in the workplace do not commit these acts maliciously or with the intent to undermine women in the workplace. In the coffee shop, young men performed many chivalrous acts, such as carrying larger loads and heavy garbage bags, instead of allowing female co-workers to do it. Even though the women were physically able to carry the large loads of garbage, when they worked with a male co-worker, the man automatically did the carrying.

The second mechanism of discrimination that we observe in the workplace is benevolent exploitation. Benevolent exploitation refers to small, innocent assumptions made in the workplace that result in job assignment. In the coffee shop, many times, young men told women that they were much better at making the foam or dealing with people. Women are assumed to be naturally good with people and therefore better at service, dealing with people, and helping others. Such assumptions result in differential job placements and potential differences in pay. Young women who had been complimented on their social abilities or in their abilities to deal with customers were often happy to receive the comments. Many took pride in the fact that they accomplished these tasks. In fact, their special skills shaped their identities in the workplace: "I make the best foam"; "I am good with customers." However, such assumptions often caused them to become stuck in these specific positions.

Alternative Masculinities

While early labor-force experiences create and sustain important forms of gender inequality, such as the gender wage gap, they also create some positive gender outcomes. Unlike many workplaces, the coffee shops where I conducted my ethnography created and reinforced a gender-supportive environment. Instead of promoting hegemonic masculinities (to borrow from R. W. Connell), the coffee shop promoted an alternative masculinity. Hegemonic masculinity, which refers to cultural and social norms governing male behavior, captures socially acceptable behavior for men and often prescribes a misogynistic, aggressive, and homophobic outlook for them. In his book *Guyland* (2008), which is based on four hundred in-depth interviews with young men between ages sixteen and twenty-four, Kimmel observes a sense of entitlement, a refusal to transition from adolescence into adulthood, and a retreat to a homosocial existence, unadulterated by work, demands of adult life, and girlfriends. Surrounded by this culture, the environment at the coffee shop offered an alternative masculinity to young men. The behavior of the young men working at the coffee shop differed greatly from ideas of hegemonic masculinity and challenged such patriarchal views.

For starters, the "look" for the men at the coffee shop was more feminized. Theresa, a nineteen-year-old, described the boys at the coffee shop as "artsy and somewhat nerdy. The guys that work there usually play the guitar. Smart people usually work at the Coffee Bean." For nineteen-year-old Will, men at the coffee shop could be described as "liberal, artsy, upper to middle class, earrings, tattoos, drives a green car, hates war, and loves trees." As Greg Bortnichak explains in "Starbucks Intervention," "I am the kind of twenty-something guy you expect to work at the coffee shop. I play guitar and cello in an experimental punk band and have some cool downloads in MySpace. I am tall and lean, with an explosive mess of dark hair that makes me look like the love child of Edward Scissorhands and Blacula. Most people correctly guess that I am artistic and a bit to the political left" (2009: 171). Sally agreed that young people working at the coffee shop followed that pattern: Men tended to be more artsy and more feminine, deviating greatly from hegemonic masculinity: "The typical Coffee Bean employee is someone who is hardworking and always polite. They tend to be the 'artsy' type to make it easier to work in a coffeehouse environment, where people interested in the arts tend to gravitate. They also tend to be college students, working part-time or full-time in order to fund some type of endeavor."

While looking artsy was one of the ways men at the coffee shop deviated from hegemonic masculinity, they were also described as nerdy. Nathalie, a nineteen-year-old student, said, "A typical Coffee Bean employee is someone who reads books for fun and more on the nerdy side. Their looks are very dull, mostly brown or very dark hair color. Also mostly a high school or college student."

Many male workers I spoke with at the coffee shop self-identified as feminist and had feminine self-presentations. Many were interested in arts and music and adorned themselves in body art and longer hair styles.

For Noah, his job at the coffee shop was not just a job but an expression of his gender identity. For him, the coffee shop offered a space for alternative masculinities. Especially in the suburbs, he believed that the coffee shop allowed him to be himself and express his gender identity. He felt more comfortable with the coffee-shop culture, where he talked openly with his friends. His longer hair and jewelry, which often attracted criticism from others, were welcome at the coffee shop, and he felt surrounded by other men like him. This feeling went beyond simple looks and stylistic choices, such as long hair, jewelry, or body art. The coffee shop attracted boys with specific interests: more liberal arts majors and interests in art, the environment, and music. The culture at the coffee shop also encouraged talking and sharing. Contrary to ideals of hegemonic masculinity, the friendships at the coffee shop involved many cross-sex relationships and encouraged these friendships. Groups of friends at the coffee shop included both males and females, and there were close friendships between everyone. Many hung out during and after the shifts. Furthermore, the men at the coffee shop often talked with the others about their school, family, and relationship problems, as encouraged by the culture at the shop.

Overall, the coffee shop became a gender refuge for young people, especially men, who differed from hegemonic masculinity. Because the coffee shop promoted and encouraged alternative masculinities, gender relationships at the coffee shop differed somewhat from the traditional accounts of the workforce. For example, the male workers at the coffee shop did not practice collegial exclusion, where male workers socialize and exclude women. Most friendships at the workplace were across borders of gender, as male and female workers of the coffee shop socialized together during and after their shifts.

Overall, the youth labor force offers a wide range of opportunities in the study of gender. The equal labor-force participation of women and the prevalence of women in the service sector are welcome developments. In addition, owing to aesthetic-labor considerations, many places promote and reinforce alternative masculinities, creating and reinforcing more feminine images for men. But despite such welcome changes in gender relations, early work experiences also create the gender wage gap. Such pay differences emerge in the youth labor force and widen with age.

The analysis of the youth labor force, like a social laboratory, offers a time when most traditional explanations of the gender wage gap are not applicable and almost every individual characteristic, such as education and experience, are equal. The absence of these potentially confounding variables makes youth labor the ideal laboratory for the study of the gender wage gap. Previous explanations of the gender wage gap have attempted to account for the gap through differences in individual characteristics between men and women, such as education, experience, skills, domestic obligations, or child care practices. None of these explanations applies to youth labor, yet the gender wage gap remains. Although a cursory examination of youth employment patterns shows almost no difference in labor-force participation rates and even seems to favor girls, a detailed analysis of the data shows the origins of the gender wage gap. In this chapter, I have traced the creation of the gender gap through youth employment and the contribution of early market experiences of youth to the pay disparity. My findings show that demographic variables, such as race, age, and income, significantly increase the gender wage gap and that the type of work significantly explains the pay disparity between boys and girls. However, despite controlling for all possible explanations and testing for differences in values, the gender wage gap persists.

8

Conclusion

The Economic Recession and the Future of Youth Labor

began my examination of the current state of the American youth labor force by noting its unique composition. Contrary to romanticized images of poor students working to put themselves through school, the current and counterintuitive composition of the youth labor force is overwhelmingly dominated by affluent students. Unfortunately, many traditional accounts consider "youth" and the "youth labor force" as monolithic categories, without real inner differences. This book explores the inner differences among the student employees in the United States—showing two distinct populations: affluent students and poor dropouts. Lower-income dropouts' decision to work is not surprising, but affluent students' overwhelming desire to work in traditionally working-class jobs is.

What makes the members of this population so special or different is not only their high labor-force participation rates or their unique—mostly affluent—socioeconomic composition but also the reasons and motivations behind their desire to work. While economically deprived school dropouts work for the money, these affluent students work to fulfill their social needs. Affluent youth's part-time employment while still in school, therefore, has become a "social problem." Often viewed as a character builder, as a way to keep teenagers out of trouble, and especially as a way for economically disadvantaged young people to support themselves through school, youth employment has not been seen as an activity that creates inequality or an act that disadvantages relatively less affluent youth. These perceptions are predominantly based on the previous composition of the youth labor force, consisting mainly of relatively less affluent youth. However, the current composition of the youth labor force does not reflect these assumptions. Although in previous years, economically disadvantaged youth would be more likely to work, during the past decade, the youth labor force has become dominated by relatively more affluent youth, rendering jobs less and less available to those who economically need these jobs the most. This is not to say that economically disadvantaged youth do not participate in the labor force at all, but it is important to note that they are a minority in the current youth labor market, and their options are becoming increasingly scarce.

Work experience begins before the actual job is found, starting with the job search. The job-search patterns of youth have important implications for the perception and experience of the work experience and help deconstruct the meaning of work from their perspective. The ways they get jobs indicate that most "shop around" for them by flipping through magazines, going through information about available jobs and companies themselves, and then go directly to the shops and get a job as they would any other product. Alternately, they get jobs through their close friends by working in the same or similar places as the people whom they are socially close to. In both cases, the work experience is obtained to enjoy the company's brand and/or to enjoy time with friends in that social space. The search for jobs reveals the meaning and the social function of jobs for young people. Just like products that young people consume, jobs are *branded*. Taking jobs at certain stores also becomes a way to associate with the desired brand. Apple, Abercrombie and Fitch, the Gap, Anthropologie, and Starbucks emerge as desirable brands for young people, while some supermarkets, fast-food chains, and restaurants are less desirable. Paralleling the desires of young people to be associated with cool brands, more and more employers wish to hire young and mostly affluent workers to better reflect the lifestyle they want to associate with the brand. Aesthetic labor has become an important consideration in hiring decisions.

Moreover, from the perspective of the workers, these low-paying, routinized jobs are considered fun, becoming forms of branded consumption for many young people. Many see jobs as an opportunity to meet new people and see their existing friends. Especially in centerless suburbs that are social wastelands with limited opportunities for social interactions, jobs fulfill this function.

What makes this even more interesting is that it is not happening in the rest of the developed world. In the youth labor literature, the U.S. youth labor market is identified as unique, and youth employment is considered predominantly as an American phenomenon. Interestingly, the youth labor markets in the United States and in other industrialized countries are bifurcated similarly into student and nonstudent samples. Just as in the United States, in other industrialized countries, the youth labor market is not homogenous but has two distinct segments: students and nonstudents. The nonstudents in other industrialized countries are similar to their counterparts in the United States in terms of their backgrounds and their motivations for working: Nonstudents in other industrialized countries, too, work for economic reasons. Student populations, on the other hand, make the American youth labor force unique. First, students who work are an exclusively American phenomenon: An overwhelming majority of students in the United States work while still in school, whereas in other industrialized countries, this situation is relatively rare. Also, the socioeconomic backgrounds of student workers in the United States are very different from their counterparts in other industrialized countries. While student workers in the United States are predominantly from higher socioeconomic backgrounds, student workers in other industrialized countries tend to come from lower socioeconomic backgrounds. Furthermore, the motivations behind their work are very different: Students in the United States work for social reasons, such as meeting new people, but for the students in other industrialized countries, work is primarily an economic activity rather than a social function.

Underlying these findings is a failure, or at least a perceived failure, of the American education system and how it influences the decision of affluent youth to seek employment. If American students opt to enter the labor market to fulfill social needs, why can they not meet these needs at school? The findings show that for students in the United States, their level of confidence in the education system strongly predicts their decision to enter the labor market while still in school. For American students, the likelihood of working increases substantially with a lack of confidence in the education system, regardless of socioeconomic status, gender, or race.

This desire to work could be interpreted as American students' attempt at creating an alternative to school that provides economically relevant skills, opportunities to meet people, and a socially cohesive environment for youth. The mechanisms through which these perceptions translate into decisions to enter the labor market are ripe for future examination, as are the factors that contribute to their perception of the education system. Whether there has been a change in schools' ability to fulfill such needs requires further research, but it is important to note that, regardless of the characteristics of schools, many students see schools as being unable to provide social connections.

Focusing on the early employment practices has important implications for understanding critical characteristics of the labor markets, such as the gender wage gap. The analysis of the youth labor force offers a time when most traditional explanations of the gender wage gap are not applicable and almost every individual characteristic, such as education and experience, are equal. The absence of these potentially confounding variables makes youth labor the ideal laboratory for the study of the gender wage gap.

Previous explanations of the gender wage gap have attempted to account for it through differences in individual characteristics between men and women, such as education, experience, skills, domestic obligations, or child care practices. None of these explanations applies to youth labor, yet the gender wage gap remains. In Chapter 7, I traced the creation of the gender gap through youth employment and the contribution of early market experiences of youth to the pay disparity. In this chapter, I find that the types of jobs young people are employed in strongly affect gender wage disparity. In addition, factors such as race, age, and income exacerbate the wage inequality between boys and girls. However, even after controlling for individual and occupational characteristics, the wage gap still persists.

My analysis of youth labor eliminates a number of frequent explanations for the wage gap, but further research needs to unravel the mechanisms through which this gap is created, internalized, and translated into the gender wage gap in full-time employment. Just as many feminist scholars argue that organizations are gendered in full-time work, the next step would be to unravel the mechanisms through which the early labor-market experiences translate to and contribute to the adult gender wage gap and to unravel the everyday experience of the gender wage gap for youth.

This study of the youth labor market is important because it sheds light on the creation and the experience of these inequalities. As the youth labor market becomes an important part of the current labor force, understanding the barriers in entering such jobs based on socioeconomic status and decreased pay due to gender provides a more accurate understanding of the labor market. Furthermore, it is important to understand such inequalities in the youth labor market, as they are also durable and persistent characteristics of adult labor markets. Understanding the creation and early experience of these inequalities contributes to our understanding of these inequalities in the adult labor market.

In addition, as work is an important activity for both student and non-student youth in the United States, understanding such a prevalent activity increases our understanding of youth in the United States. The finding that many students choose to work because they want to meet new people and use work as a social space illuminates our understanding of students' lives in the United States and the important role that work plays in their lives as a result of the social function it fulfills.

These findings also increase our understanding of the perceived image of the education system. The perception of many students that schools do not provide enough opportunities for meeting new people and offer job-related training raises important questions about the role of education and expectations of schools, which require further research.

Youth Work after the Economic Recession

Recent years have brought vast changes to the youth labor force. Jobs that young people work in while still in school tend to be service sector jobs: retail, service, food. These jobs have been characterized as low-paying and readily available, with limited skill requirements. In previous years, these jobs may have been abundant and easy to get. However, finding these jobs is becoming more and more difficult. The recent recession might have affected the manufacturing industry more, but growth in service sector jobs has also been stagnant. Many corporations have been cautious in expanding and hiring, and many have closed some underperforming branches.

When they do open new branches, many are located in the affluent suburbs rather than in the inner cities. With increasing unemployment levels, the existing pool of applicants is also in competition with other potential workers who have lost their jobs.

According to Casey B. Mulligan's (2011) analysis using the U.S. Census Bureau's Household Survey, although all age groups (except for seniors) have experienced a severe reduction in the number of hours worked, younger workers have especially been affected. Mulligan (2011) shows that an average sixteen-year-old in 2011 works 40 percent fewer hours than an average sixteen-year-old did in 1997. According to the U.S. Department of Labor, among sixteen- to nineteen-year-olds, unemployment had reached unprecedented levels of 20.3 percent in July 2013 (compared with 13 percent in May 2000).

Traditionally, retail jobs were characterized by their abundant supply. As Chris Tilly and Françoise Carré (2011: 298) observe, many employers referred to the "pulse test" (does the candidate have a pulse?) or the "mirror test" (does the candidate's breath fog up a mirror?) in their hiring decisions. However, they note a vast difference in hiring practices. For many retail jobs, emerging studies show that employers will not hire just anybody (Tilly and Carré 2011). In addition to the limited supply of jobs due to the recent economic recession, evidence from numerous advanced economies emphasizes the importance of self-presentation, soft skills, aesthetic skills, and social/cultural capital (Gatta 2011; Nickson et al. 2011). Young people could have a marked advantage here. Compared to the traits of older workers, youth itself is a soft skill and an appearance requirement. Young, energetic workers are preferred to be the face of a company rather than older workers. Students in particular are preferred, because they often desire infrequent and irregular hours to accommodate their school schedules, as opposed to nonstudent youth, who need to work more hours to make ends meet. Not all students have the same advantages. Young people with more middle- and upper-class self-representations have a real edge. Retail employers screen at the initial interview for soft skills, particularly aesthetic skills. As Nickson and colleagues (2011) argue, for style jobs, middle-classness is sought by retailers as a skill.

This has important social implications. Katherine Newman argues:

> Minimum-wage jobs cannot buy real economic independence; they cannot cover the cost of living, including rent, food, and the rest of an adult's monthly needs. What Jessica can do with her earnings is cover the marginal cost of her presence in the household, leaving something out every week to contribute to the core cost of maintaining the household. Youth workers, particularly those who are parents themselves, generally do turn over part of their pay to the head of the household as a kind of rent. In this fashion, working-poor participate in a pooled income strategy that makes it possible for households—as opposed to individuals—to sustain themselves. (1999: 68)

In other words, when low-income youth are unable to find jobs, the overall household income suffers. In the 1990s, Democrats repeatedly turned down opportunities to raise the minimum wage, choosing to focus instead on programs that give tax breaks to low-income households, on the theory that increasing the minimum wage helps teen workers but does not really do anything to help poor families.

With the importance of aesthetic labor in hiring, being middle class or even affluent becomes a skill requirement. If job skills are defined through looking or sounding a certain way, this also has important implications for skills learned on the job. Despite the perceptions of young people that jobs train them and teach them valuable skills, Nickson and colleagues (2011) show that young people are taught mostly aesthetic labor, such as voice and accent coaching and make-up and personal grooming.

Policy Implications

Three important policy implications surface from this study. First, as aesthetic labor becomes an important component of retail jobs, it is important to equip economically disadvantaged youth with such soft skills so that they are able to find these jobs they need economically. Many scholars (Gatta 2011; Tilly and Carré 2011) advocate for both public and nonprofit training systems to educate youth in soft skills to help mitigate class inequality. However, such organizations could be problematic, as the assumption suggests that middle-class-ness can be learned or taught as a job requirement—often referred to as the Eliza Doolittle Syndrome (Gatta 2011). Often, this view reduces existing class inequalities and income differences to simple stylistic changes. By telling youth they can improve their soft skills and self-presentations, we put the pressure on the disadvantaged youth and blame them for not finding jobs.

Despite criticism, some scholars have argued that learning soft skills is not just a form of Eliza Doolittle Syndrome, but rather a pragmatic approach to gain an advantage in the job market. Chris Warhurst and Dennis Nickson argue:

> Twenty thousand people are unemployed in Glasgow, but there exists 5,500 unfulfilled jobs. Our contention is that a proportion of these jobs are likely to remain unfulfilled unless long-term unemployed people are equipped with aesthetic skills. Such jobs, such as hospitality, clearly demand employees to affect the appropriate role-required bodily dispositions, adopting "masks for tasks" or simply "surface acting," and the employed should be aware of this need. (2009: 11)

Unfortunately, coaching of soft skills is limited in its approach and success if not supported by commensurate income and consumption. Lack of access to quality health care, along with stressful life circumstances, often contributes to physical signs of poverty, such as damaged teeth, skin, and hair (Gatta 2011). These visible signs of poverty can be difficult, and in some cases impossible, to cover.

A component of aesthetic labor also involves the use of the products sold by the corporation. Many young people have reported using the products of the corporation they worked for as an advantage in getting jobs. Therefore, using and knowing about the products—which requires money—is a central part of the soft skills that is intertwined with income. As Vicki Smith (2006) observes in her study of the support groups provided to white-collar, unemployed workers in California, many soft-skill coaching classes include such tips as having new, clean, and pressed suits for interviews, clean cars, and other consumption habits that require a hefty financial investment.

Furthermore, aesthetic requirements often create potential racial inequality. Because aesthetic judgments and soft-skill evaluations are highly subjective, recent research links such hiring practices to employer discrimination against African Americans (Zamudio and Lichter 2008). If social and aesthetic considerations become influential factors in hiring decisions, many corporations can turn down candidates if they fail to fit the corporate image.

The second policy implication concerns the hiring process. Because aesthetic and stylistic concerns are central for some jobs, the hiring process appears to be more arbitrary. As many scholars have documented (Gatta 2011), many retailers make what Mary Gatta refers to as "blink decisions": hiring decisions based on their initial impressions of the physical and social self-presentation of the candidate. Because self-presentation is highly correlated to class and race, Philip Moss and Chris Tilly (2001) find many discriminatory practices in the hiring process based on such informal hiring criteria. Carré and co-authors (2010) also document the underrepresentation of people of color and immigrants in retail jobs. Therefore, more regulation and more standardized hiring practices will inevitably help mitigate such inequality. Although regulation and standardization are important, they are not sufficient without the awareness and education of the employers. As Gatta argues, the gut reactions or bias in itself is not as harmful if it does not translate into action. To borrow from Pierre Bourdieu and Loïc Wacquant: "What depends on us is not the first move, but the second. It is difficult to control the first inclination of habitus, but reflective analysis, which teaches us that we are the ones who endow the situation with part of the potency it has over us, allows us to alter our perceptions of the situation and thereby our reaction to it" (1992: 136).

From a legal perspective, Dianne Avery and Marion Crain (2007) show that in the United States, labor laws increasingly recognize issues of aesthetic labor. However, they point out that the existing laws reaffirm employers' rights to demand aesthetic labor from potential employees. Their detailed study shows that employees have very few legal rights in terms of challenging appearance rules in the workplace. For instance, clothing, hair, tattoos, piercings, nails, talk, speech, accent, clothing, and manners can be influential in personnel decisions. Although the law provides protection against racial discrimination, aesthetic-labor discrimination can often be challenging to prove.

Finally, many young people want to work for social reasons. From their perspectives, many find it difficult to socialize in centerless suburbs and thus they use jobs to fulfill these needs. As suburban lives offer few options for interaction and schools fail to offer alternative venues for social interaction, young people turn to work to fill this social void. Creating more social options for young people so they can spend their time doing valuable, productive tasks is very important.

Future of Youth Work and Future Research: Youth as Consumer and Consumed

Retail jobs are on their way up. According to the U.S. Bureau of Labor Statistics's employment projections for 2004–2014, "Among the 10 major occupational groups, employment in the two largest in 2004—professional and related occupations and service occupations—is projected to increase the fastest and add the most jobs from 2004–2014" (Hecker 2005: 71). Proliferation of service sector jobs inevitably brings more competition.

As the number of these service sector jobs increases, we also see a shift in the ideology behind these jobs. These jobs, typically associated with unfriendly workers, standardized scripts, and speedy impersonal service, are giving way to more personalized, customer-oriented service (Darr 2011; Duffy 1999). The environment of competition coupled with the shift to a more customer-oriented ideology will result in more aesthetic-labor requirements in the hiring process. These jobs, which were once abundant and easy to get, will become more and more difficult to land as companies search for the right personality (Callaghan and Thompson 2002), attitude (Huddleston and Hirst 2004), and physical appearance (Nickson et al. 2001; Warhurst and Nickson 2007). This gives young people an incomparable advantage in the new labor market, as they have at least one of the right qualities: youth (Buchanan, Evesson, and Dawson 2003; Gatta 2009). However, as opportunities are created for young people, this will continue to create more inequalities. Even today, we see more competition for youth jobs. As manufacturing jobs are lost, many displaced workers, elderly people, and immigrants are forced to compete against young people for the same service sector jobs. Nonstudent youth have always experienced unemployment, but for the first time, part-time student workers are also experiencing higher unemployment rates. Among sixteen- to nineteen-year-old students, we see higher unemployment rates (15.7 percent), partially because we see higher school enrollment among youth: In 2007, according to the U.S. Bureau of Labor Statistics (2008), 82.5 percent of youth were employed while in school.

In the upcoming years, we will see increased competition for youth jobs coupled with an increased preference for affluent youth. We can also expect to see young people consuming brands through work. Other studies have pointed to young people relating to social phenomena, such as political causes, or social issues, such as environmentalism, as branded products; we expect to see more branding in jobs in the near future. As young people consume work as a branded product, they themselves are consumed by others as a part of the product experience, in a vicious cycle of consumption and work. The next step would be to focus on the realities of many senior workers and immigrants who work side by side with affluent youth at these minimum-wage jobs.

APPENDIX
Notes on Methodology

I n addition to my own interviews and observations, data from published surveys were used in my analyses. Here I provide background information on these published surveys, as well as chapter-specific comments on my methods. The names of all informants discussed in the text are pseudonyms. The names and identifying characteristics have been changed to protect the privacy of the respondents.

Methodological Notes for Chapter 2

The National Longitudinal Study of Youth 1997 is one of a series of surveys of the labor market conducted by the Bureau of Labor Statistics of the U.S. Department of Labor over a span of more than four decades. NLSY97 consists of a representative sample of the noninstitutionalized U.S. population born between 1980 and 1984, including 8,984 youth respondents who were between the ages of twelve and sixteen as of December 31, 1996. (An oversample of black and Hispanic individuals required the use of sample weighting.) Interviews for NLSY97 were conducted in five waves. The first interviews (Round 1) for the survey took place in 1997, when both the eligible youth and one of that individual's parents participated in hour-long personal interviews. In addition, during the screening process, an extensive two-part questionnaire was administered to gather demographic information on members of each youth's household and on his or her immediate family members living elsewhere. Youth were reinterviewed annually, and data from Rounds 1–5 of NLSY97 were released in May 2003. The aim of NLSY97 was to document the transition of youth from school to work and into adulthood through the collection of extensive information about the behavior of youth in the labor market and their educational experiences over time. Employment data included details on methods employed for job searches and on the demographic background of the youth.

The data employed in Chapter 2 are from the first round of interviews for NLSY97. For my analysis, I used the full range of ages from NLSY97 (twelve through sixteen years) and NLSY97 data on the methods the youth employed for obtaining a job. In the survey, the employed youth were presented with a series of questions concerning their choice of method for finding a job. The questions were selected on the basis of the results of a pretest and were in line with the standard phrasing of questions employed by the Current Population Survey. (The Current Population Survey is conducted monthly and consists of personal and telephone interviews of adults and youth aged fifteen years and older. It is sponsored jointly by the U.S. Census Bureau and the U.S. Bureau of Labor Statistics and provides the data for a variety of major economic statistics, including the national unemployment rate.)

The ways youth find jobs have been operationalized in different ways: The respondents were asked about their typical methods of finding jobs as well as the methods used to find their current jobs or in their current job search. The variable employed for the purposes of my study was their general method of finding jobs rather than one in reference to a specific job. However, it is important to note that these job-search indicators are highly correlated. This is not surprising: The way an individual finds a job one time is probably the same way that he or she will look for the next job. The employed respondents were asked the following questions about their job searches:

Do you contact the employer directly?
Do you contact a public agency?
Do you contact a private agency?
Do you contact friends/relatives?
Do you contact a school/university's employment center?
Do you answer job ads?
Do you contact a professional organization or a union?
Do you passively view job ads?

The respondents were allowed to answer "yes" to as many of the questions as were applicable. A "yes" answer was coded as 1 and a "no" answer was coded as 0.

To better discern the racial/ethnic differences within the youth labor market, respondents were coded as to their racial/ethnic group. The race/ethnicity variable was combined in NLSY97, and respondents were asked to select their race/ethnicity from a list that was coded as the follows: 1, black; 2, Hispanic;

3, mixed-race (non-Hispanic); 4, non-black/non-Hispanic. For the purposes of my study, the coding was simplified such that white respondents were coded as 2 and all others were coded as 1. This coding not only is in line with the existing literature but also provides the opportunity to compare the most pronounced differences in employment between nonwhites and whites. The NLSY97 sample was bifurcated to separate male and female subsamples to facilitate observation of gender differences within my study's youth sample (coded 1 male and 2 for female in my study). The NLSY97 sample was also divided into high- and low-income groups to trace the effects of income differences in the youth sample. However, this bifurcation of the sample did not show differential patterns of job searching. Instead of simply dividing all youth into high- and low-income groups, the sample was divided into four income quartiles: lowest quartile, second quartile, third quartile, and highest quartile. For this breakdown, income was measured as annual income in dollars and as a percentage of the respondent's family income relative to the local poverty line to control for area differences.

Methodological Notes for Chapter 4

For the purposes of my analysis, young workers are defined as being between sixteen and nineteen years of age and engaged in wage labor. This is in line with the U.S. Department of Labor's definition of an "employed person" as a civilian, age sixteen years or older, who does a minimum of one hour of work for pay or profit or fifteen hours or more without pay in a family enterprise (Entwisle, Alexander, and Olson 2000). The lower age cutoff was set at sixteen years in accord with U.S. Department of Labor's minimum legal age for nonagricultural work. This age group not only fits the legal definition of labor but also consists of teenagers exclusively. A large portion of the youth labor literature typically includes sixteen- to nineteen-year-olds, whether they are in high school or college, because they show similar work patterns. Work, for the purposes of Chapter 4, includes all work done for pay outside the home.

The data for Chapter 4 are from the World Values Study (Abramson and Inglehart 1995), which provides comparable and reliable survey data on economic and social work-related factors for the population of interest—youth between the ages of sixteen and nineteen—for forty-five societies. The study was conducted among 1,839 Americans and 89,908 respondents throughout the world, in two waves. My data come from the second, most recent wave of the study, which was carried out by the Gallup organization in the United States. This data set has been used widely, especially among economists, political scientists, and sociologists, for examining differential beliefs about social institutions, government, and values, such as postmaterialism, individualism, and the role of women. It provides the ideal data set for measuring the relative impacts of economic and social factors in decisions to enter the labor market, because it offers a wide array of work-related variables, including economic and social factors for working among a large, nationally representative sample.

The World Values Study also defines work in much the same way this book does: paid labor done outside the home, not including unpaid work, domestic labor, or agricultural labor. Most importantly, the data set was constructed from ethnographic, in-depth, face-to-face interviews with the respondents conducted by social scientists on the basis of questions devised by survey methodologists according to the results of several waves of pilot studies. I subdivided the U.S. age group of interest, ages sixteen to nineteen, into student and nonstudent samples. Even though the focus of my study is on the student population, nonstudents in the same age cohort are included for comparative purposes.

Interestingly, the biggest bifurcation in my findings is based on student status. Whether a respondent is identified as a student (high school or college) is an important predictor in understanding why youth work. As is documented in the literature, student youth in this age group do not show considerable differentiation in their labor-force entry decisions, with the composition of the workforce remaining constant between educational levels. To account for any potential confounding factors, however, the model described below was run separately for college and high school students, and the resulting coefficients were then compared with F-tests against the null hypothesis that the coefficients are equivalent (and, thus, that the effects of the reasons for working do not vary across the groups). The analyses failed to reject the null hypothesis of no difference between college and high school students for all coefficients. However, students and nonstudents in the same age bracket behave quite differently in terms of their labor-market entry decisions. Within the age bracket of interest, student status is highly correlated with socioeconomic status. Almost all sixteen- to nineteen-year-old nonstudents are economically deprived, although not all economically deprived youth leave school early. This creates a confounding factor in analyses of labor-market entry decisions, because student status and socioeconomic status are often highly correlated, muting the independent effects of one or both of the factors. Unfortunately, the measurement of variables such as socioeconomic status is typically not precise enough in surveys to capture the relative degree of deprivation. Although such measurements are useful in accounting for more pronounced effects, they fail to capture more nuanced ones. However, adopting the student/nonstudent indicator provides a more fine-tuned measure of economic deprivation and low socioeconomic status. Although many teenagers are economically deprived, coming from lower socioeconomic backgrounds, only those who are extremely deprived do not go to school.

To better capture the differential reasons for working, the sample was separated into student and nonstudent subsamples for comparison. Within these groups, I could control for the effect of socioeconomic status, allowing me to examine how socioeconomic status affects students and nonstudents differentially. In the World Values Study, youth—and all other respondents—were asked, "Did you work for money or benefits at least for one hour last week?" The answer is dichotomous; it was coded as 1 if the respondent worked for money or benefits for at least an hour in the reference week or 0 otherwise. There are several reasons for the choice of a dichotomous dependent variable over modeling the number of hours worked. Prior research has shown (Entwisle, Alexander, and Olson 2000) that the number of hours worked does not have significant effects on many aspects of employment. This makes sense: It is unlikely that the factors that lead a teenager to take a job for ten hours a week differ considerably from those that lead a teenager to work twenty hours a week. Also, the number of hours worked in a week by teenagers is often highly inconsistent, varying by as many as ten hours from week to week. This not only renders measures of central tendency ineffective but also raises questions about the use of threshold effects. If we believe that taking a job of twenty hours per week is different from taking a job of fifteen hours per week, what should be done with a student who works more than twenty hours one week but fewer the next? Furthermore, the only findings that seem to show a difference based on the number of hours worked appear to indicate a threshold effect such that academic performance is hurt only after individuals work more than thirty hours per week.

In addition to questions about work status, respondents to the World Values Study were asked which factors they thought were the most important when choosing a job. They were then given fifteen cards, each representing a factor that they were told some people believe to be important in a job, and asked to choose which of the factors they personally thought were important. Respondents could choose as many or as few of the cards as they felt were applicable. It is important to note that *all* respondents were asked these questions, regardless of their work status. Moreover, the question was asked regarding respondents' beliefs about work in general and not in reference to any particular job. This is especially important because of the high turnover rates endemic to many youth-oriented jobs. The job factors listed were

Good pay
Not too much pressure
Good job security
Good chances for promotion
A job respected by people in general
Good hours

An opportunity to use initiative
A useful job for society
Good holidays
A job in which you feel you can achieve something
A responsible job
A job that is interesting
A job that meets one's abilities
Meeting people
Pleasant people to work with

In my study, each of the categories was treated as a separate variable, coded as 1 if the subject chose the reason and 0 otherwise. The majority of the independent variables in the model were constructed, as discussed earlier, from the respondents' beliefs about the importance of different aspects of jobs, both social and economic. The aspects of a job respondents were able to choose from includes both economic (such as good pay, chances of promotion, and job security) and social factors (such as meeting people and having pleasant people to work with). The inclusion of such factors allowed me to compare the social and economic aspects of a job that respondents report as important in their decision to work.

In comparing the labor-market entry decisions of student and nonstudent youth, in addition to the potential social and economic reasons for working, some control variables were included. First, a socioeconomic status measure was included. The World Values Study measures socioeconomic status based on the parents' type of occupation. The question presented to the respondents (not asked verbally by the interviewer, but to be filled out on the written portion of the survey) asked them to classify their socioeconomic background in one of four categories: upper/upper middle class, middle class/nonmanual labor, manual skilled labor/nonmanual skilled labor, and unskilled manual labor. This breakdown was based on the definitions provided in the World Values Study and is in line with the common practice in academic studies on youth employment (Greenberger and Steinberg 1986). The exact specification in my model is discussed in detail at the end of this section. Another important distinction that must accounted for is whether youth live with their parents or not. The World Values Study provides a variable specifically to measure that. The respondents were asked, "Do you live with your parents?" The answers were coded 1 if the respondents reported living with their parents and 0 otherwise. Preliminary findings show no main effect of living with parents for U.S. students and nonstudents but significant effects for youth in other industrialized countries. The names of the variables were abbreviated for presentation of the model. Their definitions are as follows:

Y: The dependent variable, whether an individual works or does not

Decision to work: Respondent's answer of "yes" or "no" to the question of whether he or she works or not

Good pay: Importance of good pay for both working and nonworking respondents in the decision to work in general

No pressure: Importance of having a no-pressure job for both working and nonworking respondents in the decision to work in general

Security: Importance of job security for both working and nonworking respondents in the decision to work in general

Promotions: Importance of possibility of promotions for both working and nonworking respondents in the decision to work in general

Respected: Importance of having a respected job for both working and nonworking respondents in the decision to work in general

Good hours: Importance of good hours for the respondent for both working and nonworking respondents in the decision to work in general

Initiative: Importance of having the opportunity to use initiative in the job for both working and nonworking respondents in the decision to work in general

Useful: Importance of usefulness of the job for both working and nonworking respondents in the decision to work in general

Good holidays: Importance of good holidays for both working and nonworking respondents in the decision to work in general

Achievement: Importance of the possibility of achievement for both working and nonworking respondents in the decision to work in general

Responsibility: Importance of having responsibilities at work for both working and nonworking respondents in the decision to work in general

Interesting: Importance of having an interesting job for both working and nonworking respondents in the decision to work in general

Meets abilities: Importance of having a job that meets the respondents' abilities for both working and nonworking respondents in the decision to work in general

Meet people: Importance of having a job that provides the respondent with opportunities to meet new people

Pleasant people: Importance of having pleasant people to work with for both working and nonworking respondents in the decision to work in general

Live with parents: A dummy variable that identifies respondents living with their parents; respondents living with their parents are coded as 1, and 0 otherwise

Because of the dichotomous nature of the dependent variable—an individual either works or does not—I employed logistic regression techniques to predict a respondent's likelihood of working, given the variables listed above as predictive variables. The model was run separately for student and nonstudent youth to demonstrate the uniqueness of the student population within the United States. Because the coefficients attached to logistic regression coefficients tell us very little about the effect of an independent variable other than its size and its significance, it was necessary to use Monte Carlo simulation to fully analyze the results. To this end, Gary King's CLARIFY plug-in for STATA was used (King, Tomz, and Wittenberg 2000). Monte Carlo simulations estimate unweighted, predicted probabilities at random one thousand draws. They offer expected values for each independent variable. To simulate the parameters, they use the point estimates of variance/covariance matrices of the estimates to randomly draw a multivariate normal distribution that enables determination of predicted probabilities. The numbers show the amount of change in the dependent variable for every change, from the lowest category to the highest category. In other words, the Monte Carlo values for each independent variable show how much the likelihood of working increases or decreases, moving from the lowest category of the independent variable to its highest value. Simply put, the Monte Carlo simulation allowed me to present numerically precise estimates of the effects of parameters of interest in a way that requires minimal statistical knowledge on the part of the reader. Certainly the procedure was more complicated than some other approaches, such as odds ratios, but the interpretation and the visual representation of the results are much simpler with the aid of Monte Carlo simulations. As King, Tomz, and Wittenberg (2000) argue, with Monte Carlo simulations, the interpretation of the size and the magnitude of the effects is much simpler and easier to follow for readers, and the results are comparable across different models. Also, with Monte Carlo simulations, it is easier to visually observe the size and the magnitude of the changes.

Methodological Notes for Chapter 5

The data employed for the analyses in Chapter 5 come from the World Values Study (Abramson and Inglehart, 1995), which is described in detail in the Methodological Notes for Chapter 3.

One of the main predictors of labor-market entry decisions is confidence in the education system. The World Values Study offers a variable that measures this attitude. As part of a battery of questions examining confidence in various organs of government and society (such as the church, the media, the military, the police, and NATO), respondents were asked to indicate their confidence in the education system of their nation, with four possible responses ranging from "none whatsoever" to "complete confidence." The responses were recoded to make the lowest level of confidence correspond to 1 for the variable and the highest level of confidence correspond to 4. The employment of this representation for the measurement of attitudes not only is widely practiced in many fields, including sociology, economics, and political science, but also parallels the existing literature. The data set allows inclusion of economic, social, and value variables as possible predictors of youth labor-market entry decisions. As possible explanations of these decisions, both economic and noneconomic/social factors were included. Respondents were asked, "What do you think is an important factor in your decision to work?" Responses were collected via the card system described in the methodology discussion for Chapter 4. Also, again, because of the high turnover rates endemic to many youth-oriented jobs, all respondents were asked the question regardless of their work status and with reference to their beliefs about work in general and not in reference to any particular job. The aspects of a job listed on the cards considered for Chapter 5 were "good pay," "good holidays," and "meeting people." Each of the categories was treated as a separate variable, coded as 1 if the respondent chose the reason but 0 otherwise. These particular variables seemed to be the best representatives of value types. "Good pay" is representative of monetary motivations for work; "good holidays" indicates good working, or quality-of-life, considerations; and "meeting people" is representative of social considerations. The inclusion of such factors allowed me to compare the social and economic aspects of a job that respondents report as important in their decision to work.

Two additional socioeconomic factors were evaluated. First, the socioeconomic status of the respondent was determined as described in the methodology discussion for Chapter 4. In the analyses for Chapter 5, socioeconomic status was broken into three categories: upper/upper middle class and middle class/nonmanual labor (combined), manual skilled labor/nonmanual skilled labor, and unskilled manual labor. The second socioeconomic factor included was whether youth live with their parents or not (evaluated as described in the methodology discussion for Chapter 4).

Controls for race and gender were introduced to acknowledge that different groups in society have different levels of confidence in the education system. Prior research has identified class, gender, and race as three major areas in which education has differential impacts (Postman 1996; Powell, Farrar, and Cohen 1985), and, thus, areas in which one could expect that confidence in the education system might have differential effects on the likelihood of working. Thus, the model included the possibility that confidence in the education system has differential impacts on working for students based on their race and gender through the inclusion of dummy variables. Race was coded as white or nonwhite (1 or 0, respectively), and gender was coded as male or female (1 or 2, respectively).

The dichotomous nature of the dependent variable—an individual either works or does not—logistic regression techniques and Monte Carlo simulation were again used (as described in the methodology discussion for Chapter 4) to predict a respondent's likelihood of working, given certain values of the predictive variables.

Methodological Notes for Chapter 7

My first source of data in this line of enquiry in Chapter 7 is findings from the first year of the National Longitudinal Study of Youth 1997, which is described in detail in the Methodological Notes for Chapter 2. The youth respondents of NLSY97 were between the ages of twelve and sixteen for this period of data collection. Comparable data for older youth, ages sixteen to nineteen, were derived from the Current Population Survey. The same definitions and questions were used for both age groups. For my analyses, the data sets were aggregated by age to facilitate analysis and explore changes over time among three cohorts: twelve- to thirteen-year-olds, fourteen- to fifteen-year-olds, and sixteen- to nineteen-year-olds. Organized in this manner, the data were particularly valuable in terms of not only providing detailed, nationally representative data on the employment characteristics of youth but also including twelve- to fifteen-year olds, who are traditionally omitted from analyses of youth labor. Although such early labor-market practices remain outside the scope of this book, such detailed data on early employment provide extensive information that illuminated gender relations in the labor market of sixteen- to nineteen-year-olds.

References

Abbott-Chapman, Joan, and Margaret Robertson. 2009. "Leisure Activities, Place and Identity." In *Handbook of Youth and Young Adulthood: New Perspectives and Agendas,* edited by Andy Furlong, 243–248. London: Routledge.

Abowd, John, Francis Kramarz, Thomas Lemieux, and David Margolis. 1999. "Minimum Wage and Youth Employment in France and the United States." In *Youth Unemployment and Employment in Advanced Countries,* edited by David G. Blanchflower and Richard Freeman, 427–472. Chicago: University of Chicago Press.

Abraham, Katherine G., and Henry S. Farber. 1987. "Job Duration, Seniority and Earnings." *American Economic Review* 77:278–297.

Abramson, Paul, and Ronald Inglehart. 1995. *Value Change in Global Perspective.* Ann Arbor: University of Michigan Press.

Acker, Joan. 1990. "Hierarchies, Jobs, Bodies: A Theory of Gendered Organizations." *Gender and Society* 4:139–158.

Adler, Seymour. 2001. "Review: The Employment Interview Handbook." *Personnel Psychology* 54:251–254.

Adorno, Theodor W. 1994. *The Stars down to Earth and Other Essays in Irrational Culture.* London: Routledge.

———. 2001. *The Culture Industry: Selected Essays on Mass Culture.* New York: Routledge.

Adorno, Theodor W., and Max Horkheimer. [1979] 1997. *Dialectic of Enlightenment.* Trans. J. Cumming. London: Verso.

Ahn, Thomas, Peter Arcidiacono, Alvin Murphy, and Omari Swinton. 2010. "Explaining Cross-Racial Differences in Teenage Labor Force Participation: Results from a Two-Sided Search Model." *Journal of Econometrics* 156:201–211.

Akabayashi, Hideo, and George Psacharopoulos. 1999. "The Trade-Off between Child Labour and Human Capital Formation: A Tanzanian Case Study." *Journal of Development Studies* 35 (5): 120–140.

Aldrich, Mark, and Robert Buchele. 1989. "Where to Look for Comparable Worth: The Implications of Efficiency Wages." In *Comparable Worth Analyses and Evidence,* edited by M. A. Hill and M. Killingsworth, 11–28. Ithaca, NY: ILR Press.

Allais, Federico Blanco, and Frank Hagemann. 2008. "Child Labor and Education: Evidence from SIMPOC Surveys." Working Paper, Geneva, ILO, IPEC, SIMPOC.

Altonji, Joseph, and Robert Shakotko. 1987. "Do Wages Rise with Job Seniority?" *Review of Economic Studies* 54:437–459.

Alvim, Rosilene. 2000. "Debates on Poor Children in Brazil: Between Marginalization and Premature Labour." In *The Exploited Child*, edited by Bernard Schlemmer, 160–175. London: Zed Books.

Andrews, Martyn, Steve Bradley, and Richard Upward. 1999. "Estimating Youth Training Wage Differentials during and after Training." *Oxford Economic Papers* 51 (3): 517–544.

Arnott, Richard. 1998. "Economic Theory and the Spatial Mismatch Hypothesis." *Urban Studies* 35:1171–1185.

Avery, Dianne, and Marion G. Crain. 2007. "Branded: Corporate Image, Sexual Stereotyping, and the New Face of Capitalism." *Duke Journal of Gender Law and Policy* 14 (13): 13–123.

Bailey, Thomas. 1993. "Can Youth Apprenticeship Thrive in the United States?" *Educational Researcher* 22:4–10.

Bair, Jennifer, and Sam Bernstein. 2006. "Labor and the Wal-Mart Effect." In *Wal-Mart World: The World's Biggest Corporation in the Global Economy*, edited by Stanley D. Brunn, 99–113. London: Routledge.

Balding, John. 1991. "A Study of Working Children in 1990." *Education and Health* 9 (1): 4–6.

Ballou, Dale, and Michael Podgursky. 1998. "Teacher Recruitment and Retention in Public and Private Schools." *Journal of Policy Analysis and Management* 17:393–417.

Banerjee, Biswajit, and Gabriella A. Bucci. 1995. "On-the-Job Search in a Developing Country: An Analysis Based on Indian Data on Migrants." *Economic Development and Cultural Change* 43:565–583.

Banpasirichote, Chantana. 2000. "Rapid Economic Growth: The Social Exclusion of Children in Thailand." In *The Exploited Child*, edited by Bernard Schlemmer, 135–145. London: Zed Books.

Barnes, William F. 1975. "Job Search Models, the Duration of Unemployment, and the Asking Wage: Some Empirical Evidence." *Journal of Human Resources* 10:230–240.

Bauman, Zygmunt. 2000. *Liquid Modernity*. New York: Polity.

Bayard, Kimberly, Judith Hellerstein, David Neumark, and Kenneth Troske. 2003. "New Evidence on Segregation and Sex Difference in Wages from Matched Employee-Employer Data." *Journal of Labor Economics* 21 (4): 887–922.

Beck, E. M., Patrick M. Horan, and Charles M. Tolbert II. 1980. "Industrial Segmentation and Labor Market Discrimination." *Social Problems* 28:113–130.

Becker, Brian E., and Stephen Hills. 1983. "The Long-Run Effects of Job Changes and Unemployment among Male Teenagers." *Journal of Human Resources* 18 (2): 197–212.

Becker, Gary. 1985. "Human Capital, Effort, and Sexual Division of Labor." *Journal of Labor Economics* 3:S33–S58.

———. 1993. *Human Capital: A Theoretical and Empirical Analysis with Special Reference to Education*. Chicago: University of Chicago Press.

Bell, Daniel. 1973. *The Coming of Post-industrial Society*. New York: Basic Books.

Benhayoun, Gilbert. 1994. "The Impact of Minimum Wages on Youth Employment in France Revisited: A Note on the Robustness of the Relationship." *International Journal of Manpower* 15 (2): 82–85.

Bennett, Andy. 2003. "Subculture or Neo-tribes? Rethinking the Relationship between Youth, Style and Musical Taste." In *The Consumption Reader,* edited by David B. Clarke, Marcus A. Doel, and Kate M. L. Housiaux, 152–156. London: Routledge.

Benokraitis, Nijole V., and Joe R. Feagin. 1986. *Modern Sexism: Blatant, Subtle, and Covert Discrimination.* Englewood Cliffs, NJ: Prentice Hall.

Berk, Richard A., and Sarah Fenstermaker Berk. 1979. *Labor and Leisure at Home: Content and Organization of the Household Day.* Newbury Park, CA: Sage.

Besen, Yasemin. 2004. "It's Not Like a Job." *Contexts* 3:60–61.

———. 2005. "Consumption of Production: A Study of Part-Time Youth Labor in Suburban America." *Berkeley Journal of Sociology* 49:58–75.

Besen, Yasemin, and Michael S. Kimmel. 2006. "At Sam's Club, No Girls Allowed: The Lived Experience of Sex Discrimination." *Equal Opportunities International* 25 (3): 172–187.

Besen-Cassino, Yasemin. 2008. "The Study of Youth Labor: The Shift toward a Subject-Centric Approach." *Sociology Compass* 2:352–365.

Best, Amy. 2006. *Fast Cars, Cool Rides: The Accelerating World of Youth and Their Cars.* New York: New York University Press.

———. 2009. "Young People and Consumption in Handbook of Youth and Young Adulthood." In *Handbook of Youth and Young Adulthood: New Perspectives and Agendas,* edited by Andy Furlong, 255–268. London: Routledge.

Beynon, Huw. 1985. *Working for Ford.* Harmondsworth, UK: Penguin.

Bielby, Denise D., and William T. Bielby. 1988. "She Works Hard for the Money." *American Journal of Sociology* 93:1031–1059.

Bills, David B. 2004. *The Sociology of Education and Work.* Malden, MA: Wiley Blackwell.

Bills, David B., Lelia B. Helms, and Mustafa Ozcan. 1995. "The Impact of Student Employment on Teachers' Attitudes and Behaviors toward Working Students." *Youth and Society* 27:169–193.

Bishop, John H. 1999. "Nerd Harassment and Grade Inflation: Are College Admissions Policies Partly Responsible?" Center for Advanced Human Resources Studies, New York State School of Industrial and Labor Relations. Working Paper Series #99-14.

Black, Matthew. 1981. "An Empirical Test of the Theory of On-the-Job Search." *Journal of Human Resources* 16:129–140.

Blau, David M. 1992. "An Empirical Analysis of Employed and Unemployed Job Search Behavior." *Industrial and Labor Relations Review* 45:738–752.

Blau, Francine D. 1977. *Equal Pay in the Office.* Lexington, MA: Heath.

Blau, Francine D., Marianne Ferber, and Anne Winkler. 2006. *The Economics of Women, Men and Work.* 5th ed. Upper Saddle River, NJ: Pearson Prentice Hall.

Blumer, Herbert. 1969. *Symbolic Interactionism.* Englewood Cliffs, NJ: Prentice Hall.

Bonar, Hugh S. 1942. "High-School Pupils List Their Anxieties." *School Review* 50:512–515.

Bortnichak, Greg. 2009. "Starbucks Intervention." In *Men's Lives,* edited by Michael S. Kimmel, 171–176. New York: Allyn Bacon.

Bound, John, and Richard B. Freeman. 1992. "What Went Wrong? The Erosion of Relative Earnings and Employment among Young Black Men in the 1980s." *Quarterly Journal of Economics* 107 (1): 201–232.

Bound, John, Richard B. Freeman, and Jeff Grogger. 1992. "Arrests, Persistent Youth Joblessness, and Black/White Employment Differentials." *Review of Economics and Statistics* 74 (1): 100–106.

Bourdieu, Pierre. 1984. *Distinction: A Social Critique of Judgement in Taste.* Cambridge, MA: Harvard University Press.

———. 1998. *Acts of Resistance: Against the Tyranny of the Market.* New York: New Press.

———. 2000. "The Politics of Protest. An Interview by Kevin Ovenden," *Socialist Review* 242:18–20.

Bourdieu, Pierre, and Loïc Wacquant. 1992. *An Invitation to Reflexive Sociology.* Chicago: University of Chicago Press.

Bourdillon, Michael, Deborah Levinson, William Myers, and Ben White. 2010. *Rights and Wrongs of Children's Work.* New Brunswick, NJ: Rutgers University Press.

Bozkurt, Ödül, and Irena Grugulis. 2011. "Why Retail Work Demands a Closer Look." In *Retail Work,* edited by Irena Grugulis and Ödül Bozkurt, 1–21. London: Palgrave Macmillan.

Braddock, Jomills Henry, and James M. McPartland. 1987. "How Minorities Continue to Be Excluded from Equal Opportunities: Research on Labor Market and Institutional Barriers." *Journal of Social Issues* 43:5–39.

Bradshaw, Thomas F., and Janet L. Scholl. 1976. "The Extent of Job Search during Layoff." *Brookings Papers on Economic Activity* 1976 (2): 515–526.

Brady, David. 2004. "Reconsidering the Divergence between Elderly, Child and Overall Poverty." *Research on Aging* 26 (5): 487–510.

Breen, Richard. 1992. "Job Changing and Job Loss in the Irish Youth Labour-Market: A Test of a General Model." *European Sociological Review* 8:113–125.

Brenner, O. C., and Joseph Tomkiewicz. 1979. "Job Orientation of Males and Females: Are Sex Differences Declining?" *Personnel Psychology* 32 (4): 741–750.

Brumberg, Joan Jacobs. 1997. *The Body Project: The Intimate History of American Girls.* New York: Random House.

Buchanan, John, Justine Evesson, and M. Dawson. 2003. "Retail Trade." In *Beyond VET: The Changing Skill Needs of the Victorian Services Industries,* edited by J. Buchanan and D. Hall. Sydney: ACIRRT, University of Sydney.

Burawoy, Michael. 1979. *Manufacturing Consent: Changes in the Labor Process under Monopoly Capitalism.* Chicago: University of Chicago Press.

Burdett, Kenneth. 1978. "Employee Search and Quits." *American Economic Review* 68: 212–220.

Burgess, Paul L. 1992. "Compliance with Unemployment-Insurance Job-Search Regulations." *Journal of Law and Economics* 35:371–396.

Burtless, Gary. 1996. "Does Money Matter?" Washington, DC: Brookings Institution Press.

Callaghan, George, and Paul Thompson. 2002. "We Recruit Attitude": The Selection and Shaping of Routine Call Centre Labour." *Journal of Management Studies* 39:233–254.

Canny, Angela. 2002. "Flexible Labour? The Growth of Student Employment in the UK." *Journal of Education and Work* 15 (3): 277–301.

Card, David. 1992. "Do Minimum Wages Reduce Employment? A Case Study of California, 1987–89." *Industrial and Labor Relations Review* 46:38–54.

Card, David, and Thomas Lemieux. 2000. "Adapting to Circumstances: The Evolution of Work, School and Living Arrangements among North American Teenagers." In *Youth Employment and Joblessness in Advanced Countries,* edited by David G. Blanchflower and Richard B. Freeman, 171–214. Chicago: University of Chicago Press.

Carré, Françoise, Chris Tilly, Maarten van Klaveren, and Dorothea Voss-Dahm. 2010. "Retail Jobs in Comparative Perspective." In *Low-Wage Work in the Wealthy World,* edited by Jérôme Gautié and John Schmitt, 211–268. New York: Russell Sage Foundation.

Cassino, Dan, and Yasemin Besen-Cassino. 2009. *Consuming Politics: Jon Stewart, Branding, and the Youth Vote in America*. Madison, NJ: Rowman and Littlefield/FDU Press.

Chen, Yu-Hisia. 1991. "Youth Labour Supply and the Minimum Hour Constraint: The Case of Single Males." *Applied Economics* 23 (1B): 229–235.

Chinoy, Eli. 1955. *Automobile Workers and the American Dream*. New York: Doubleday.

Chubb, John, and Terry Moe. 1990. "Politics, Markets, and America's Schools." Washington, DC: Brookings Institution Press.

Cleveland, Douglas B. 1999. *The Role of Services in the Modern US Economy*. U.S. Department of Commerce, Office of Service Industries. Available at http://trade.gov/td/sif/PDF/ROLSERV199.pdf.

Cohen, David K., Stephen W. Raudenbush, and Deborah L. Ball. 2003. "Resources, Instruction, and Research." *Educational Evaluation and Policy Analysis* 25 (2): 119–142.

Coleman, James S. 1984. "The Transition from School to Work." *Research in Social Stratification and Mobility* 3:27–59.

Collins, Randall. 1979. *The Credential Society: A Historical Sociology of Education and Stratification*. New York: Academic Press.

Cooksey, Elizabeth Constance, and Ronald R. Rindfuss. 2001. "Patterns of Work and Schooling in Young Adulthood." *Sociological Forum* 16:731–755.

Corbett, William R. 2007. "The Ugly Truth about Appearance Discrimination and the Beauty of Our Employment Discrimination Law." *Duke Journal of Gender Law and Policy* 14:153–178.

Corcoran, Mary, and Greg J. Duncan. 1979. "Work History, Labor Force Attachments, and Earning Differences between the Races and Sexes." *Journal of Human Resources* 14 (1): 3–20.

Corcoran, Mary, Richard Gordon, Deborah Laren, and Gary Solon. 1992. "The Association between Men's Economic Status and Their Family and Community Origins." *Journal of Human Resources* 27 (4): 575–601.

Coverdill, James E. 1988. "The Dual Economy and Sex Differences in Earnings." *Social Forces* 66:970–993.

Currie, Janet, and Bruce C. Fallick. 1996. "The Minimum Wage and the Employment of Youth: Evidence from the NLSY." *Journal of Human Resources* 31 (2): 404–428.

Curtis, Susan, and Rosemary Lucas. 2001. "The Coincidence of Needs? Employers and Full-Time Students." *Employee Relations* 23 (1): 38–51.

D'Amico, Ronald. 1984. "Does Employment during High School Impair Academic Progress?" *Sociology of Education* 57:152–164.

D'Amico, Ronald, and Paula Baker. 1984. *Pathways to the Future*. Columbus: Center for Human Resource Research, Ohio State University.

Darr, Asaf. 2011. "Humour in Retail Work: Jokes Salespeople Tell about Their Clients." In *Retail Work*, edited by Irena Grugulis and Ödül Bozkurt, 235–252. London: Palgrave Macmillan.

Daymont, Thomas N., and Paul J. Andrisani. 1984. "Job Preferences, College Major, and the Gender Gap in Earnings." *Journal of Human Resources* 19 (3): 408–428.

Dee, Thomas S., and Helen Fu. 2004. "Do Charter Schools Skim Students or Drain Resources?" *Economics of Education Review* 23:259–271.

Defleur, Lois B., and Ben A. Menke. 1975. "Learning about the Labor Force: Occupational Knowledge among High-School Males." *Sociology of Education* 48:324–345.

De Vise, Pierre. 1976. "The Suburbanization of Jobs and Minority Employment." *Economic Geography* 52:348–362.

Dreeben, Robert. [1968] 2002. *On What Is Learned in Schools*. Clinton Corners, NY: Percheron Press.

Drentea, Patricia. 1998. "Consequences of Women's Formal and Informal Job Search Methods for Employment in Female-Dominated Jobs." *Gender and Society* 12:321–338.

Duffy, Jan. 1999. *Harvesting Experience: Reaping the Benefits of Knowledge*. Prairie Village, KS: ARMA International.

Dvorkin, Spencer J. 1941 "Youth Looks at Careers." *Journal of Educational Sociology* 14:462–466.

Edmonds, Eric V. 2008. "Child Labor." In *Handbook of Development Economics,* edited by T. Paul Schultz and John Strauss, 4 (5): 5–57. Amsterdam: Elsevier Science.

Ehrenreich, Barbara. 2001. *Nickel and Dimed: On (Not) Getting By in America*. New York: Basic Books.

Elder, Glen H., Jr. 1974. *Children of the Great Depression: Social Change in Life Experience*. Chicago: University of Chicago Press.

Ellwood, David T. 1982. "Teenage Unemployment: Permanent Scars and Temporary Blemishes?" In *The Youth Labor Market Problem: Its Nature, Causes, and Consequences,* edited by Richard B. Freeman and David A. Wise, 349–390. Chicago: University of Chicago Press.

Engel, Mary, Gerald Marsden, and Sylvie Woodaman. 1968. "Orientation to Work in Children." *American Journal of Orthopsychiatry* 68:137–143.

England, Paula. 1997. "The Sex Gap in Pay." In *Workplace/Women's Place,* 1st ed., edited by Paula J. Dubeck and Dana Dunn, 74–87. Los Angeles: Roxbury Publishing.

Entwisle, Doris R., Karl L. Alexander, and Linda Steffel Olson. 2000. "Early Work Histories of Urban Youth." *American Sociological Review* 65:279–297.

Ewing, Bradley T. 1995. "High School Athletics and the Wages of Black Males." *Review of Black Political Economy* 24 (1): 65–78.

Farkas, George, D. Alton Smith, and Ernst W. Stromsdorfer. 1983. "The Teenage Entitlement Demonstration: Subsidized Employment with a Schooling Requirement." *Journal of Human Resources* 18 (4): 557–573.

Feldberg, Roslyn L., and Evelyn Nakano Glenn. 1979. "Male and Female: Job versus Gender Models in the Sociology of Work." *Social Problems* 26:524–538.

Ferber, Marianne A., and Joe L. Spaeth. 1984. "Work Characteristics and the Male-Female Earnings Gap." *American Economic Review* 74:260–264.

Ferguson, Kathy E. 1984. *The Feminist Case against Bureaucracy*. Philadelphia: Temple University Press.

Filer, Randall K. 1983. "Sexual Differences in Earnings: The Role of Individual Personalities and Tastes." *Journal of Human Resources* 18:82–99.

Finch, Michael D., Michael J. Shanahan, Jeylan T. Mortimer, and Seongryeol Ryu. 1991. "Work Experience and Control Orientation in Adolescence." *American Sociological Review* 56:597–611.

Findeis, Jill L., and Leif Jensen. 1998. "Employment Opportunities in Rural Areas: Implications for Poverty in a Changing Policy Environment." *American Journal of Agricultural Economics* 80:1000–1007.

Finkelstein, Barbara. 1991. "Dollars and Dreams: Classrooms and Fictive Message Systems, 1790–1930." *History of Education Quarterly* 31:463–487.

Finn, Dan. 1987. *Training without Jobs: New Deals and Broken Promises.* Basingstoke: Macmillan.

Fischel, W. A. 2002. *An Economic Case against Vouchers: Why Local Public Schools Are a Local Public Good.* Dartmouth Economics Department Working Paper 02-01, Hanover, NH: Dartmouth College.

Fleener, Hannah. 2005. "Looks Sell, but Are They Worth the Cost: How Tolerating Looks-Based Discrimination Leads to Intolerable Discrimination." *Washington University Law Quarterly* 83:1295–1330.

Frank, Karen A., and Quentin Stevens, eds. 2007. *Loose Space: Possibility and Diversity in Urban Life.* London: Routledge.

Freeman, Richard B. 1982. "Economic Determinants of Geographical and Individual Variation." In *The Youth Labor Market Problem: Its Nature, Causes, and Consequences,* edited by Richard B. Freeman and David A. Wise, 115–148. Chicago: University of Chicago Press.

———. 1987. "The Relation of Criminal Activity to Black Youth Employment." *Review of Black Political Economy* 16 (1): 99–108.

Fukui, Lia. 2000. "Why Is Child Labor Tolerated? The Case of Brazil." In *The Exploited Child,* edited by Bernard Schlemmer, 118–134. London: Zed Books.

Fuller, Bruce. 1983. "Youth Job Structure and School Enrollment, 1890–1920." *Sociology of Education* 56:145–156.

Fyfe, Alec. 1989. *Child Labour.* Cambridge, UK: Polity Press.

Gaines, Donna. 1998. *Teenage Wasteland: Suburbia's Dead-End Kids.* Chicago: University of Chicago Press.

Gardecki, Rosella M. 2001. "Racial Differences in Youth Employment." *Monthly Labor Review* 124 (8): 51–67.

Gardecki, Rosella M., and David Neumark. 1998. "Order from Chaos? The Effects of Early Labor Market Experiences on Adult Labor Market Outcomes." *Industrial and Labor Relations Review* 51:299–322.

Garet, Bernard. 2000. "Apprenticeship in France: A Parallel Case in an Industrialized Society." In *The Exploited Child,* edited by Bernard Schlemmer, 248–260. London: Zed Books.

Gatta, Mary. 2009. "Restaurant Servers, Tipping, and Resistance." *Qualitative Research in Accounting and Management* 6 (1–2): 70–82.

———. 2011. "In the 'Blink' of an Eye—American High-End Small Retail Businesses and the Public Workforce System." In *Retail Work,* edited by Irena Grugulis and Ödül Bozkurt, 49–67. London: Palgrave Macmillan.

Geertz, Clifford. 1973. *The Interpretation of Cultures.* New York: Basic Books.

Gill, Andrew M., and Robert J. Michaels. 1992. "Does Drug Use Lower Wages?" *Industrial and Labor Relations Review* 45 (April): 419–434.

Gill, Brian P., Michael Timpane, Karen E. Ross, and Dominic J. Brewer. 2001. *Rhetoric Versus Reality: What We Know and What We Need to Know about Vouchers and Charter Schools.* Santa Monica, CA: RAND Corporation.

Ginzberg, Eli. 1977. "The Job Problem." *Scientific American* 237:43–57.

Gladwell, Malcolm. 2005. *Blink: The Power of Thinking about Thinking.* New York: Little, Brown.

Glaser, Barney. 1992. *The Basics of Grounded Theory Analysis*. Mill Valley, CA: Sociology Press.

Glazer, Nona. 1993. *Women's Paid and Unpaid Labor: The Work Transfer in Health and Retailing*. Philadelphia: Temple University Press.

Goffman, Erving. 1959. *The Presentation of Self in Everyday Life*. New York: Anchor.

———. 1961. *Asylums: Essays on the Social Situation of Mental Patients and Other Inmates*. New York: Doubleday.

Goldin, Claudia. 1990. *Understanding the Gender Gap: An Economic History of American Women*. New York: Oxford University Press.

Goldstein, Bernard, and Jack Oldham. 1979. *Children and Work*. New Brunswick, NJ: Transaction.

Goss, Ernst P., and Niles C. Schoening. 1984. "Search Time, Unemployment, and the Migration Decision." *Journal of Human Resources* 19:570–579.

Granovetter, Mark. 1983. "The Strength of Weak Ties: A Network Theory Revisited." *Sociological Theory* 1:201–233.

Greenberger, Ellen, and Laurence Steinberg. 1983. "Sex Differences in Early Work Experience: A Harbinger of Things to Come." *Social Forces* 62 (2): 467–486.

———. 1986. *When Teenagers Work: The Psychological and Social Costs of Adolescent Employment*. New York: Basic Books.

Greve, Henrich R., and Takako Fujiwara-Greve. 2003. "Job Search with Organizational Size as a Signal." *Social Forces* 82:643–669.

Grogger, Jeffrey. 1995. "The Effect of Arrests on the Employment and Earnings of Young Men." *Quarterly Journal of Economics* 110 (February): 51–71.

Groshen, Erica L. 1991. "The Structure of Female/Male Wage Differential: Is It Who You Are, What You Do, or Where You Work?" *Journal of Human Resources* 26 (3): 457–472.

Grossberg, Adam J., and Paul Sicilian. 1999. "Minimum Wages, On-the-Job Training, and Wage Growth." *Southern Economic Journal* 65 (3): 539–556.

Guarchello, Lorenzo, Scott Lyon, Furio Rosati, and Cristina Valdivia. 2007. "Children's Non-market Activities and Child Labour Measurement: A Discussion Based on Household Survey Data." Geneva: International Labor Organization.

Guarchello, Lorenzo, Furio Rosati, Scott Lyon, and Cristina Valdivia. 2005. "Impact of Children's Work on School Attendance and Performance: A Review of School Survey from Evidence from Five Countries." Geneva: International Labor Organization, UNICEF, World Bank.

Gubrium, Jaber F., and James A. Holstein. 1997. *The New Language of Qualitative Method*. New York: Oxford University Press.

Gulrajani, Mohini. 2000. "Child Labor and the Export Sector in the Indian Carpet Industry." In *The Exploited Child*, edited by Bernard Schlemmer, 51–66. London: Zed Books.

Gustman, Alan L., and Thomas L. Steinmeyer. 1988. "A Model for Analyzing Youth Labor Market Policies." *Journal of Labor Economics* 6 (3): 376–396.

Hansen, David M., and Patricia Jarvis. 2000. "Adolescent Employment and Psychological Outcomes: A Comparison of Two Employment Contexts." *Youth and Society* 31 (4): 417–436.

Harris, Scott R. 2000. "The Social Construction of Equality in Everyday Life." *Human Studies* 23:371–393.

———. 2001. "What Can Interactionism Contribute to the Study of Inequality? The Case of Marriage and Beyond." *Symbolic Interaction* 24:455–480.

———. 2003. "Studying Equality/Inequality: Naturalist and Constructionist Approaches to Equality in Marriage." *Journal of Contemporary Ethnography* 32:200–232.

Hebdige, Dick. 1979. *Subculture: The Meaning of Style.* London: Routledge.

Hecker, Daniel. 2005. *Occupational Employment: Projections to 2014.* Washington, DC: U.S. Bureau of Labor Statistics.

Heinz, Walter R. 2000. "Education and Employment in Germany: Changing Chances and Risks for Youth." *International Social Science Journal* 52 (164): 161–170.

Herman, Alexis. 2000. *Report on the Youth Labor Force.* Washington, DC: U.S. Bureau of Labor Statistics.

Hersch, Joni, and Leslie S. Stratton. 1997. "Housework, Fixed Effects, and Wages of Married Workers." *Journal of Human Resources* 32 (2): 285–307.

Herz, Diane, and Karen Kosanovich. 2000. "Trends in Youth Employment: Data from the Current Population Survey." In *Report on the Youth Labor Force,* edited by Alexis Herman, 30–51. Washington, DC: U.S. Bureau of Labor Statistics.

Herzog, A. Regula. 1982. "High School Students' Occupational Plans and Values: Trends in Sex Differences 1976 through 1980." *Sociology of Education* 55:1–13.

Hine, Thomas. 1999. *The Rise and Fall of the American Teenager: A New History of the Adolescent Experience.* New York: Perennial.

Hirschman, Charles, and Irina Voloshin. 2007. "The Structure of Teenage Employment: Social Background and the Jobs Held by High School Seniors." *Research in Social Stratification and Mobility* 25:189–203.

Hobbs, Sandy, Michael Lavalette, and Jim McKechnie. 1992. "Part-Time Employment and Schooling." *Scottish Education Review* 25:116–126.

Hochschild, Arlie Russell. 1983. *The Managed Heart: The Commercialization of Human Feeling.* Los Angeles: University Foundation.

———. 1989. *The Second Shift.* New York: Viking Penguin.

———. 2001. *Time Bind: How Work Becomes Home and Home Becomes Work.* New York: Owl Books.

Hodson, Randy, and Paula England. 1986. "Industrial Structure and Sex Differences in Earnings" *Industrial Relations* 25:6–32.

Holden, Chris. 2003. "Decommodification and the Workfare State." *Political Studies Review* 1:303–316.

Horan, Patrick M., and Peggy G. Hargis. 1991. "Children's Work and Schooling in the Late Nineteenth-Century Family Economy." *American Sociological Review* 56:583–596.

Horkheimer, Max, and Theodor W. Adorno. 1969. *Dialectic of Enlightenment.* New York: Continuum.

Howieson, Cathy, Jim McKechnie, and Shiela Semple. 2006. *The Nature and Implications of Part-time Employment of Secondary Pupils. Scouting Executive Social Research.* Glasgow: Scottish Executive Social Research, Department of Enterprise, Transport and Lifelong Learning.

Huddleston, Prue. 2011. "'It's All Right for Saturdays but Not Forever': The Employment of Part-Time Student Staff within the Retail Sector." In *Retail Work,* edited by Irena Grugulis and Ödül Bozkurt, 109–127. London: Palgrave Macmillan.

Huddleston, Prue, and Christine Hirst. 2004. "Are You Being Served? Skills Gaps and Training Needs within the Retail Sector." Research Paper 53. Oxford, UK: Centre on Skills, Knowledge and Organizational Performance, Oxford and Warwick Universities.

Huyssen, Andreas. 1986. *The Great Divide: Modernism, Mass Culture and Post-Modernism*. London: Macmillan.

Ihlanfeldt, Keith R., and David L. Sjoquist. 1990. "Job Accessibility and Racial Differences in Youth Employment Rates." *American Economic Review* 80 (8): 267–276.

Jacobs, Jerry A. 1989. *Revolving Doors: Sex Segregation and Women's Careers*. Stanford, CA: Stanford University Press.

Jacobs, Jerry A., and Ronnie J. Steinberg. 1990. "Compensating Differentials and the Male-Female Wage Gap: Evidence from the New York State Comparable Worth Study." *Social Forces* 69:439–468.

James, Victoria. 2007. "Lost in the Concrete Jungle." *Geographical* 79 (11): 34–38.

Johnson, David S., and Mark Lino. 2000. "Teenagers: Employment and Contributions to Family Spending." *Monthly Labor Review* 123 (9): 15–25.

Johnson, Jerome, and Jerald G. Bachman. 1973. *The Transition from High School to Work*. Ann Arbor: Institute of Social Research, University of Michigan.

Jones, Jacqueline. 1985. *Labor of Love, Labor of Sorrow*. New York: Vintage.

Jovanovic, Boyan. 1979. "Job Matching and the Theory of Turnover." *Journal of Political Economy* 87:972–990.

Kaestner, Robert. 1991. "The Effect of Illicit Drug Use on the Wages of Young Adults." *Journal of Labor Economics* 9 (October): 381–412.

Kahn, Lawrence M., and Stuart A. Low. 1982. "The Relative Effects of Employed and Unemployed Job Search." *Review of Economics and Statistics* 64:234–241.

Kahn, Shulamit, and Harriet Griesinger. 1989. "Female Mobility and the Returns to Seniority: Should EEO Policy Be Concerned with Promotion?" *American Economic Review* 79:300–304.

Kahne, Hilda. 1992. "Part-Time Work: A Hope and a Peril." In *Working Part-Time: Risks and Opportunities*, edited by Barbara D. Warme, Katherina L. P. Lundy, and Larry A. Lundy, 295–309. New York: Praeger.

Kalleberg, Arne L. 2011. *Good Jobs, Bad Jobs: The Rise of Polarized and Precarious Employment Systems in the United States, 1970 to 2000s*. New York: Russell Sage Foundation.

Kanter, Rosabeth Moss. 1977. *Men and Women of the Corporation*. New York: Basic Books.

Katz, Jack. 2001. "How to Why: On Luminous Description and Causal Inference in Ethnography." *Ethnography* 2:443–473.

Keith, Kristen, and Abigail McWilliams. 1999. "The Returns to Mobility and Job Search by Gender." *Industrial and Labor Relations Review* 52:460–477.

Kemple, James J., and Jason C. Snipes. 2001. *Career Academies: Impact on Students' Engagement and Performance in High School*. New York: Manpower Demonstration Research Corporation.

Kenkel, Donald S., and David C. Ribar. 1994. "Alcohol Consumption and Young Adults' Socioeconomic Status." *Brookings Papers on Economic Activity: Microeconomics,* 119–175.

Kerckhoff, Alan C., ed. 1996. *Generating Social Stratification: Toward a New Research Agenda*. Boulder, CO: Westview Press.

Kessler-Harris, Alice. 1986. "Women's History Goes to Trial: EEOC vs. Sears, Roebuck, and Co." *Signs* 11 (Summer): 767–779.

Khandker, Rezaul K. 1992. "A Model of Layoff, Search and Job Choice and Its Estimation." *Review of Economics and Statistics* 74:269–275.

Kilbourne, Barbara Stanek, Paula England, George Farkas, Kurt Beron, and Dorothea Weir. 1994. "Return to Skill, Compensating Differentials, and Gender Bias: Effects of

Occupational Characteristics on the Wages of White Women and Men." *American Journal of Sociology* 100 (3): 689–719.

Kimmel, Michael S. 2004. *The Gendered Society*. Oxford, UK: Oxford University Press.

———. 2008. *Guyland: The Perilous World Where Boys Become Men*. New York: Harper Perennial.

King, Gary, James Honaker, Anne Joseph, and Kenneth Scheve. 2001. "Analyzing Incomplete Political Science Data." *American Political Science Review* 95:49–69.

King, Gary, Michael Tomz, and Jason Wittenberg. 2000. "Making the Most of Statistical Analyses: Improving Interpretation and Presentation." *American Journal of Political Science* 44 (2): 341–355.

Kirschenman, Joleen, and Kathryn Neckerman. 1991. "We'd Love to Hire Them, but . . . : The Meaning of Race for Employers." In *The Urban Underclass*, edited by Christopher Jencks and Paul E. Peterson, 203–232. Washington, DC: Brookings Institution Press.

Klein, Naomi. 2002. *No Logo*. New York: Picador.

Klepinger, Daniel, Shelly Lundberg, and Robert Plotnick. 1999. "How Does Adolescent Fertility Affect the Human Capital and Wages of Young Women?" *Journal of Human Resources* 34 (3): 421–448.

Korczynski, Marek, and Cameron Macdonald. 2008. *Service Work: Critical Perspectives*. New York: Routledge.

Krishna, Sumi. 1996. *Restoring Childhood*. Delhi: Konark.

Krueger, Alan B., and Diane M. Whitmore. 2001. "The Effect of Attending a Small Class in the Early Grades on College-Test Taking and Middle School Test Results: Evidence from Project STAR." *Economic Journal* 111 (468): 1–28.

Ladd, Diane. 2003. "School Vouchers and Student Achievement: What We Know So Far." *Education Reform*, 3 (1): 1–4.

Lange, Marie-France. 2000. "The Demand for Labour within the Household: Child Labour in Togo." In *The Exploited Child*, edited by Bernard Schlemmer, 268–277. London: Zed Books.

Lavalette, Michael. 1991. *The Forgotten Work Force*. Glasgow: Scottish Low Pay Unit.

———. 1994. *Child Employment in the Capitalist Labour Market*. Aldershot, UK: Avebury.

———. 2000. "Child Employment in a Capitalist Labour Market: The British Case." In *The Exploited Child*, edited by Bernard Schlemmer, 214–230. London: Zed Books.

Leidner, Robin. 1993. *Fast Food, Fast Talk: Service Work and the Routinization of Everyday Life*. Berkeley: University of California Press.

———. 1996. "Rethinking Issues of Control." In *Working in the Service Society*, edited by Cameron Lynne Macdonald and Carmen Sirianni, 29–49. Philadelphia: Temple University Press.

———. 2006. "Identity and Work." In *Social Theory at Work*, edited by Marek Korczynski, Randy Hodson, and Paul K. Edwards, 424–463. Oxford, UK: Oxford University Press.

Leslie, Deborah. 2002. "Gender, Retail Employment and the Clothing Commodity Chain." *Gender, Place and Culture* 91:61–76.

Leventhal, Tama, Julia A. Graber, and Jeanne Brooks-Gunn. 2001. "Adolescents' Transition to Adulthood: Antecedents, Correlates, and Consequences of Adolescent Employment." *Journal of Research on Adolescence* 11:297–323.

Levine, Phillip B., Tara A. Gustafson, and Ann D. Velenchik. 1997. "More Bad News for Smokers? The Effects of Cigarette Smoking on Wages." *Industrial and Labor Relations Review* 50 (3): 493–509.

Levy, Frank. 1998. *The New Dollars and Dreams: American Incomes and Economic Change.* New York: Russell Sage Foundation.

Lewin-Epstein, Noah. 1981. *Youth Employment during High School.* Chicago: National Center for Education Statistics.

Liebel, Manfred. 2004. *A Will of Their Own: Cross-Cultural Perspectives on Working Children.* London: Routledge.

Light, Audrey. 1995. "The Effects of Interrupted Schooling on Wages." *Journal of Human Resources* 30 (3): 472–502.

Light, Audrey, and Manuelita Ureta. 1995. "Early Career Work Experience and the Returns to Schooling." *Journal of Labor Economics* 13 (1): 121–154.

Lindeboom, Maarten, Jan Van Ours, and Gusta Renes. 1994. "Matching Employers and Workers: An Empirical Analysis on the Effectiveness of Search." *Oxford Economic Papers,* New Series 46:45–67.

Linnehan, Frank. 1996. "Measuring the Effectiveness of a Career Academy Program from the Employer's Perspective." *Educational Evaluation and Policy Analysis* 18 (1): 73–89.

Lueptow, Lloyd B. 1980. "Social Change and Sex-Role Change in Adolescent Orientations toward Life, Work and Achievement 1964–1975." *Social Psychology Quarterly* 43: 48–59.

Lynch, Lisa M. 1992. "Private-Sector Training and the Earnings of Young Workers." *American Economic Review* 82 (1): 299–312.

Lynott, Patricia P., and Barbara J. Logue. 1993. "The Hurried Child: The Myth of Lost Childhood in Contemporary American Society." *Sociological Forum* 8:471–491.

Macdonald, Cameron Lynne, and Carmen Sirianni. 1996. *Working in the Service Society.* Philadelphia: Temple University Press.

MacKinnon, Catherine A. 1979. *Sexual Harassment of Working Women.* New Haven, CT: Yale University Press.

MacLennan, Emma, John Fitz, and Jill Sullivan. 1985. *Working Children.* London: Low Pay Unit.

Major, Brenda, and Ellen Konar. 1984. "An Investigation of Sex Differences in Pay Expectations and Their Possible Causes." *Academy of Management Journal* 27:777–792.

Manegold, Catherine S. 1994. "Clinton Tells Educators Youth Are Not Getting Practical Skills for Jobs." *New York Times,* February 23.

Mangan, John, and John Johnston. 1999. "Minimum Wages, Training Wages and Youth Employment." *Economics* 26 (1/2/3): 415–429.

Manning, Wendy D. 1990. "Parenting Employed Teenagers." *Youth and Society* 22:184–200.

Marguerat, Yves. 2000. "The Exploitation of Apprentices in Togo." In *The Exploited Child* edited by Bernard Schlemmer, 239–247. London: Zed Books.

Marsh, Herbert W. 1991. "Employment during High School: Character Building and Subversion of Academic Goals." *Sociology of Education* 64:172–189.

Mason, Geoff, and Matthew Osborne. 2008. "Business Strategies, Work Organisation and Low Pay in the United Kingdom Retailing." In *Low-Wage Work in the United Kingdom,* edited by Caroline Lloyd, Geoff Mason, and Ken Mayhew, 131–167. New York: Russell Sage Foundation.

Mattila, Peter J. 1974. "Job Quitting and Frictional Unemployment." *American Economic Review* 64:235–239.

Maxwell, Nan L., and Victor Rubin. 2000. *High School Career Academies: Pathways to Educational Reform in Urban Districts?* Kalamazoo, MI: W. E. Upjohn Institute.

Mbaye, Serigne Mor, and Abdou Salam Fall. 2000. "The Disintegrating Social Fabric: Child Labor and Socialization in Senegal." In *The Exploited Child,* edited by Bernard Schlemmer, 292–299. London: Zed Books.

McCafferty, Stephen. 1978. "A Theory of Semi-Permanent Wage Search." *Southern Economic Journal* 45:46–62.

McKechnie, Jim, Sandra Lindsay, and Sandy Hobbs. 1993. *Child Employment in Cumbria: A Report to Cumbria County Council.* Paisley, Scotland: University of Paisley Press.

———. 1994. *Still Forgotten: Child Employment in Rural Scotland.* Glasgow: Scottish Low Pay Unit.

McMorris, Barbara, and Christopher Uggen. 2000. "Alcohol and Employment in Transition to Adulthood." *Journal of Health and Social Behavior* 41:276–294.

McNeal, Ralph B., Jr. 1997. "Are Students Being Pulled Out of High School? The Effect of Adolescent Employment on Dropping Out." *Sociology of Education* 70:206–220.

Meillassoux, Claude. 2000. "The Economy and Child Labor: An Overview." In *The Exploited Child,* edited by Bernard Schlemmer, 41–50. London: Zed Books.

Meyer, Robert H., and David A. Wise. 1982. "High School Preparation and Early Labor Force Experience." In *The Youth Labor Market Problem: Its Nature, Causes, and Consequences,* edited by Richard B. Freeman and David A. Wise, 277–348. Chicago: University of Chicago Press.

———. 1983. "The Effects of the Minimum Wage on the Employment and Earnings of Youth." *Journal of Labor Economics* 1 (1): 66–100.

Michael, Robert T., and Nancy Brandon Tuma. 1984. "Youth Employment: Does Life Begin at 16?" *Journal of Labor Economics* 2:464–476.

Mihalic, Sharon W., and Delbert Elliot. 1997. "Short- and Long-Term Consequences of Adolescent Work." *Youth and Society* 28:464–498.

Mills, C. Wright. 1956. *White Collar: The American Middle Classes.* New York: Oxford University Press.

Mincer, Jacob. 1962. "On the Job Training: Costs, Returns and Some Implications." *Journal of Political Economy* 70 (5): 50–79.

Mincer, Jacob, and Boyan Jovanovic. 1981. "Labor Mobility and Wages." In *Studies in Labor Markets,* edited by Sherwin Rosen, 21–64. Chicago: University of Chicago Press.

Mincer, Jacob, and Haim Ofek. 1982. "Interrupted Work Careers: Depreciation and Restoration of Human Capital." *Journal of Human Resources* 17:3–24.

Mincer, Jacob, and Solomon Polacheck. 1974. "Family Investments in Human Capital: Earnings of Women." *Journal of Political Economy* 82:S76–S108.

Moorehead, Caroline. 1987. *School Age Workers in Britain Today.* London: Anti-Slavery Association.

Morisi, Teresa. 2008. "Youth Enrollment and Employment during the School Year." *Monthly Labor Review* 131 (2): 51–63.

———. 2010. "The Early 2000s: A Period of Declining Teen Summer Employment Rates." Washington, DC: U.S. Bureau of Labor Statistics.

Morrison, Toni. 1994. *The Bluest Eye.* New York: Plume.

Mortimer, Jeylan T. 2003. *Working and Growing Up in America.* Cambridge, MA: Harvard University Press.

———. 2007. "Working and Growing up in America: Myths and Realities." In *Working to Be Someone: Child-Focused Research and Practice with Working Children,* edited by Beatrice Hungerland, Manfred Liebel, Brian Milne, and Anne Wihstutz, 117–132. London: Jessica Kingsley.

Mortimer, Jeylan T., and Michael D. Finch. 1986. "The Effects of Part-Time Work on Self-Concept and Achievement." In *Becoming a Worker,* edited by Kathryn M. Borman and Jane Reisman, 66–89. Norwood, NJ: Ablex.

Mortimer, Jeylan T., Michael Finch, Katherine Dennehy, Chaimun Lee, and Timothy Beebe. 1994. "Work Experience in Adolescence." *Journal of Vocational Education Research* 19:39–70.

Moss, Philip, and Chris Tilly. 1995. *Getting a Job: A Study of Contacts and Careers.* Chicago: University of Chicago Press.

———. 1996. "'Soft' Skills and Race: An Investigation of Black Men's Employment Problems." *Work and Occupation* 23 (3): 252–276.

———. 2001. *Stories Employers Tell: Race, Skill and Hiring in America.* New York: Russell Sage Foundation.

Mosteller, Frederick. 1995. "The Tennessee Study of Class Size in the Early School Grades: The Future of Children." *Critical Issues for Children and Youths* 5 (2): 113–127.

Muirhead, Russell. 2004. *Just Work.* Cambridge, MA: Harvard University Press.

Mulligan, Casey B. 2011. "Who Lost Work During the Great Recession?" *New York Times, Economix,* September 7. Available at http://economix.blogs.nytimes.com/2011/09/07/who-lost-work-during-the-great-recession/?_r=0.

Nambissan, Geetha B. 2003. "Social Exclusion, Children's Work and Education: A View from the Margins." In *Child Labour and the Right to Education in South Asia,* edited by Naila Kabeer, Geetha B. Nambissan, and Ramya Subrahmanian, 109–142. New Delhi: Sage.

Namboodiri, Krishnan. 1987. "The Floundering Phase of the Life Course." In *Research in the Sociology of Education and Socialization,* edited by Ronald G. Corwin. Vol. 17, 59–86. Greenwich, CT: JAI Press.

Neumark, David. 1995. *The Effects of Minimum Wages on Teenage Employment, Enrollment, and Idleness.* ERIC Document No. ED397241; Clearinghouse No. CE072034.

Neumark, David, and William Wascher. 1992. "Employment Effects of Minimum and Subminimum Wages: Panel Data on State Minimum Wage Laws." *Industrial and Labor Relations Review* 46:55–81.

Newman, Katherine S. 1999. *No Shame in My Game: Working Poor in the Inner City.* New York: Vintage Books and Russell Sage Foundation.

Nickson, Dennis, Scott A. Hurrell, and Chris Warhurst. 2007. "A New Labour Aristocracy? Aesthetic Labor and Routine Interactive Service." *Work, Employment and Society* 21:785–798.

Nickson, Dennis, Scott A. Hurrell, Chris Warhurst, and Johanna Commander. 2011. "Labour Supply and Skills Demand in Fashion Retailing." In *Retail Work,* edited by Irena Grugulis and Ödül Bozkurt, 66–87. London: Palgrave Macmillan.

Nickson, Dennis, Chris Warhurst, and Eli Dutton. 2004. "Aesthetic Labour and the Policy-Making Agenda: Time for a Reappraisal of Skills?" Research Paper 48. Warwick Business School. Coventry, UK: SKOPE Publications.

Nickson, Dennis, Chris Warhurst, Cliff Lockyer, and Eli Dutton. 2004. "Flexible Friends? Lone Parents and Retail Employment." *Employee Relations* 26 (3): 255–273.

Niuwenhuys, Olga. 2000. "The Household Economy and the Commercial Exploitation of Children's Work: The Case of Kerela." In *The Exploited Child*, edited by Bernard Schlemmer, 287–291. London: Zed Books.

Oklah, Montaser J. 1987. "The Effects of Labor Unions on the Wages of Youth." Ph.D. diss., University of Oklahoma.

O'Neill, June. 1985. "The Trend in the Male-Female Gender Wage Gap in the United States." *Journal of Labor Economics* 3:S91–S116.

O'Regan, Katherine M., and John M. Quigley. 1996a. "Spatial Effects upon Employment Outcomes: The Case of New Jersey Teenagers." University of California, Berkeley Working Paper Series.

———. 1996b. "Teenage Employment and the Spatial Isolation of Minority and Poverty Households." *Journal of Human Resources* 31:692–702.

Ostermann, Paul, and Maria Ianozzi. 1993. "Youth Apprenticeship and School to Work Transitions: Current Knowledge and Legislative Strategy." Working Paper 14. National Center on the Educational Quality of the Workforce, University of Pennsylvania.

Pabilonia, Sabrina W. 2001. "Evidence on Youth Employment, Earnings, and Parental Transfers in the NLSY 1997." *Journal of Human Resources* 36 (4): 795–822.

Parsons, Donald O. 1991. "The Job Search Behavior of Employed Youth." *Review of Economics and Statistics* 73:597–604.

Paternoster, Raymond, Shawn D. Bushway, Robert Brame, and Robert Apel. 2003. "The Effect of Teenage Employment on Delinquency and Problem Behaviors." *Social Forces* 82:297–335.

Pease, John, and Lee Martin. 1997. "Want Ads and Jobs for the Poor: A Glaring Mismatch." *Sociological Forum* 12:545–564.

Peng, Samuel S., William B. Fetters, and Andrew J. Kolstad. 1981. *High School and Beyond: A Capsule Description of High School Students*. Washington, DC: National Center for Education Statistics.

Pettinger, Lynne. 2004. "Brand Culture and Branded Workers: Service Work and Aesthetic Labour in Fashion Retail." *Consumption, Markets and Culture* 7 (2): 165–184.

Pissarides, Christopher A. 1984. "Search Intensity, Job Advertising, and Efficiency." *Journal of Labor Economics* 2:128–143.

Polacheck, Solomon W. 1975. "Discontinuous Labor Force Participation and Its Effect on Women's Market Earnings." In *Sex, Discrimination and the Division of Labor*, edited by Cynthia B. Lloyd, 90–124. New York: Columbia University Press.

———. 1981. "Occupational Self-Selection: A Human Capital Approach to Sex Differences in Occupational Structure." *Review of Economics and Statistics* 63 (1): 60–69.

Pond, Chris, and Anne Searle. 1991. *The Hidden Army: Children and Army Children at Work in the 1990's*. London: Low Pay Unit.

Post, David. 2001. *Children's Work, Schooling and Welfare in Lain America*. Boulder, CO: Westview Press.

Post, David, and Suet-Ling Pong. 2009. "Student Labor and Academic Proficiency in International Perspective." *International Labour Review* 148:93–122.

Postman, Neil. 1996. *The End of Education: Redefining the Value of School*. New York: Vintage Books.

Powell, Arthur G., Eleanor Farrar, and David K. Cohen. 1985. *The Shopping Mall High School: The Winners and Losers in the Educational Marketplace*. New York: Houghton Mifflin.

Presser, Harriet B. 2006. "Toward a 24-Hour Economy: The U.S. Experience and Implications for the Family." In *Working in America: Continuity, Conflict, and Change,* edited by Amy S. Wharton, 459–465. New York: McGraw-Hill.

Psacharopoulos, George. 1997. "Child Labor versus Educational Attainment: Some Evidence from Latin America." *Journal of Population Economics* 10 (4): 377–386.

Ramanathan, Usha. 2000. "The Public Policy Problem: Child Labor and The Law in India." In *The Exploited Child,* edited by Bernard Schlemmer, 146–159. London: Zed Books.

Raphael, Steven. 1998. "Inter- and Intra-ethnic Comparisons of the Central City-Suburban Teenage Employment Differential: Evidence from the Oakland Metropolitan Area." *Industrial and Labour Relations Review* 51:505–524.

Ray, Manabendranath, and Asha N. Iyer. 2006. *Abuse among Child Domestic Workers: A Research Study in West Bengal.* Calcutta: Save the Children, UK.

Rees, Albert, and Wayne Gray. 1982. "Family Effects in Youth Employment." In *The Youth Labor Market Problem: Its Nature, Causes, and Consequences,* edited by Richard B. Freeman and David A. Wise, 453–464. Chicago: University of Chicago Press.

Register, Charles A., and Donald R. Williams. 1990. "Wage Effects of Obesity among Young Workers." *Social Science Quarterly* 71:130–141.

Reid, Graham L. 1972. "Job Search and the Effectiveness of Job-Finding Methods." *Industrial and Labor Relations Review* 25:479–495.

Reskin, Barbara, and Irene Padavic. 1994. *Women and Men at Work.* Newbury Park, CA: Pine Forge Press.

Reubens, Beatrice. 1983. *Youth at Work: An International Survey.* New York: Rowman and Littlefield.

Ritzer, George. 2000. *The McDonaldization of Society.* Newbury Park, CA: Pine Forge Press.

Roberts, Steven. 2011. "'The Lost Boys': An Overlooked Detail in Retail?" In *Retail Work,* edited by Irena Grugulis and Ödül Bozkurt, 128–148. London: Palgrave Macmillan.

Robertson, Margaret E., and Michael Williams, eds. 2004. *Young People, Leisure and Place: Cross-Cultural Perspectives.* New York: Nova Scientific.

Robinson, Richard, and David Hurst. 1997. "College Education for Any and All." *Teachers College Record* 99:62–65.

Ross, Catherine E. 1987. "The Division of Labor at Home." *Social Forces* 65:816–833.

Ruhm, Christopher. 1997. "Is High School Employment Consumption or Investment?" *Journal of Labor Research* 15:735–776.

Sandell, Steven H. 1980. "Is the Unemployment Rate of Women Too Low? A Direct Test of the Economic Theory of Job Search." *Review of Economics and Statistics* 62: 634–638.

Sandell, Steven H., and David Shapiro. 1978. "The Theory of Human Capital and the Earnings of Women: A Reexamination of the Evidence." *Journal of Human Resources* 13:103–117.

Sastre, Béatriz S. Céspedes, and María-Isabel Zarama V. Meyer. 2000. "Living and Working Conditions: Child Labour in the Coal Mines of Colombia." In *The Exploited Child,* edited by Bernard Schlemmer, 83–92. London: Zed Books.

Schaefer, Kayleen. 2010. "New Policies Exterminating Teen Mall Rats." *ABC News.* September 23.

Schiller, Bradley R. 1994. "Moving Up: The Training and Wage Gains of Minimum-Wage Entrants." *Social Science Quarterly* 753:131–144.

Schlemmer, Bernard. 2000. *The Exploited Child.* New York: Zed Books.

Schlosser, Eric. 2002. *Fast Food Nation: The Dark Side of the All-American Meal.* New York: Harper Perennial.

Schneider, Barbara, and David Stevenson. 1999. *The Ambitious Generation: America's Teenagers, Motivated but Directionless.* New Haven, CT: Yale University Press.

Schoenhals, Mark, Marta Tienda, and Barbara Schneider. 1998. "The Educational and Personal Consequences of Adolescent Employment." *Social Forces* 77:723–761.

Schor, Juliet. 1993. *The Overworked American: The Unexpected Decline of Leisure.* New York: Basic Books.

———. 2000. "Towards a New Politics of Consumption." In *The Consumer Society Reader,* edited by Juliet B. Schor and Douglas B. Holt, 446–462. New York: New York University Press.

Schultz, Theodore W. 1960. "Investment in Human Capital." *American Economic Review* 51 (1): 1–17.

Scott, William Richard. 1995. *Institutions and Organizations.* Thousand Oaks, CA: Sage.

Sennett, Richard. 1998. *The Corrosion of Character: The Personal Consequences of Work in the New Capitalism.* New York: Norton.

Shaefer, H. Luke. 2009. "Part-time Workers: Some Key Differences between Primary and Secondary Earners." *Monthly Labor Review* 132 (10): 3–15.

Shapiro, D. 1979. "Working Students." In *Pathways to the Future: Preliminary Report to Youth and the Labor Market,* edited by M. E. Borus, 161–167. Columbus, OH: Center for Human Resources.

Skillsmart. 2007. *Sector Skills Agreement Stage One: Assessment of Current and Future Skills Needs.* London: Skillsmart.

Slater, Don. 1997. *Consumer Culture and Modernity.* Cambridge, UK: Polity Press.

Smith, Clifton L., and Jay W. Rojewski. 1993. "School to Work Transition: Alternatives for Educational Reform." *Youth and Society* 25:225–250.

Smith, Dorothy E. 1979. "A Sociology for Women." In *The Prism of Sex: Essays in the Sociology of Knowledge,* edited by Julia A. Sherman and Evelyn Torton Beck, 135–187. Madison: University of Wisconsin Press.

Smith, Marvin M. 1985. "Early Labor Market Experiences of Youth and Subsequent Wages." *American Journal of Economics and Sociology* 44 (4): 391–400.

Smith, Vicki. 2006. "Structural Unemployment and the Reconstruction of the Self in the Turbulent Economy." In *Working in America: Continuity, Conflict, and Change,* edited by Amy S. Wharton. New York: McGraw-Hill.

Stack, Niamh, and Jim McKechnie. 2002. "Working Children." In *Children, Welfare and the State,* edited by Barry Goldson, Michael Lavalette, and Jim McKechnie, 87–101. London: Sage.

Steele, Claude M. 1992. "Race and Schooling of Black Americans." *Atlantic Monthly* (April): 68–78.

Steinberg, Laurence, and Sanford M. Dornbusch. 1991. "Negative Correlates of Part-Time Employment during Adolescence: Replication and Elaboration." *Developmental Psychology* 27:304–313.

Steinberg, Laurence, Suzanne Fegley, and Sanford Dornbusch. 1993. "Negative Impact of Part-Time Work on Adolescent Adjustment: Evidence from a Longitudinal Study." *Developmental Psychology* 29 (2): 171–180.

Steinberg, Laurence, and Susan B. Silverberg. 1986. "The Vicissitudes of Autonomy in Early Adolescence." *Child Development* 57 (4): 841–851.

Steinberg, Ronnie J. 1990. "Social Construction of Skill: Gender, Power and Comparable Worth." *Work and Occupations* 17:449–482.

Stella, Alessandro. 2000. "Introduction: A History of Exploited Children in Europe." In *The Exploited Child,* edited by Bernard Schlemmer, 21–38. London: Zed Books.

Stephenson, Stanley P., Jr. 1976. "The Economics of Youth Job Search Behavior." *Review of Economics and Statistics* 58:104–111.

———. 1980. "In School Work and Early Post-School Labor Market Dynamics." Working Paper. Department of Economics. State College: Pennsylvania State University.

Stern, David, and Yoshi-fumi Nakata. 1989. "Characteristics of High School Students' Paid Jobs, and Employment Experience after Graduation." In *Adolescence and Work,* edited by David Stern and Dorothy Eichorn, 189–211. Hillsdale, NJ: Erlbaum.

Stevens, David. 1967. "Racial Differences in Migration and Job Search: A Case Study: Comment." *Southern Economic Journal* 33:574–576.

Stewart, Rosemary. 1982. "A Model for Understanding Managerial Jobs and Behavior." *Academy of Management Review* 7:7–13.

Strauss, Anselm. 1987. *Qualitative Analysis for Social Scientists.* Cambridge, UK: Cambridge University Press.

Suremain, Charles-Eduard. 2000. "Coffee Beans and the Seeds of Labour: Child Labor on Guatemalan Plantations." In *The Exploited Child,* edited by Bernard Schlemmer, 231–238. London: Zed Books.

Sweet, Richard. 1995. "The Naked Emperor: Training Reform, Initial Vocational Preparation and Youth Wages." *Australian Economic Review* 28 (2): 101–108.

Tannery, Frederick J. 1983. "Search Effort and Unemployment Insurance Reconsidered." *Journal of Human Resources* 18:432–440.

Tannock, Stuart. 2001. *Youth at Work: The Unionized Fast-Food and Grocery Workplace.* Philadelphia: Temple University Press.

Tarancena, Elvira, and Maria-Luisa Tavera. 2000. "Stigmatization versus Identity: Child Street-Workers in Mexico." In *The Exploited Child,* edited by Bernard Schlemmer, 93–106. London: Zed Books.

Tarrant, Mark, Adrian C. North, Mark D. Edridge, Laura E. Kirk, Elizabeth A. Smith, and Roisin E. Turner. 2001. "Social Identity in Adolescence." *Journal of Adolescence* 24:597–609.

Tarrant, Mark, Adrian C. North, and David J. Hargreaves. 2001. "Social Categorization, Self-Esteem, and the Estimated Music Preferences of Male Adolescents." *Journal of Social Psychology* 141 (5): 565–581.

Taylor, Phil, and Peter Bain. 1999. "'An Assembly Line in the Head': Work and Employee Relations in the Call Centre." *Industrial Relations Journal* 30 (2): 101–117.

Teske, Paul, and Mark Schneider. 2001. "What Research Can Tell Policy Makers about School Choice?" *Journal of Policy Analysis and Management* 20:609–631.

Thornton, Sarah. 1995. *Club Cultures: Music, Media and Subcultural Capital.* Cambridge, UK: Polity Press.

Tienda, Marta, and Haya Stier. 1996. "Generating Labor Market Inequality: Employment Opportunities and the Accumulation of Disadvantage." *Social Problems* 43:147–165.

Tilly, Chris. 1995. *Half a Job: Bad and Good Part-Time Jobs in a Changing Labor Market.* Philadelphia: Temple University Press.

Tilly, Chris, and Françoise Carré. 2011. " Endnote: Perceptions and Reality." In *Retail Work,* edited by Irena Grugulis and Ödül Bozkurt, 297–306. London: Palgrave Macmillan.

Tiwari, Jyotsna. 2004. *Child Abuse and Human Rights.* New Delhi: Isha Books.

Tomaskovic-Devey, Donald. 1993. "The Gender and Race Composition of Jobs and the Male/Female, White/Black Wage Pay Gap." *Social Forces* 72:45–76.

Torres, Lisa, Matt Huffman, and Steven Velasco. 1998. "Comment on Patricia Drentea's 'Consequences of Women's Formal and Informal Job Search Methods for Employment in Female-Dominated Jobs.'" *Gender and Society* 12:466–468.

Treiman, Donald J., and Heidi I. Hartmann. 1981. *Women, Work and Wages.* Washington, DC: National Academy Press.

Ullman, Joseph C., and Thomas G. Gutteridge. 1974. "Job Search in the Labor Market for College Graduates: A Case Study of MBAs." *Academy of Management* 17:381–386.

Umana, Aniefiok J. 1992. "Postsecondary Vocational Training and Its Relationship to Labor Force Participation and Wages among Youth in the United States." Ph.D. diss., Pennsylvania State University.

Urquiola, Miguel, David Stern, Ilana Horn, Carolyn Dornsife, Bernadette Chi, Lea Williams, Donna Merritt, Katherine Hughes, and Thomas Bailey. 1997. *School to Work, College and Career: A Review of Policy, Practice, and Results 1993–1997.* Berkeley: National Center for Research in Vocational Education, University of California.

U.S. Bureau of Labor Statistics. 2012a. *Occupational Employment and Wages.* March 27. Washington, DC: U.S. Department of Labor.

———. 2012b. *Occupational Outlook Handbook, 2012–13 Edition.* Projections Overview. March 29. Washington, DC: U.S. Department of Labor. Available at http://www.bls .gov/ooh/about/projections-overview.htm.

Vallance, Elizabeth. 1973. "Hiding the Hidden Curriculum." *Curriculum Theory Network* 4:5–21.

Vartanian, Thomas P. 1999. "Adolescent Neighborhood Effects on Labor Market and Economic Outcomes." *Social Science Review* 73 (2): 142–167.

Verlet, Martin. 2000. "Growing Up in Ghana: Deregulation and the Employment of Children." In *The Exploited Child,* edited by Bernard Schlemmer, 67–82. London: Zed Books.

Veum, Jonathan R., and Andrea B. Weiss. 1993. "Education and the Work Histories of Young Adults." *Monthly Labor Review* 116:11–20.

Villermé, L. R. [1840] 1989. Tableau de l'état physique et moral des ouvriers employés dans les manufactures de coton, de laine et de soie. New ed. Paris: EDI.

Vulcan, Beatrice. 1968. "American Social Policy towards Youth and Youth Employment." In *Work, Youth, and Unemployment,* edited by Melvin Herman, Stanley Sadofsky, and Bernard Rosenberg, 76–90. New York: Thomas Y. Crowell.

Wacquant, Loïc. 1995. "The Pugilistic Point of View: How Boxers Think about Their Trade." *Theory and Society* 24:489–535.

———. 1998. "Negative Social Capital: State Breakdown and Social Destitution in America's Urban Core." *Netherlands Journal of Housing and Built Environment* 13:25–39.

Wadsworth, Jonathan. 1991. "Unemployment Benefits and Search Effort in the UK Labour Market." *Economica* 58:17–34.

Waldfogel, Jane. 1998. "The Family Gap for Young Women in the United States and Britain: Can Maternity Leave Make a Difference?" *Journal of Labor Economics* 16 (30): 505–545.

Waldinger, Roger. 1996. "Who Cleans the Rooms? Who Washes the Dishes? Black/ Immigrant Competition Reassessed." In *Immigrants and Immigration Policy: Individual Skills, Family Ties, and Group Identities,* edited by Harriet Orcutt Duleep and Phanindra V. Wunnava, 265–288. Vol. 79, Contemporary Studies in Economic and Financial Analysis. Greenwich, CT: JAI Press.

Walker, Jon E., Curt Tausky, and Donna Oliver. 1982. "Men and Women at Work: Similarities and Differences in Work Values within Occupational Groupings." *Journal of Vocational Behavior* 21:17–36.

Walls, Stephen. 2007. "Are You Being Served? Gendered Aesthetics among Retail Workers." Ph.D. diss., Durham University, Durham, UK.

Ward, Thomas. 2003. "The Meaning of Race to Employers: A Dynamic Qualitative Perspective." *Sociological Quarterly* 44: 227–42.

Warhurst, Chris, and Dennis Nickson. 2007. "Employee Experience of Aesthetic Labour in Retail and Hospitality." *Work, Employment and Society* 21:103–120.

———. 2009. "Becoming a Class Act? Reflections on Aesthetic Labour." Paper presented at the 23rd Annual Labour Process Conference, University of Strathclyde, Glasgow.

Warhurst, Chris, Paul Thompson, and Dennis Nickson. 2009. "The Labour Process Theory: Putting the Materialism Back into the Meaning of Service Work." In *Service Work: Critical Perspectives,* edited by Cameron L. Macdonald and Marek Korczynski, 91–112. New York: Routledge.

Warren, John R., and Emily Forrest. 2001. "Trends in the Selectivity and Consequences of Adolescent Employment, 1966–1997." Unpublished manuscript. Seattle: University of Washington, Department of Sociology.

Weinberg, Bruce, Patricia Reagan, and Jeffrey J. Yankow. 1999. "Do Neighborhoods Matter? Evidence from the NLSY79." Columbus: Center for Human Resources, Ohio State University.

Weinberger, Catherine J. 1998. "Race and Gender Wage Gaps in the Market for Recent College Graduates." *Industrial Relations* 37 (1): 67–84.

———. 1999. "Mathematical College Majors and the Gender Gap in Wages." *Industrial Relations* 38 (3): 407–413.

Welch, Finis, and James Cunningham. 1978. "Effects of Minimum Wages on the Level and Age of Youth Employment." *Review of Economics and Statistics* 60 (1): 140–145.

Wellington, Alison J. 1991. "Effects of the Minimum Wage on the Employment Status of Youths: An Update." *Journal of Human Resources* 26:27–46.

White, Rob. 1999. *Australian Youth Subcultures, on the Margins and in the Mainstream.* Hobart: Australian Clearinghouse for Youth Studies.

Whittaker, A. 1986. "Child Labour and Its Causes." *Third World Now* (Spring).

Williams, Christine L., and Catherine Connell. 2010. "Looking Good and Sounding Right: Aesthetic Labor and Social Inequality in the Retail Industry." *Work and Occupations* 37:349–377.

Wilson, Kathryn. 2001. "The Determinants of Educational Attainment: Modeling and Estimating the Human Capital and Education Production Functions." *Southern Economic Journal* 67 (3): 518–551.

Wilson, William Julius. 1978. *The Declining Significance of Race.* Chicago: University of Chicago Press.

———. 1996. *When Work Disappears: The World of the New Urban Poor.* New York: Alfred A. Knopf.

Witz, Anne, Chris Warhurst, and Dennis Nickson. 2003. "The Labour of Aesthetics and Aesthetics of Organization." *Organization* 10:33–54.

Wolkowitz, Carol. 2006. *Bodies at Work.* London: Sage.

Wright, David. 2005. "Commodifying Respectability: Distinctions at Work in the Bookshop." *Journal of Consumer Culture* 5 (3): 295–314.

Yoon, Bong Joon. 1981. "A Model of Unemployment Duration with Variable Search Intensity." *Review of Economics and Statistics* 63:599–609.

Zamudio, Margaret M., and Michael I. Lichter. 2008. "Bad Attitudes and Good Soldiers: Soft Skills as a Code for Tractability in the Hiring of Immigrant Latina/os over Native Blacks in the Hotel Industry." *Social Problems* 55:573–589.

Zelizer, Viviana. 1994. *Pricing the Priceless Child: The Changing Social Value of Children.* Princeton, NJ: Princeton University Press.

Zemsky, Robert. 1998. "Labor Markets and Educational Restructuring." *Annals of the American Academy of Political and Social Sciences* 559:77–90.

Index

Yasemin Besen-Cassino is an Associate Professor of Sociology at Montclair State University. She is the coauthor (with Dan Cassino) of *Consuming Politics: Jon Stewart, Branding, and the Youth Vote in America* and coeditor (with Michael S. Kimmel) of *The Jessie Bernard Reader*.